Servants of Wealth

Polemics

Stephen Eric Bronner, Series Editor

The books in the Polemics series confront readers with provocative ideas by major figures in the social sciences and humanities on a host of controversial issues and developments. The authors combine a sophisticated argument with a lively and engaging style, making the books interesting to even the most accomplished scholar and appealing to the general reader and student.

Media Wars
News at a Time of Terror
By Danny Schechter

The Collapse of Liberalism
Why America Needs a New Left
By Charles Noble

Imperial Delusions
American Militarism and Endless War
By Carl Boggs

Murdering Myths
The Real Story Behind the Death Penalty
By Judith Kay

Primetime Politics
The Truth about Conservative Lies, Corporate Control, and Television Culture
By Philip Green

Gay Marriage and Democracy
Equality for All
By R. Claire Snyder

Servants of Wealth
The Right's Assault on Economic Justice
By John Ehrenberg

Servants of Wealth

The Right's Assault on Economic Justice

John Ehrenberg

ROWMAN & LITTLEFIELD PUBLISHERS, INC.
Lanham • Boulder • New York • Toronto • Plymouth, UK

ROWMAN & LITTLEFIELD PUBLISHERS, INC.

Published in the United States of America
by Rowman & Littlefield Publishers, Inc.
A wholly owned subsidiary of The Rowman & Littlefield Publishing Group, Inc.
4501 Forbes Boulevard, Suite 200, Lanham, Maryland 20706
www.rowmanlittlefield.com

Estover Road
Plymouth PL6 7PY
United Kingdom

British Library Cataloguing in Publication Information Available

Library of Congress Cataloging-in-Publication Data

Ehrenberg, John, 1944–
    Servants of wealth : the right's assault on economic justice / John Ehrenberg.
       p.   cm— (Polemics)
    Includes bibliographical references and index.
    ISBN-13: 978-0-7425-4204-4 (cloth : alk. paper)
    ISBN-13: 978-0-7425-4205-1 (pbk. : alk. paper)
    ISBN-10: 0-7425-4204-1 (cloth : alk. paper)
    ISBN-10: 0-7425-4205-X (pbk. : alk. paper)
       1. United States—Economic policy.   2. Conservatism—United States—History.
    I. Title.
    HC103.E37   2006
    330.973—dc22   2006020728

Printed in the United States of America

♾ ™ The paper used in this publication meets the minimum requirements of American
National Standard for Information Sciences—Permanence of Paper for Printed Library
Materials, ANSI/NISO Z39.48-1992.

To Cassie and David

Contents

Preface

We Americans live in the most unequal advanced country in the world. When compared with similar societies, ours has the greatest inequities in the distribution of income and wealth, the provision of basic health care, the relationship between CEO salaries and average wages, the influence of money on office-holders, and the level of political participation. This didn't happen overnight and is not the unforeseen product of economic growth. It's the direct result of twenty-five years of public policy that has favored wealth, rewarded property, and encouraged the concentration of both.

General prosperity notwithstanding, the vast amount of money that's gone to the few has come at the expense of the many. Disappearing pensions and weakened social protections, longer hours at work and more stress on the job, a large class of the permanently impoverished, the world's largest population of prison inmates, less upward mobility, and stagnant wages are only a few of the social pathologies that have worsened over the past twenty-five years. Nor is a corrective in sight. One of the most right-wing governments in American history has intensified the assault on social welfare and accelerated a drive toward empire that is more formally acknowledged and explicitly embraced than at any time in recent memory. As radical as it is, the Bush administration doesn't stand alone. Its policy of even more tax cuts on wealth, even more deregulation of business, and even more privatization of governmental functions continues the general pattern of the past twenty-five years. As the Right continues its long project of concentrating wealth in a small section of the population and developing a political apparatus openly dedicated to serving the needs of the rich, the United States is beginning to look more and more like the diseased state that the ancient Greeks called "plutocracy."

How did this happen in a country whose history has been powerfully shaped by democratic movements and periods of social reform? Cycles of economic concentration have always alternated with the diffusion of wealth, but contemporary polarization has been developing since the late 1970s. Originating as a reaction to military defeat in Vietnam, racial turmoil, and social chaos, a comprehensive right-wing political program to shift wealth and power upward has slowly taken shape over the past quarter of a century. Its momentum partly shaped by the need to win a measure of popular consent, it has accelerated and gotten more radical over the past few years. Economic crisis, the political mobilization of business, international difficulties, domestic disorder, the collapse of Keynesianism, a conservative religious Great Awakening—all played important parts in setting the stage for what's been happening, but the power of ideas was enormous. As an influential grouping of conservative intellectuals, columnists, religious leaders, political figures, and writers began to develop a broad attack on the liberal assumptions that had accompanied thirty years of America's "middle-class republic," they also crafted a "positive," forward-looking political program and addressed problems that were troubling millions of people. An increasingly ideological Republican Party won broad support for a program of military strength, moral restoration, social order, individual freedom, and economic opportunity. As they came to dominate public life, right-wing spokesmen worked hard to change the way Americans think about equality, democracy, and freedom.

This book is about how they did it. Partly a history of ideas, it's also about current affairs. Many of the particular conditions that gave rise to a new "populist" conservatism have changed, but neither the ideological assault on equality nor the politics of plutocracy shows any sign of slowing down. The Right advanced across a very wide front and its key arguments continue to resonate in times of anxiety and fear. No particular chronological order imposes itself, for the neo-conservative assault on President Carter's foreign policy came at roughly the same time as the beginning of the Christian Right's campaign to defend "traditional family values" and the backlash appeal to racial fear accompanied tax revolts and an attack on the regulatory state. Nevertheless, five broad interconnected themes suggest themselves. The Right developed blistering critiques of liberalism in matters of foreign policy, social authority, race relations, the welfare state, and economic equality. As it did so, it crafted a more "muscular" approach to international relations, called for moral renewal and a restoration of authority in all areas of life, suggested that the government end racial preferences and encourage a "color-blind society," extolled the creative and democratic power of unfettered capitalism, and articulated a broad celebration of personal freedom, individual opportunity, and economic growth. Through all the turmoil of the past twenty-five years, it has remained faithful to this fixed set of core ideas and paid close attention to ideology.

Something important happened in the late 1970s that transformed conservatism into a coherent political tendency, but the modern Right has never been a monolithic enterprise. Its constituent parts agree about a great deal and disagree about almost as much. Christian conservatives are often nervous about the free market's indifference to morality. Cultural authoritarians worry about laissez-faire economics. Neo-conservatives don't often get involved in the culture wars. Appeals to racial anxiety are less useful than they used to be, and hardly anyone supports the militias, clinic bombers, and race warriors. But even if they disagree with one another, the Right's often-divergent tendencies are united by two sides of a single project that rests at the heart of everything they've been saying and doing for a quarter of a century. When all is said and done, the contemporary Right is about attacking equality and serving wealth.

A variety of foundations, think-tanks, newspapers, publishers, and institutes were important in developing this program. Many of them worked together, some were more prominent than others, most benefited from the near-total collapse of liberalism, and they've largely succeeded in getting the country to debate elementary principles of equality and democracy on their terms. This book doesn't pretend to offer a full account of how the Right was put together or how it came to dominate national life. It presents a broad survey of its important ideological currents, looks at several books that have contributed to its growth, establishes the attack on equality as its central project, and places social justice at the center of political democracy and individual freedom. If we're to understand twenty-five years of aggressive right-wing support for the unprecedented concentration of economic and political power, let's start at the beginning: with the ideas that helped make it work.

Acknowledgments

Many people helped me with this book, but a few stand out. My wife Kathleen has urged me for years to write something that would help explain what's been going on in the country. Steve Bronner helped refine the original idea. Mark Naison made important contributions throughout the project. David Cohen, Charlotte and Jon Collett, Jeff Frieden, Fran Furey, Ed Nathan, and Mike Spiegel have been very generous with their time and contributed many helpful suggestions. Long Island University's Provost Gale Haynes and Vice President Jeffrey Kane were extraordinarily supportive. It's not often that one gets a chance to thank loved ones, friends, and colleagues so publicly. I am delighted to do so now.

CHAPTER ONE

~

Crisis and Consolidation

Halfway through his first term, President Eisenhower wrote his brother a letter that sharply expressed the limits of acceptable political discourse. "Should any political party attempt to abolish social security, unemployment insurance, and eliminate labor laws and farm programs, you would not hear of that party again in our political history," he said. "There is a tiny splinter group, of course, that believes you can do these things. Among them are H. L. Hunt (you possibly know his background), a few other Texas oil millionaires, and an occasional politician or businessman from other areas. Their number is negligible and they are stupid."[1]

Fifty years later, Eisenhower's "tiny splinter group" has come to dominate American politics and is raising questions about matters that earlier generations had settled. Far from having disappeared, they have created a serious debate about whether Social Security should exist, whether evolution should be taught in school, whether the federal government should guarantee a minimum of health care, whether there should be any taxes on wealth at all, whether the United States should openly declare itself a "Christian nation," and whether Washington should obey the international laws of war or honor its treaty obligations. These questions have been resolved in most modern societies. But in the home of the world's most advanced economy and its most powerful military, they're on the table once again.

How did this happen? Why are these questions being seriously discussed? How did Eisenhower's "negligible number" of "stupid people" become so powerful? Why do we have to take them seriously?

It all began thirty years ago with a broad reaction to the social movements of the 1960s and 70s, defeat in Vietnam and the long crisis of Keynesian macroeconomic policy. As a set of intractable political problems came

1

together to doom Jimmy Carter's presidency, the foundations of the American postwar liberal consensus began to unravel. A forceful rejection of Carter's belief that the United States was in a period of decline gave rise to a strategy of national renewal that promised to restore strength to a country that was supposedly becoming dangerously enfeebled. It wasn't long before conservative ideologists were blaming national weakness on domestic policies that promoted social welfare and economic equality. A series of right-wing arguments acquired new traction even as they renounced important strands of American history and conflicted with many citizens' stated preferences.

As the 1970's economic crisis accelerated and the New Deal coalition began to splinter into a fractious coterie of "special interests," old arguments that aimed at reducing the state's welfare function became more credible than they had been for many years. Conservatives began to claim that public solidarity and social welfare sap national, community, and individual strength. A series of more focused arguments set the conditions for a broad assault on liberalism. Military requirements were more important than social welfare, so the democratic and egalitarian impulses of the late 1960s and early 70s had to be brought under control. The welfare state had become an incompetent and unjust obstacle to progress and freedom, so public policy must restore the market to its rightful place as the central organizing institution of a free society. Economic revival, moral renewal, social peace, and political integrity now meant resisting selfish women, disciplining irresponsible blacks, lowering taxes, and encouraging private investment. Liberty, individualism, and opportunity must be privileged over equality, solidarity, and redistribution. Inequality is an unavoidable feature of freedom, but economic growth can transform it into an instrument of progress, freedom, and vitality.

These arguments had been correctly dismissed as patently false and self-serving in an earlier period, but things were not the same at the end of the 1970s. The long-term crisis of Keynesian macroeconomics was undermining liberals' happy expectation that an expanding economy would enable them to organize political life around a set of mildly egalitarian policies. As the postwar social order's foundations began to shift, a newly emboldened Right developed a set of "positive" positions that supplemented its traditional attacks on social welfare. Conservatives had always defended wealth and privilege, but they began to craft a populist language of national renewal and individual strength during the late 70s. A forward-looking vision emphasized economic growth, political liberty, and individual opportunity for hard-working, besieged middle-class Americans. This view merged with a familiar negative critique of a grasping and ignorant state bureaucracy that had supposedly yielded to the blackmail of unproductive and parasitical minorities. Former reactionaries suddenly became visionaries, all the more so because much of the leadership and many of the institutions that had been associated with social welfare simply collapsed.

The long decline of the New Deal coalition paralyzed Carter's presidency and prepared the ground for the contemporary Right. But a powerful group of immediate events helped undermine the postwar consensus that had stabilized the national hegemony of the Democratic Party. A thirty-year period of social policy came to an end in a toxic environment of political scandal, racial tension, economic stagnation, runaway inflation, shattered dreams, national distress, and tax revolt.

The Keynesian Dead End

Until the great economic expansion of the early 20th century, most economic thought had revolved around overcoming scarcity and producing enough to satisfy basic human needs. But the appearance of a modern industrial economy began to shift the earlier emphasis on production to a preoccupation with consumption. This process that had been under way for some time before the Great Depression reshuffled the nation's political deck of cards.[2] After flirting with the idea of reforming and supervising the economy's basic economic institutions, President Roosevelt had settled on using fiscal and monetary policy to stimulate consumption so as to increase production and spread prosperity to wider sections of the population. The "second New Deal" was shaped by his conviction that the best way to encourage consumption was through government spending. It was clear that the economy had more than enough productive power; the great problem of the Depression's early years had been the irrational combination of scarcity amidst surplus capacity. Some economists talked about "overproduction," but the term that really captured things was the obverse: "underconsumption."

Economists and politicians had always recognized the importance of consumption; what was new was the central place that it came to occupy. John Maynard Keynes challenged economic orthodoxy with his claim that consumption drove production and not the other way around. It followed, he said, that government policy should aim at increasing purchasing power instead of stimulating saving and investment. Keynes tied economic recovery, long-term stability, and general prosperity to the fortunes of consumers and the economic sectors associated with them. This position was relatively new. For decades, orthodox economists had relied on Say's Law of Markets to argue that consumption was the result of production. The very act of producing goods, they said, created purchasing power and stimulated demand. It followed that economic policy should favor producers. Tight money, low inflation, high interest rates, hostility to labor, regressive taxation, economic inequality, and opposition to social spending followed. But economic reality had the final say, and by the early 1930s it had become clear that consumption did not automatically follow production and that increased industrial output did not necessarily increase payments to the consuming population. Too much private and corporate savings and too much economic inequality could restrict purchasing power and delay recovery. If Keynes was right and consumption called forth production rather than the other way around, it followed that the chief remedy for economic hard times was more purchasing power.

Since the rich tended to save and not spend, the problem was how to get money into the hands of middle- and working-class consumers. Resolving this problem explained why Keynesianism had an implicitly egalitarian core. It drove FDR's economic thinking even after he abandoned the more aggressive regulatory and redistributionist impulses of the "first New Deal." Public works, federal loans to homeowners and small businesses, progressive taxation, federal credit mechanisms, unemployment insurance, Social Security, deficit spending, and similar measures created enormous constituencies for the New Deal's program of distributing wealth downward. Since the economy had the capacity to produce enough to meet everyone's needs, national economic policy was organized around reducing inequality and moving toward a regime of high wages, full employment, low prices, and mass purchasing power. For the next thirty years, federal policy tended to favor consumers over investors, accept progressive taxation and encourage the downward distribution of disposable income.

By the end of World War II, the government had committed itself to stimulating consumption by creating purchasing power and expanding the money supply. Broadly speaking, these fiscal and monetary policies came to be known as Keynesianism. Supplemented by direct spending on infrastructure and light supervision of some of the economy's core institutions, it provided the underpinnings for a remarkably successful political regime that continued for four decades after the Depression had ended. Large modern economies need a good deal of government regulation and public oversight, and Keynesianism was so durable because many powerful domestic constituencies rallied to its support. Trade unions, farmers, businesses organized around the mass production of consumer goods, retailers, the entertainment industry, real estate, and the financial institutions associated with them were important elements of the New Deal coalition and supported the long political dominance of the national Democratic Party.

Full employment, economic growth, and mass consumption rested at the heart of the federal government's domestic policy. They helped organize the long period of mild social reform and economic egalitarianism that characterized the "Golden Age." From the end of World War II through the mid-1970s, steady expansion created a large middle class of white Americans, assimilated newcomers, facilitated social mobility, eased tensions, spread prosperity, and blunted the edge of class conflict. A relatively open social structure, an ideology of individual advancement, a political system devoted to economic growth, and an understanding of democracy as access to the fruits of consumption defined "the American Way of Life." It didn't matter much whether the Democrats or Republicans dominated national politics. A bipartisan commitment to a high-wage, low-price economy meant reliable federal support for creating and extending mass purchasing power, the most important tools with which government planners could counter-act the tendency to recession. The European social democracies focused on social welfare, but it was consumption that provided the glue for American social cohesion and collective identity. Labor and capital agreed to organize a democracy of consumers, even if they fought pitched battles about protective legislation, the right to organize, tax policy, health insurance, and the organization of the workplace. None of this required racial or gender equality, but a mass consumers' republic did have a democratizing effect—so long as the economy delivered the goods.[3]

This postwar American social contract brought unprecedented prosperity and security to its enormous white middle class, a situation captured by John Kenneth Galbraith's 1958 characterization of "the affluent society." A growing consumer economy, a stable bipartisan political consensus, full employment, a patriotic and pacified working class, and a relatively generous set of welfare provisions characterized the period—all made possible by intelligent and moderate Keynesian macroeconomic policies. Everyone seemed to benefit. Employers were willing to pay relatively high wages so long as putting spending money in the hands of working-class consumers did not eat into profits or investment; labor got higher wages, important fringe benefits, access to the fruits of production, and a generous set of social protections; government got an expanding economy, higher tax revenues, social peace, and political stability. As long as economic expansion could be sustained, white Americans could look forward to a harmonious future of full employment, rising real incomes, relative economic equality, and substantial social welfare. The key to all this, though, was maintaining the right balance between production and consumption. Dramatic and prolonged inflation could threaten everything.

Government management of the business cycle meant deficit spending, reducing taxes, and financing public works in periods of recession or sluggish growth. The risk was limited, for a modest increase in inflation was a small price to pay for stimulating the economy and getting people back to work. The other side of Keynesianism was just as useful, for reducing consumer spending and raising government revenues through tax increases would stabilize the economy when it started growing too fast. That risk was a limited one, for a modest increase in unemployment was a small price to pay for cooling the economy down and avoiding inflation. Such methods were admirably suited to a liberal consensus that blended mild redistribution and social stability. After all, spreading purchasing power to wide sections of the population gave powerful support to what egalitarians had always wanted to believe.

Everything was fine so long as the underlying conditions for managing the economy remained stable. Keynesian stimulus methods, which every President had used since the Depression, would not be available if high rates of inflation and high levels of unemployment occurred together—something that had never happened. But the 1970s turned out to be different. The decade's high rates of inflation *and* unemployment—a phenomenon so new that analysts had to invent the term "stagflation"—undid the postwar consensus because it deprived government planners of the stabilizing instruments they had been using for decades.

At first blush, it seemed that the devilish pairing of inflation and recession was caused by the Vietnam War's huge deficits and President Johnson's refusal to weaken political support for the Great Society by raising taxes. But there was more at stake, for persistent stagflation marked the end of a long period during which the American economy was able supply large quantities of both guns and butter. The political and ideological consequences of this development turned out to be far more profound than anyone knew at the time. For twenty-five years, American cold war liberalism had been able to sustain high levels of spending for social welfare and the military. When OPEC's "oil shocks" of 1973 were added to the Vietnam War's unpaid bills, an intractable crisis announced the beginning of a twenty-year reorganization of the world economy. Epidemic levels of unemployment, homelessness, deindustrialization, capital flight, and social pathology characterized the most severe economic slump since the Great Depression. As social welfare payments ate up an increasing proportion of state revenue, a persistent "fiscal crisis of the state" threatened the foundations of the postwar consensus. It wasn't long before serious ideological and political challenges to postwar liberalism took shape as an insecure and threatened population began to entertain ideas it had been rejecting for years.

All this played itself out during Carter's presidency, but the Democratic Party had been under severe strain since the end of the 1960s. Right-wing arguments that liberals were responsible for national decline because of their toothless foreign policy, pandering to irresponsible students, retreats before crazed feminists, coddling of parasitical blacks and general inability to impose order built on a foundation that had been laid down before Carter became President. But it was during his term that the country's long-simmering economic difficulties precipitated a national political crisis.

In the end, it was stagflation that doomed Carter's presidency, ruined the Democratic Party, and opened the door to the Right. High unemployment meant that the old ways of dealing with inflation were no longer available, and the longer Carter temporized and sought to retain the allegiance of traditional Democratic constituencies, the worse the problem got. After OPEC launched a new round of price increases, the inflation rate went from 6.5% in 1977 and 7.7% in 1978 to a staggering 11.3% a year later. The political and ideological fallout turned out to be far more damaging than anyone understood at the time. Keynesianism had always held that unemployment was the biggest single danger to economic stability and growth. Whatever their party, Presidents had never hesitated to spend and inflate their way out of recessions and periods of high unemployment. Stagflation made all that impossible, and the ideological consequences were profound. A single and endlessly repeated message came out of the late 1970s: inflation had replaced high unemployment as the nation's most dangerous economic enemy. The success of this claim would lead Americans to tolerate the draconian policies of tight money, recession, high unemployment, and gutted social services that marked the end of an era.

Democratic-inspired social programs had two thrusts. One, originating in the New Deal, benefited the organized working class, was universal in its coverage, and tried to reward the vast majority of productive citizens. The other, which roughly corresponded to Lyndon Johnson's War on Poverty, was aimed at the poor and seemed to benefit blacks in disproportionate numbers. As long as the rosy glow of the civil rights movement could be sustained by an expanding economy and higher incomes, many Americans supported the Great Society's social programs. But the stagflation of the late 70s attacked that willingness at its root. In a period of anemic growth the Right was able to drive a wedge between the white working class and the black poor by attacking anti-poverty programs as inefficient and immoral failures. Republicans could make good on their argument that the Democrats had mismanaged the economy and that their long love affair with state programs and social welfare made them unable to resolve a whole new set of problems.

All this shaped the period's great tax revolts. Beginning with Proposition 13 in 1978, tax-cutting and service-slashing initiatives swept the nation as more than twenty states followed California's lead. Inflation pushed them all to the right as a new generation of conservative activists demanded tax cuts, discipline, and austerity. Inexorable economic pressures were fracturing the Keynesian political coalition. Rising taxes were directly affecting millions of middle-class families and making them susceptible to right-wing arguments that the welfare state was taking money from the overtaxed and productive and giving it to the idle and undeserving. The entire argument was heavily coded for race and would have fallen on deaf ears in an earlier period, but stagflation made it possible for the attack on liberal social policy and the welfare state to develop some traction. When the tax system was flat for the Democrats' working- and middle-class constituencies, when incomes and productivity were growing, and when both unemployment and inflation were low, it was possible to maintain the alliance between the working and middle classes and the poor. It was in these conditions that the Democrats had won elections and organized social welfare programs like Medicaid, AFDC, Food Stamps, and Head Start. These programs did not directly benefit those whose taxes were paying for them, but as long as economic conditions were generally getting better it was possible to finance them without incurring broad hostility. When this situation changed during the middle and late 70s, it caught the Democrats completely by surprise. They had never been in this position before, and it took them a while to react.

Political Fallout

On August 6, 1979, President Carter appointed Paul Volcker to head the Federal Reserve with a bipartisan mandate to bring inflation under control. That day announced a dramatic reorientation of American economic doctrine and domestic politics. The steady expansion that had provided the material base for Keynesian stimulus and welfare policies came to a sudden halt as Volcker initiated a determined attack on inflation. As the Fed cut back the money supply and drove interest rates to nearly 20%, a brutal austerity that had been politically impossible in an earlier period succeeded in wringing inflation out of the economy. But the economic and political price was ferocious. Two recessions, a 10% reduction in manufacturing output and median family income, and an official unemployment rate of 11% set the stage for a new political regime, an increasingly coherent set of conservative ideas, and the steady transfer of wealth to those at the top.

As recession persisted, unemployment remained high, and real wages fell, a new consensus began to take shape. It was led by an investor and creditor class that had begun to mobilize in the mid-70s because its interests were directly threatened by inflation. The domestic and international political repercussions were dramatic and reflected general patterns, for the transition to a high-interest rate, low-inflation political economy was linked to governments of the right throughout the industrialized world. Even though President Reagan quickly turned away from balanced budgets by combining tax cuts and massive increases in military spending, the interests of investors had become central to the future of every major capitalist power. This was reflected in ideology and politics, and it wasn't long before policies long associated with finance acquired a mass base they had been lacking. Retirees, white-collar workers, small businessmen, and other sectors of the population joined forces with the traditional deficit hawks on Wall Street to "Whip Inflation Now." It would have been impossible for most politicians to accept a 10% increase in unemployment as the price for satisfying Wall Street in an earlier period, but by the end of the 1970s austerity had become a viable strategy.

A powerful political and ideological project began to take shape that would become known as the "Washington consensus." Anti-inflationary fiscal and monetary policy, tax and spending cuts, privatization, and deregulation became the centerpieces of a new set of understandings that would have been inconceivable a few years earlier. If the country could no longer have it both ways and inflation was now a more serious enemy than unemployment, it followed that the interests of businessmen, investors, and those who save were to be privileged over those whose main sources of income were wages and salaries. The choice between unemployment and inflation is a choice between capital and labor, and the Right was perfectly clear about where it stood. As it became fashionable to attribute the country's many problems to inflation and the Keynesian-influenced liberalism that was associated with it, the stage was set for a wide-ranging assault on the foundations of the welfare state and economic equality.

The period's economic decline meant an erosion of corporate profits, but it turned out that there was much more at stake. Core American institutions had been weakened by years of turmoil, foreign policy seemed disorganized, international competition was sharpening, and the social compact that had regulated domestic affairs was coming under severe strain. Ever since the end of the Depression, labor had accepted its inferior standing on the shop floor and the logic of profit as the organizing principle for particular plants and for the economy as a whole. In turn, business recognized unions, sought a stable work force, provided generous benefits, and paid high wages. A large state sector stabilized the economy and managed the business cycle. A limited set of social welfare programs completed the basic architecture of the Keynesian welfare state.

Stagflation subjected that arrangement to serious strain and prompted a broad and comprehensive political mobilization of American business. Much of its animus was initially directed at the regulatory agencies that had emerged during the late 1960s and 70s. The Environmental Protection Agency, the Occupational Safety and Health Administration, the Consumer Product Safety Commission, the Mine Safety and Health Administration, and the Equal Employment Opportunity Commission were particularly offensive because they demanded that employers put political or ethical goals at the center of business decisions. High corporate and progressive income taxes to finance the Great Society, chronic government deficits, expanding income maintenance programs, and other features of the welfare state soon drew the fire of business executives. Underlying all of these specific complaints was the fear that a "rising tide of entitlements" was choking American politics and threatening the viability of free enterprise. Encouraged by business itself, Americans had come to expect a rising standard of living and greater economic security. In the new view of many executives, this behavior created a vicious cycle: displeased when the private sector could not deliver, people turned to government to fill the gap between their expectations and economic capacity. Conservative economists warned that as government spending and regulation increased, less private capital would be available, the rate of investment would slow down, and the economy would deliver less. By the mid-1970s, wide swaths of American business had decided to move against decades of public policy.

They mobilized in response to a situation that they knew was as political and ideological as it was economic. The crisis was so broad that it could not be addressed by individual corporations using their own resources or by a narrow political project that proposed discrete, limited responses to a particular set of problems. Business saw an entire social order veering out of control and concluded that only a massive and comprehensive effort could set things right. Kevin Phillips reports that "a sampling of 1,844 *Harvard Business Review* readers in 1975 found nearly three-quarters extremely pessimistic about the U.S. commitment to private property and limited government surviving the next decade. At a series of meetings held by the business-sponsored Conference Board in 1974–75, the corporate executives in attendance agreed that the future of the American free enterprise system was extremely problematic."[4] Indeed, between 1968 and 1977, the percentage of Americans who thought that businesses were pursuing a fair balance between their profits and the public interest had dropped from 70 to 15%.[5] Business reacted aggressively to this perceived crisis of legitimacy. More was involved than some bad policies, or even a particularly ineffective regime. A broad response wasn't long in coming.

Rejecting the Keynesianism that had enriched it for decades, corporate America began to mobilize behind a distinctly right-wing program. Whether it was forming the Business Roundtable, strengthening the Chamber of Commerce, dramatically increasing contributions to conservative political candidates, supporting right-wing think-tanks like the American Enterprise Institute, the Hoover Institution, and the Heritage Foundation, or funding conservative legal foundations, talk radio, and student newspapers, the mobilization of business was rapid, thorough, and effective. By 1980, corporations and trade associations operated half of all lobbying offices in Washington and contributed about 60% of all PAC money that went to House and Senate candidates.[6] The effort went far beyond trying to influence policy on a specific number of narrow issues. It aimed to change thirty years of social policy, and its target was the national government.

No one proved better able to guide the developing offensive than Irving Kristol. Written in 1978, his *Two Cheers for Capitalism* called on business to organize itself, "think politically," and save both American civilization and the cause of freedom. The "father of neo-conservatism" knew that this wouldn't be easy. Corporations had become deeply unpopular with a population that had come to judge them on the basis of broad political and social expectations. Kristol knew that things had changed. Executives could no longer claim that their job was simply making money, but that didn't mean that they had to obey a public agenda created by their fiercest critics. If the population was animated by some sense of "the public interest" and expected businesses to act accordingly, then Kristol called on corporations to shape popular expectations of just what that "interest" might be. Besieged as it was by international communism, third-world nationalism, and domestic criticism, it was high time for business to become politically active. Failure to do so risked everything, Kristol warned: "if corporations are going to be able to resist the total usurpation of their decision-making powers by government, they must create a constituency—of their stock-holders, above all—which will candidly intervene in the 'political game' of interest-group politics, an intervention fully in accord with the principles of our democratic system."[7] The future depended on the success of this effort. Kristol minced no words as he warned business leaders how high the stakes were. "In some ways," he said, "it may be the most important question confronting our liberal-capitalist society. There can be no doubt that, if business as an occupation and businessmen as a class continue to drift in popular opinion from the center of respectability to its margins, then liberal capitalism—and our liberal political system with it—has precious little chance of survival."[8]

Kristol's call to businessmen was phrased as part of a project for limited government that would protect property and facilitate the development of markets. But there was more—a dangerous and pernicious enemy was at hand, he said, and conservatives should have no illusions about the magnitude of the task that lay ahead. A "new class" of educated, anti-business intellectuals had come to maturity in the aftermath of the social and anti-war movements of the period, and it was seeking to reshape the foundations of American civilization. It intended to replace the core institution of American history—the free market—with a redistributionist state that will serve its goal of social transformation. "The elitist attitude," Kristol announced, "is basically suspicious of, and hostile to, the market precisely because the market is so vulgarly democratic—one dollar, one vote. A civilization shaped by market transactions is a civilization responsive to the common appetites, preferences, and aspirations of the common people. The 'new class'—intelligent, educated, and energetic—has little respect for such a commonplace civilization. It wishes to see its 'ideals' more effectual than the market is likely to permit them to be. And so it tries always to supersede economics by politics—an activity in which *it* is the most competent—since it has the talents and the implicit authority to shape public opinion on all larger issues."[9] Political liberalism had become a threat to prosperity and freedom.

Kristol announced that social reform was now elitist and that democracy was to be found in market relations. Since liberalism's "new class" relied on the regulatory and redistributionist state, he called for an unambiguous defense of the market. But he feared that business was laboring at a great disadvantage—one that it could reverse if only it knew what to do. The "new class" had spent years developing its position. It was expressed as environmentalism, consumer planning, and economic equality, but common to them all was a drive toward state regulation of property in the name of some higher ethical or political purpose known only to the intelligentsia. This top-down, statist managerialism was liberalism's basic impulse. If the governmental bureaucracy acquired the power to politicize the economy in this way, then "we shall move toward some version of state capitalism in which the citizen's individual liberty would be rendered even more insecure."[10] The market has its own logic, said Kristol, and freedom requires that government authorities refrain from interfering with it.

Kristol's attack on equality, regulation, and redistribution wasn't new. What was new was an environment that made it more credible than it had been for a generation. Markets and businessmen are misunderstood, he said, and it's high time to mount an ethical defense of both. It's difficult to convince people that profits are moral, but Kristol knew that a right-wing notion of liberty must go beyond a simple celebration of money and a defense of wealth. It would be a while before conservative ideologues began to claim that individualism, profit, capitalism, and competition expressed the most important categories of morality and justice, but Kristol was there at the beginning.

He had a good foundation to build on. Inflation was the burning question of the time, and Kristol was convinced that Americans had gotten spoiled. Accustomed to decades of economic expansion and successful Keynesian economic management, they had come to expect too much from economic and political institutions. It was time to call a halt to the period's demanding social movements and end all talk of economic redistribution. Because it had not been contained by "the spirit of moderation," the period's "revolution of rising expectations" was threatening economic prosperity and political stability. And the chief culprit for the constant rise in expectations was Keynesian liberalism, no longer able to deliver on the many promises it had been making since the end of World War II. Acutely aware of the possibilities that were opening up, Kristol was hopeful that economic difficulties might disabuse a naive population of the fiction that it can have everything. But that would take some convincing.

For the moment, Kristol announced that he was not opposed to the New Deal as such. He wanted a "conservative" welfare state that provided a modest level of social support, abandoned all talk of intrusive regulation, did not try to organize programs of economic redistribution, and recognized the free market as the basic organizing principle of social life. Resting on an alliance between big business, small business, farmers, homeowners, and other proprietors, Kristol's alliance could be built only on the basis of an entirely new set of political ideas. It was important not to go too far. Acutely aware of how volatile the situation was, he recommended that business respect FDR's basic policies and institutions.

But the War on Poverty and the Great Society were different. With an acute understanding of the opening created by racial tension, Kristol announced that an appropriately "conservative welfare state" should stop short of Johnson's desire to inject utopian, irrelevant, and burdensome political and moral considerations into the management of the economy. If business was going to "think politically," it should root its argument where it was strong. "I assumed," he said, "that the large corporation wished to survive as a species of 'private enterprise,' that it wanted to avoid socialization and burdensome government regulation, that its survival as a business took precedence over its profit-and-loss statement for any single year, and that it wished to retain the good opinion of the American people. I therefore concluded that, as a *business institution*, it had on occasion to think politically rather than economically."[11]

Kristol understood what many of his critics did not: the mobilization of business needed a comprehensive political goal that initially aimed at deregulation but soon embraced a much broader set of objectives. A hostile ideological climate, lower profits, broad social crisis, a shift in power toward the affluent, the weakening of labor, fractures in the Democratic Party, and an element of good fortune accompanied an attack on state regulation that quickly broadened into a wide-ranging assault on the foundations of Keynesianism. The whole project was far more successful that Kristol had ever expected. By the late 1970s and early 80s business and finance had gained a level of influence over Washington that they had not possessed since the late 1920s.

What made this all the more remarkable was that it happened without a public mandate and with virtually no public discussion. A series of elections had affirmed the broad popularity of pro-business values during the Roaring Twenties, but this was not the case when corporate executives and lobbyists began their 1970s campaign. Business first organized to change what it perceived as a hostile ideological and political environment. Its newfound political power enabled it to work on popular opinion. For the most part, the ideological triumph of the contemporary Right followed, supported, and drew strength from the political mobilization of business and wealth.

What made all this possible? A thirty-year shift in political power has accompanied the country's accelerating economic polarization, and the Right's dramatic reorganization of public policy has mirrored both. The richest 1% of the country's population—those who enjoy an average income of $1 million and boast an average net worth eight to ten times that—now command 40% of the country's total assets, and their share has been increasing steadily since 1977.[12] This accounts for the right-wing turn in American politics, but it didn't happen just because the rich got richer. The broad liberal consensus that had organized public life for three decades was abandoned because business and the wealthy became highly politicized and militantly aggressive in the late 1970s. They took advantage of Keynesianism's inability to deal with the Carter inflation and gained strength because the Great Society had failed to eliminate poverty or end social disorder. The triumph of wealth has been the triumph of the Right that has served it. Its politics have become more sharply defined and radical as it's matured. "I'm going to come out strong after my swearing in," President George W. Bush said in anticipation of a second term, "'with fundamental tax reform, tort reform, privatizing of Social Security."[13] In fiscal matters, this means even lower income taxes for the rich, abolishing the inheritance tax, lower capital gains and corporate taxes, and the possibility of a regressive flat tax on consumption. Bush's talk of freedom, democracy, "tax relief," the genius of markets, "family values," and the virtues of free enterprise describe individual pieces of a larger project, but there's much more here than meets the eye. When all is said and done, the modern Right is about the aggressive use of state power to advance the interests of the rich.

Notes

1. President Dwight David Eisenhower, letter to his brother Edgar Newton Eisenhower, November 8, 1954, www.eisenhowermemorial.org/.

2. See Alan Brinkley, *The End of Reform: New Deal Liberalism in Recession and War* (New York: Vintage, 1995) and Lizabeth Cohen, *A Consumers' Republic: The Politics of Mass Consumption in Postwar America* (New York: Vintage, 2004).

3. Olivier Zunz, *Why the American Century?* (Chicago: University of Chicago Press, 2000).

4. Kevin Phillips, *Wealth and Democracy: A Political History of the American Rich* (New York: Broadway Books, 2002), p. 83.

5. *Ibid.*, p. 147.

6. David Plotke, "The Political Mobilization of American Business" in Mark Petracca, ed., *The Politics of Interests: Interest Groups Transformed* (Boulder: Westview Press, 1992), p. 176.

7. Irving Kristol, *Two Cheers for Capitalism* (New York: Basic Books, 1978), p. 23.

8. *Ibid.*, p. 84.

9. *Ibid.*, pp. 28–29. His emphasis.

10. *Ibid.*, p. 30.

11. *Ibid.*, p. 92. His emphasis.

12. Kevin Phillips, *op. cit.*, pp. 122, 127.

13. Ron Suskind, "Faith, Certainty and the Presidency of George W. Bush," *New York Times Magazine*, October 17, 2004.

CHAPTER TWO

~

Militarism

Shortly after the end of World War II, the British government informed the United States that it could no longer be responsible for the future of the Eastern Mediterranean. Washington quickly decided to step into the breach and on February 27, 1947, President Truman met with Congressional leaders in the White House. Undersecretary of State Dean Acheson spoke for ten minutes and told the legislators that an insurrection in Greece and neutralist pressures in Turkey were pushing relations with the Soviet Union to a turning point. Truman was determined to lead the country into a global campaign against "international communism" and he wanted Congressional support. Nobody seems to have asked, but Acheson assured the legislators that the future of Western civilization hung in the balance.

The Congressmen were silent for a few moments and then Senator Arthur Vandenberg spoke up. The influential Michigan Republican told Truman that Congress would help but warned him that big tax increases to support the right-wing Greek monarchy, build up the Turkish army, and escalate tensions with the USSR would not be popular. Vandenberg knew just what to do. If the President wished to sell his program, he would have to "scare hell out of the country."

Truman got the message—and so has every President since him. His announcement of the doctrine that bears his name was only the first step in a long bipartisan campaign to convince the population that the survival of freedom, democracy, and "the American way of life" required permanent struggle against a deadly and implacable enemy. It hinged on a series of claims that the Soviet Union was at the center of a coordinated drive for world conquest—a drive that could be defeated only if the United States remained united at home, interventionist abroad, and always ready to put "national security" ahead of everything else. Endlessly repeated, this simple set of ideas supported almost fifty years of American foreign policy during the Cold War. The fall of the Soviet Union briefly changed things, but September 11 has put threat and fear back at the center of the country's view of the world. All things considered, it was a remarkably smooth transition. Al Qaeda, Saddam Hussein, and terrorism have turned out to be perfectly good substitutes for the Soviet Union, Mao Tse-tung and communism.

None of this was inevitable, for political leaders have considerable resources and can respond to any situation with a variety of policies. The Bush administration understands this very well and has moved with remarkable clarity and swiftness to reorganize the country's approach to the rest of the world. Fanning a self-righteous and belligerent nationalist response to terrorist attack, it has placed unilateralism, preemption, and a readiness to use force at the center of American foreign policy.

This development has been paralleled by dramatic domestic changes. Until the mid-1970s, American politics pivoted around the themes of mild social reform at home and militant counter-revolution abroad. As long as the economy was expanding and a broad political consensus held steady, it was possible to fund expensive social programs and support a large military apparatus at the same time. Elements of a welfare state grew up in the shadow of a permanent war economy, but prosperity provided sufficient quantities of both guns and butter. The Democratic Party organized this period; when it came to an end in the aftermath of the Vietnam War, the ensuing crisis played out as a crisis of postwar American liberalism.

The Right had attacked center-left governments for years as "soft on communism." The Democrats had managed to fend off such claims by repeatedly demonstrating their willingness to use force, but that could work only as long as foreign interventions were successful and economic expansion continued to support the welfare state. What made the mid-70s unique was a combination of economic crisis, political weakness, and ideological confusion that provided the Right with an opportunity to begin a sustained assault on liberalism itself. The campaign started slowly and haphazardly but by end of the decade a group of "neo-conservative" thinkers had begun a broad attack on the foundations of American foreign policy. It wasn't long before their critique broadened to include domestic affairs. Defeat in Vietnam and political weakness at home enabled them to successfully identify liberalism with naiveté, weakness, and confusion.

The early neo-conservatives probably had no idea how wildly successful their campaign would be. Indeed, Irving Kristol, Norman Podhoretz, Jeane Kirkpatrick and others began as traditional cold-war liberal Democrats who defended the New Deal and didn't call for important domestic changes. Their initial claim was simple: faced with a Soviet drive for world domination, the United States needed to mount a more assertive foreign policy than had been possible in an earlier period of "detente." Conservatives had frequently called for a more confrontational foreign policy and had often been rejected, but changed domestic circumstances now meant changed consequences. The results would soon be felt across a wide range of political issues. Persistent economic crisis dissolved the old ties linking domestic and foreign affairs and it wasn't long before economic austerity drove the neo-conservatives to attack social reform in the name of anti-Sovietism. Pulled to the right by its insistence that guns were more important than butter, neo-conservatism came to personify the new politics of militarism in an age of scarcity.

It all began with claims of imminent danger and accusations of weakness. The central position was that the Soviet Union had sensed an opportunity to change the global balance of power in the aftermath of the American defeat in Vietnam and was moving aggressively to attain nuclear and conventional military supremacy. The neo-conservatives charged that Washington was unprepared to meet this challenge and they began a sustained propaganda campaign to alert the country to the dangers that supposedly threatened it. It was high time to end the restraint and caution that had marked foreign policy since the early 1970s, they said; international communism was on the march, and only American power could blunt its long drive for world domination.

Truman had mobilized America's central political institutions in support of the Cold War. The neo-conservatives were sure that the same thing was needed thirty years later. It was essential, they said endlessly, to put an end to the period's economic, military, political, and ideological weakness if the Soviet march was to be stopped. The Sixties had been bad enough, but the neo-conservatives warned that a broad national crisis was brewing and that it was time to abandon President Carter's inclination toward caution. A program of national renewal would restore strength, unity, and purpose to a society that was becoming dangerously divided and enfeebled. A more muscular foreign policy would require domestic cutbacks, and the neo-conservatives set about convincing the population that security from external threat was worth the price. Borrowing a page from Vandenberg and Truman, they began by trying to "scare hell" out of the country.

The Committee on the Present Danger

First creating and then fanning popular anxieties about the Panama Canal "giveaway," the rise of OPEC, Japanese economic growth, Palestinian resistance, the Iranian revolution, and Soviet military policy, a group of Washington insiders organized to demand a change in the country's priorities. Their names they picked succinctly identified the alarm they intended to stir up. Organizations like the Committee on the Present Danger, the American Security Council, and the Coalition for Peace Through Strength called for a definitive end to the "Vietnam Syndrome," attacked arms control, the United Nations, and detente, and sought to undermine the foundation of peaceful coexistence. The Soviet Union, they announced, had abandoned the military parity that had ordered international relations for years and was seeking nuclear and conventional supremacy. President Carter had allowed a "window of vulnerability" to develop that directly jeopardized American security.

The Democratic Party in general, and Carter in particular, came in for special treatment. The Nixon-Kissinger policy of detente rested on the false assumption that long-term cooperation with the Soviet Union was possible in a number of areas, the neo-conservatives said, but at least the GOP thought of detente as a form of containment. But President Carter—captured by what Podhoretz called the "new national mood of self-doubt and self-disgust" that had followed defeat in Vietnam—was abandoning containment altogether. There was something to the charge, for Carter was disposed to move past the expensive and paralyzing impasse of the Cold War. Arguing that the axis of international affairs now lay in North-South relations and seeking to place human rights at the center of American foreign policy, he had little use for the view that the Soviet Union was an inherently expansionist and aggressive power with whom no long-term accommodation was possible. This view made him a perfect target for cold war hawks, and the neo-conservatives were quick to denounce what they saw as unilateral disarmament. They charged that a complacent, confused, and frightened foreign-policy establishment, supported by the leading centers of public opinion, had developed a policy of strategic retreat and an ideology of national decline. A long campaign of renewal and rearmament would be required before things could turn around, for it would take time to frighten the country into believing that it was facing unprecedented threats to its very existence. But an urgent response was necessary in the short run. The Soviet Union's leaders sense internal weakness, Podhoretz and others repeatedly warned, and the only way to defeat their drive for world domination was to increase American military expenditures, solidify public opinion and prepare for confrontation. A full-court ideological campaign began to take shape. Carter was the most conservative Democratic President in years, but it became important to paint liberalism as a dangerous threat to the country's future.

The neo-conservatives started with foreign affairs.[1] Podhoretz knew full well that the battle was more about domestic public opinion than about the nature of the Soviet Union, and he acknowledged that his first concern was to prevent the "Finlandization" of the United States. The time had come to make sure that defeat in Vietnam did not precipitate a tendency toward pacifism, disengagement, or neutrality. The neo-conservatives stepped forward as the mature, hard-headed realists who would convince the American people to reject the President's naive dreams and shoulder their historic responsibilities. "The failure of the Carter administration's foreign policy is now clear to everyone except its architects," said Jeane Kirkpatrick, "and even they must entertain private doubts from time to time about a policy whose crowning achievement was to lay the groundwork for a transfer of the Panama Canal from the United States to a swaggering Latin dictator of Castroite bent." But it was the Soviet Union that always occupied center stage. A foreign policy based on wishful thinking was plainly inadequate to the challenge posed by an expansionist and amoral foe. Carter's foreign policy, said Kirkpatrick, had sacrificed vital national interests to abstract moral rules that no revolutionary and lawless adversary will ever accept. The result was disastrous. "While Carter was President there occurred a dramatic Soviet military buildup, matched by the stagnation of American armed forces, and a dramatic extension of Soviet influence in the Horn of Africa, Afghanistan, southern Africa, and the Carribean, matched by a declining American position in all these areas. The United States never tried so hard and failed so utterly to make and keep friends in the Third World."[2]

The neo-conservatives attacked the foundations of the President's view of the world, charging that Carter simply didn't think right about foreign affairs. And they were quick to broaden the issue beyond the President himself. He represented the end of a long process of liberal decay in their eyes, for his naiveté about the world was shared by elite opinion in general. Carter's failure to understand the Soviet menace, they said, meant that he could not grasp the nature of the times or understand who the country's real enemies were. Less hostile to self-described revolutionaries than to less dangerous "authoritarian" allies like Nicaragua's Somoza and the Shah of Iran, he systematically undermined America's friends and wildly overestimated the possibilities of cooperation with Third World radicals and their Soviet backers. His optimistic conviction that he could encourage democracy and prosperity in the Third World led him to a series of dangerous misjudgments, said Kirkpatrick. Like others, she found in Carter a fatal combination of misplaced idealism and lack of nerve—a judgment that led her to one of her most famous, if false, claims. "Although there is no instance of a revolutionary 'socialist' or Communist society being democratized," she said, "rightwing autocracies do sometimes evolve into democracies—given time, propitious economic, social, and political circumstances, talented leaders, and a strong indigenous demand for representative government."[3]

Whether they believed all this or not, the neo-conservatives were convinced that Carter's willingness to weaken some of America's most dependable anti-communist allies came from something deeper than a mistaken analysis of this or that particular situation. His entire viewpoint was hopelessly naive and objectively dangerous, they said. Like most liberals, they charged, the President couldn't grasp the elementary truth that right-wing authoritarians were less dangerous to the United States than any sort of communist regime. They attacked his cosmopolitan vision of a peaceful, integrated world of prosperous communities by charging that he was driving the country into a ditch. But illusions about the United Nations and the Third World were the least of it. The President's most dangerous misjudgment in Kirkpatrick's eyes was his belief that the Soviet Union had become a status-quo power. His hope that Cold War tensions could be reduced were based on his view that it would be better for everyone if US-Soviet relations did not occupy the world's center stage. The neo-conservatives were enraged by Carter's intention to take advantage of a historic conjunction of interests between the two superpowers. They understood that his desire to place economic development, human rights, and political democracy at the center of American foreign policy was incompatible with their view of the world. They painted a picture of an environment that was full of danger and a country that was unable to respond to threat because it was being misled.

The problem with Carter's foreign policy wasn't that it was in the hands of amateurs, leading neo-conservative leaders repeatedly declared; the problem was one of fundamental assumptions. Like others in the liberal establishment, they charged, Carter came out of the Vietnam experience with a mixture of shame, guilt, desire to move beyond a preoccupation with the USSR, and—above all—a hope that the Cold War was effectively over. But he had it all wrong, they said. The Soviet Union remained a dangerous and expansionist power, and Kirkpatrick reiterated her strong support for unilateral American interventions to deal with undesirable regimes. The President's intention to make development an important policy objective for the United States in Latin America, to complete the Panama Canal Treaty, to place human rights at the center of foreign policy, to cut back on military aid and reduce military spending in general, to normalize relations with Cuba—Kirkpatrick took all of these as evidence of a dangerously naive turn. The United States was drawing the wrong conclusions from defeat in Vietnam, and Washington had become unable to articulate a clear and credible conception of the national interest. Unimportant issues had become central and fundamental ones were being ignored. Carter's posture of "continuous self-abasement and apology vis-à-vis the Third World is neither morally necessary nor politically appropriate. Nor is it necessary or appropriate to support vocal enemies of the United States because they invoke the rhetoric of popular liberation. It is not even necessary or appropriate for our leaders to forswear unilaterally the use of military force to counter military force. Liberal idealism need not be identical with masochism, and need not be incompatible with the defense of freedom and the national interest."[4]

The developing neo-conservative argument hinged on convincing the population that the United States was facing a mortal threat, that Carter's response was dangerously inadequate, and that fundamental changes in American foreign and defense policy were needed. Several new organizations stepped up to the challenge. The Committee on the Present Danger, formed in 1976 to undermine popular and elite support for arms control and challenge the administration's arguments for the SALT II arms control treaty, turned out to be one of the most influential and successful organizations in recent history. It announced that its purpose was "to alert American policy makers and the public at large to the ominous Soviet military buildup and all its implications, and to the unfavorable trends in the U.S.-Soviet military balance. We were all convinced that international stability and peace with freedom required a strong America—one that could and would deter Soviet adventurism and aggression."[5] Initially bipartisan and composed of the likes of Paul Nitze, Richard Pipes, Donald Rumsfeld, Jeane Kirkpatrick, Dean Rusk, William Casey, Richard Perle, and others, the Committee was a Who's-Who of Washington Cold War hardliners.

"Our country is in a period of danger, and the danger is increasing," it announced dramatically. "Unless decisive steps are taken to alert the nation, and to change the course of its policy, our economic and military capacity will become inadequate to assure peace with security." Lest the reader have any doubt about the nature or the source of this mortal threat, the Committee named the villain. "The principal threat to our nation, to world peace, and to the cause of human freedom is the Soviet drive for dominance based upon an unparalleled military buildup."[6] This drive is constant, coordinated, and proceeds from a single center. It is propelled by a new Soviet strategic doctrine that represents a sharp break with the past and poses a direct challenge to fundamental American interests. The United States now faces a direct challenge from a powerful antagonist that has decided to make a bid for military supremacy and reorder the world based on unchallengeable strength.

Adopting George Kennan's famous analysis of "The Sources of Soviet Conduct," the Committee called attention to an historic and innate Russian tendency toward expansion. The Russian Revolution had made this impulse particularly dangerous because it was now served by a messianic ideology and the secretive rule of an unaccountable single party that can pursue its goals with great unity and patience. Carter had it all wrong, the neo-conservatives warned; the Soviet Union is not interested in maintaining the status quo. It remains a revolutionary power determined to overthrow the institutions and assumptions that had ordered the world before it began its rush for military supremacy. Moscow is a permanent enemy of stability and freedom in the best of times and a mortal foe in times of stress. Any commitment it makes to arms control and peaceful coexistence is tactical and temporary, for "the notion of a stable world order in which nations based on differing political principles cooperate rather than contend is alien to Soviet psychology and doctrine."[7] Everything it does, from pursuing detente to modernizing its economy and assuring everyone of its commitment to peaceful coexistence, serves its drive for world domination.

The Committee repeatedly assured the country that Carter's hopes for a long-term accommodation rested on a dangerous illusion. The Soviet Union's leadership, it said, had identified the United States as its chief enemy and is seeking "visible preponderance by outflanking and isolating Washington." This will enable Moscow "to transform the conditions of world politics and determine the direction of its development."[8] Soviet military doctrine, the Committee's experts repeatedly claimed, had changed dramatically. Buoyed by recent developments and encouraged by the lack of a firm American response, the Kremlin's first goal is to attain nuclear superiority:

This Soviet literature—not propaganda written for the West but Russians talking to Russians—tells us that the Soviets do *not* agree with the Americans that nuclear

war is unthinkable and unwinnable and that the only objective of strategic doctrine must be mutual deterrence. On the contrary, it tells us that they look at the
world quite differently; that war is an extension of diplomacy; that nuclear superiority is politically usable and that the Soviets must prepare for war-fighting, war-
surviving, and war-winning. The goal of their strategic nuclear program is not necessarily to start a war, but to attain a position of such nuclear superiority as to be
able to coerce our policy through a credible array of unacceptable risks. Yet they
also believe that the United States and its allies may well turn and fight when they
are driven into the ultimate corner. The Soviets therefore plan on the assumption
that war is quite possible even though not desirable or inevitable. They believe the
best deterrent is the capability to win and survive were deterrence to fail.[9]

Showing its keen understanding of Vandenberg's advice, the Committee
repeatedly claimed that the Soviets had developed a strategic doctrine of
winnable nuclear war. But that wasn't all. If the USSR had embarked on a
comprehensive strategy of worldwide domination, it had to do much more
than attain nuclear supremacy. Its conventional buildup also had to be seen
in light of its drive for world domination. Paul Nitze outlined the enemy's
grand strategy in such a way that no one could deny the need for an across-
the-board response. "For many years the focus of Soviet strategy has been on
Western Europe," he announced. "By achieving dominance over the Middle
East, they aim to outflank Europe. They propose to outflank the Middle East
by achieving controlling positions in Afghanistan, Iran, and Iraq on one
side, South and North Yemen, Eritrea, Ethiopia, and Mozambique on the
other, and by achieving the neutrality of Turkey to the north. Concurrently,
they are attempting to encircle China by pressure on Pakistan and India, by
alliance with Vietnam, and dominance over North Korea. The United States
is the only power in a position potentially to frustrate these aims. It is therefore seen as the principal enemy."[10]

Europe, the Middle East, Asia, Africa—the Russians were on the march
everywhere, and the United States had to confront them everywhere. Neither arms control nor American restraint had affected Soviet military doctrine or political behavior, said the neo-conservatives. If the enemy could
restructure world affairs on the basis of military supremacy, then nothing
would stand in the way of communist world domination. The Committee
repeatedly assured the country that a time of mortal danger was fast
approaching. "We are convinced," said former ambassador and longtime
Washington insider Max Kampelman, "and there is widespread agreement
among knowledgeable experts, that *if past trends continue, the USSR will
within several years achieve strategic superiority over the United States*."[11] This

would be a catastrophe of historic dimensions and would allow the USSR to apply "decisive pressure" on the US in situations of conflict. The survival of freedom around the world was at stake and American military power was the only guarantor of democracy. "Soviet pressure, when supported by strategic and conventional military superiority, would be aimed at forcing our general withdrawal from a leading role in world affairs, and isolating us from other democratic societies, which could not then long survive."[12] It was time for Washington to wake up from its self-induced torpor. None of the structures or policies associated with detente had weakened the Soviet drive for world-wide dominance. It was high time to jettison them—and the leaders associated with them. The insidious ally of an external communist menace was internal political weakness born of ideological softness and wishful thinking.

That meant the President first and the liberalism that supported him second. Carter's presidency energized a new and aggressive conservatism that rejected his embrace of limits, found his caution to be obnoxious, and prepared to do ideological battle for a reorganization of American domestic politics and foreign policy. By 1977, the neo-conservatives had turned violently against Carter and, with Podhoretz's *Commentary* as one of their chief organs, began a relentless attack on him, his policies, and his advisors. Their estimate of Soviet intentions turned out to be almost completely false, but accuracy wasn't the point. Creating an atmosphere of danger and threat would serve a variety of purposes. The Committee's initial anti-Sovietism was soon extended to defending Israel's occupation of the West Bank and rejecting Third World attempts to change the distribution of worldwide economic and political power. Its earlier complaints that Carter and other cold war skeptics like Cyrus Vance, Paul Warne, and Andrew Young were leading the Democratic Party to disaster became steadily more radical. Now the liberals were leading the whole country to disaster and betraying freedom around the world. Neo-conservative attacks were clear and concise: Carter and his advisors were selling the country short. They coddled Third World tyrants, allowed the Soviets to threaten democracy everywhere, exposed Israel to danger, cared more for America's adversaries than for the country itself, substituted fantasy for reality, invented a weak policy on human rights, and failed to see that arms control and SALT II were deadly traps that would result in a loss of will and the gradual impotence of the world's best hope for freedom. Since many of them were also becoming more conservative on social and racial issues, the split with Carter led many of them out of the Democratic Party altogether and by 1980 most were supporting Reagan.

The Committee knew that fear would not be enough for its campaign to succeed, so it fell back on patriotism to summon Americans to do their duty and make the required sacrifices. It was important to destroy the illusion that compromise and understanding with the Soviet Union were possible. The United States was not just another country, and no claims to moral equivalency would be tolerated. This was a struggle between good and evil. "There is a crucial moral difference between the superpowers in their character and their objectives," the Committee proclaimed in its very first document. "The United States—imperfect as it is—is essential to the hopes of those countries which desire to develop their societies in their own ways, free of coercion." Citizens of Guatemala, Iran, Zaire, Vietnam, Chile, Cuba and a host of other beneficiaries of Washington's attention during earlier administrations might have had something to say about this assertion, but Podhoretz knew that an alarmist call to arms would be more palatable if it were supplemented by appeals to American exceptionalism, national greatness, and historic mission. The neo-conservatives were developing a "new nationalism" to contest the old "culture of appeasement" and were convinced that the outcome of their drive to reshape American politics would be critical to the future of freedom and peace around the world. Since everything depended on political will and military power, it was essential that a new set of leaders help the country shed all liberal illusions about world affairs. Max Kampelman was optimistic. "If the soporific forces among us remain powerful, there is on the other hand a contrary tendency, and a very strong one, which has also been developing in the United States alongside the culture of appeasement. It is a tendency toward what might be called a new nationalism, and it carries with it the main hope we have now for saving ourselves from the alternatives of war or Finlandization that an unimpeded culture of appeasement is certain in the end to yield."[13] This wasn't the first time, nor would it be the last, when the Right charged liberals with appeasement. The United States was at a crucial point in her history, and the neo-conservatives defined that point ideologically. More was at stake than momentary disagreements or periodic attempts to seize advantage. "The two superpowers have utterly opposing conceptions of world order. The United States, true to its traditions and ideals, sees a world moving toward peaceful unity and cooperation within a regime of law. The Soviet Union, for ideological as well as geopolitical reasons, sees a world riven by conflict and destined to be ruled exclusively by Marxism-Leninism." There was only one conclusion to be drawn:

The Soviet Union, driven both by deep-rooted Russian imperial impulses and by Communist ideology, insists on pursuing an expansionist course. In its endless, probing quest, it attempts to take advantage of every opportunity to expand its influence. And military strength is more than ever the foundation underlying its policy. In order to maintain and increase the momentum of its expansion, the Soviet Union seeks to outstrip the United States and its allies in every category of military power, both in numbers and in technological sophistication. The strategists and political planners of the Soviet Union are trained to understand that military power is the essential guarantor to expanding political influence. It is therefore the first object of their policy to assure that guarantee.

Thus, it would be irrational as well as imprudent to ignore the military element in the Soviet-American relationship. Although the political, economic, and human aspects are each important, the military dimension is fundamental and potentially decisive.[14]

The "fundamental and decisive" nature of military force has been the heart and soul of neo-conservatism for twenty-five years. Convinced that it was time to move past "the tragic experience of Vietnam," the Committee insisted that the military balance between the United States and the Soviet Union was becoming dangerously one-sided. Large increases in American military spending and strengthening of the country's "commitment to leadership" were required if democracy was to survive. It had become essential to shed illusions, grow up, and spend a lot more money on arms. "If we continue to drift," it warned, "we shall become second best to the Soviet Union in overall military strength; our alliances will weaken; our promising rapprochement with China could be reversed. Then we could find ourselves isolated in a hostile world, facing the unremitting pressures of Soviet policy backed by an overwhelming preponderance of power. Our national survival itself would be in peril, and we should face, one after another, bitter choices between war and acquiescence under pressure."[15] The road back to a sane foreign policy was paved with national resolve, a willingness to use force, and a lot more weapons.

That meant that it was also paved with attacks on social welfare and economic justice. Many of the early neo-conservatives began their journey to the right from a familiar Cold War position of liberal anti-communism. Their foreign policy views would not have driven them out of the Democratic Party in an earlier period, but by the mid-1970s many were moving toward the GOP because they wanted rearmament more than anything else. The general economic slowdown of the mid- and late 70s drove them to resist all calls for increased social spending and economic redistribution. Increasingly organized around calls for domestic order and international anti-Sovietism, they worried that too many demands were being placed on too few resources.

Their suspicion of social reform—particularly of Johnson's Great Society—was driven by the fear that increased social spending would interfere with a more aggressive foreign policy. As journals like *Commentary* and a host of new right-wing organizations continued their attacks on alleged liberal weakness and appeasement, foreign and domestic affairs came together. Fewer resources required reductions in social spending. Former veterans of the "vital center" school of American politics, many of the first neo-conservatives were ready to abandon the old commitment to anticommunism abroad and mild social reform at home. If the country could no longer afford guns and butter, it would have to do with less butter.

Their attention to public opinion marked the neo-conservatives' growing sophistication. Earlier elements of the Right hadn't bothered to appeal to the population, aware of their political unpopularity and secure in the knowledge that established wealth and privilege would quietly carry the day. Defeat in Vietnam signaled a short-term change in the way Americans thought of themselves in the world, but a distinctly conservative appeal to militarism and its "new nationalism" was gaining legitimacy. As public opinion began to register slowly-increasing support for more military spending, President Carter responded with a more bellicose foreign policy toward the end of his term. The Iranian Revolution and the Soviet invasion of Afghanistan were important catalysts, but the Right's relentless ideological campaign had popularized the view that the United States faced imminent peril and that military force remained the prime determinant of a nation's international influence. All this proved too much for Carter. As his administration entered its final year, an unmistakable pattern of yielding to the Right appeared. By 1980 his stated goals of nuclear disarmament and arms control, non-intervention, and reductions in military spending had disappeared. Military spending was rising, the Carter Doctrine legitimized foreign intervention, and a number of other measures were in the works. Carter could have articulated a stronger policy of interdependence and internationalism, but he tried to compromise with a far more ideological and tenacious foe and ended up losing the struggle.

Ronald Reagan's election marked the Committee on the Present Danger's formal accession to power and the triumph of the ideological framework within which it operated. Thirty-three officials of his first administration were members—including the President himself, who had joined in 1979. For all intents and purposes, it was during the Reagan years that the Committee won the debate it had begun in the late 1970s. The Great Communicator was just the man to make its arguments. The Committee's attacks on SALT

II and its urgent warnings that a "window of vulnerability" had opened turned out to be as false as Kennedy's earlier claims about a Soviet "missile gap"—but it didn't matter. As the White House pushed the most dramatic military rearmament since JFK's administration, it signaled how much things had changed by turning decisively against the welfare state. Reagan came to temper his militancy on both counts but he had long accepted the basic neo-conservative argument about the connection between foreign and domestic policy. He ended up pursuing a rather classical foreign policy with respect to the Soviet Union, but his willingness to sacrifice social welfare announced the end of Cold War liberalism. If increased spending for domestic programs would make the international struggle against the Soviet Union and its proxies more difficult, it had to be abandoned. If notions of economic redistribution were becoming popular, they had to be defeated. The Committee's work of creating an environment of fear and threat had been wildly successful.

The neo-conservatives were quick to claim credit for the collapse of the Soviet Union and the end of the Cold War on American terms. A reexamination of foreign policy was inevitable in the new environment created by a unipolar world, and it wasn't long before the Committee on the Present Danger's call to battle was succeeded by a second round of analysis. The world had changed, and neo-conservatism had changed with it. Breathless warnings of imminent danger now yielded to confident assertions of American power. Standing fast against communist threat now gave way to aggressively reordering the world. Hard-headed embrace of "authoritarians" now became spreading markets and democracy all over the world. Containment and roll-back now meant taking advantage of historic opportunity and reaping the fruits of victory. For all this evolution, though, a common project holds neo-conservatism together. The shared conviction that American military force is indispensable to world order and a willingness to speak of imminent peril link its two most successful institutions.

The Project for the New American Century

The Project for the New American Century is the direct heir to the Committee on the Present Danger and serves as one of the most important voices of contemporary neo-conservatism. Founded in 1997, it began its life with the same allegations of liberal weakness and vacillation as its predecessor—but now the international context had changed. Where the Committee made its living by warning of an imminent Soviet threat, the Project adapted to an international environment in which the United States stood unchallenged. Rearmament was no longer portrayed as a defensive measure necessary to save a threatened country; now the collapse of the Soviet Union gave Washington the chance to remake the entire world. Just as Jimmy Carter had been the Committee's target of opportunity, so Bill Clinton would serve as the Project's convenient foil. Personifying the continuity between new and old, Chairman William Kristol, son of Irving, introduced the new organization on its website. "The Project for the New American Century," he announced, "is a non-profit educational organization dedicated to a few fundamental propositions: that American leadership is good both for America and for the world; that such leadership requires military strength, diplomatic energy and commitment to moral principle; and that too few political leaders today are making the case for global leadership. The Project for the New American Century intends, through issue briefs, research papers, advocacy journalism, conferences, and seminars, to explain what American world leadership entails," he continued. "It will also strive to rally support for a vigorous and principled policy of American international involvement and to stimulate useful public debate on foreign and defense policy and America's role in the world."[16]

The leading lights of the Project for the New American Century, whose more aggressive name befits its more aggressive agenda, now sit at the very center of the American government. Elliott Abrams, Gary Bauer, John Bolton, William Bennett, Jeb Bush, Dick Cheney, Frank Gaffney, Donald Kagan, Zalman Khalilzad, Lewis "Scooter" Libby, Donald Rumsfeld, Paul Wolfowitz—they're all there, along with a sprinkling of first-generation neoconservatives like Midge Decter, Norman Podhoretz, and Paul Ikle. This continuity with an earlier generation of cold warriors notwithstanding, its basic position is far more radical than that of the Committee on the Present Danger. A changed international environment, it announced, means that the United States can—and should—do what is required to remake the world. Dramatic increases in military spending, confrontation with hostile regimes, preemptive action, contempt for international institutions, and a readiness to act unilaterally are the foundations of contemporary neo-conservatism. Like the rest of the modern Right, it has gotten steadily more radical as it's gotten older. This tendency was under way well before September 11, 2001. The "war against terror" has simply accelerated a trend that was already before anyone outside of Washington had heard of Osama bin Laden or Al Qaeda.

The Project's Statement of Principles purports to outline a "Reaganite policy of military strength and moral clarity." The collapse of the Soviet Union had raised widespread hopes that a "peace dividend" would permit increased spending for social welfare, but the Project quickly made its priorities clear and announced its intention to "rally support for American global leadership." Once again, the Right organized for ideological war against liberal weakness. American conservatives, the Project said, had to articulate a credible argument for increasing defense spending in a time of peace and prosperity. It announced its intention to convince the population to put arms before all else. As always, fear and threat were the trump cards.

Such an argument was difficult to sustain between 1997 and 2001, since the international environment was fairly calm and there wasn't a clear external danger to which the neo-conservatives could point. But the Project began to set the conditions for further developments. If it wasn't possible to "scare hell out of the country" yet, it could hint at unnamed menace and summon Americans to shoulder the burdens of leadership anyway. Borrowing a page from the Committee on the Present Danger, the Project began to point fingers and apportion blame. President Clinton's cuts in military spending and general inattention to international opportunities, it said, raised the danger that "we are jeopardizing the nation's ability to meet present threats and to deal with potentially greater challenges that lie ahead." These challenges were not specified, but the Project worried that "we seem to have forgotten the essential elements of the Reagan administration's success: a military that is strong and ready to meet both present and future challenges; a foreign policy that boldly and purposefully promotes American principles abroad; and national leadership that accepts the United States' global responsibilities." And, lest the nascent arguments for preemptive war be lost, the Project made them explicit. "If we shirk our responsibilities," it warned, "we invite challenges to our fundamental interests. The history of the 20th century should have taught us that it is important to shape circumstances before crises emerge, and to meet threats before they become dire."

Years before Al Qaeda was a gleam in George W. Bush's eye, the Project for the New American Century was laying the groundwork for his unilateralism, preemptive war, and militarism. It called for increasing defense spending, aggressively promoting national interests, and accepting "America's unique role in preserving an international order friendly to our security, our prosperity, and our principles." Since the United States faced no significant rivals and would be the only superpower for some time, the country's strategy should be one of maintaining its dominant position. But this didn't mean a conservative defense of the status quo. The Project's tone was belligerent, aggressive, and militant from the very beginning. But first it was important to settle matters domestically.

Lest the connection to the Committee on the Present Danger be lost, the Project published a long report, "Rebuilding America's Defenses," in September 2000—just before the Supreme Court decision that brought George W. Bush, and it, to the White House. The fall of the Soviet Union, ten years of prosperity and peace, and the absence of serious foreign threats did not deter it. "From its inception," the report reminded its readers, "the Project has been concerned with the decline in the strength of America's defenses, and in the problems this would create for the exercise of American leadership around the globe and, ultimately, for the preservation of peace."[17] Unfortunately, no single unitary threat like the USSR threatened the United States, so the Report had to limit itself to a series of vague threats and problems that would shape the future. A golden opportunity to "scare hell out of the country" wasn't far away, but the Committee made its immediate priorities clear. "Preserving the desirable strategic situation in which the United States now finds itself," it announced, "requires a globally preeminent military capability both today and in the future. But years of cuts in defense spending have eroded the American military's combat readiness, and put in jeopardy the Pentagon's plans for maintaining military superiority in the years ahead. Increasingly, the U.S. military has found itself undermanned, inadequately equipped and trained, straining to handle contingency operations, and ill-prepared to adapt itself to the revolution in military affairs. Without a well-conceived defense policy and an appropriate increase in defense spending, the United States has been letting its ability to take full advantage of the remarkable strategic opportunity at hand slip away."

It was the same old story with a slightly changed cast of characters. Calls for strong will, an activist government, and an assertive foreign policy linked the neo-conservatives' first two generations. Just as the Committee on the Present Danger had always used the Soviet Union to talk about the United States, so the Project for the New American Century addressed itself to widespread hopes that the huge budget surpluses of President Clinton's second term could be used for domestic purposes. The neo-conservatives had claimed that Carter's naive liberal blindness had led the nation to the brink of catastrophe. Reagan had saved the day, but history had come full circle. Once again, said the Project, a naive and confused Democratic President was letting a decisive advantage slip away. The "peace dividend" began to disappear in a blizzard of vague warnings about unspecified future threats. It wouldn't be long before it was formally laid to rest and the search for a malignant, threatening foreign enemy to replace the Soviet Union ended with the perfect candidate.

Barely six months after it was organized, the Project had its man. On January 26, 1998, Elliott Abrams, William J. Bennett, John Bolton, Francis Fukuyama, Zalmay Khalilzad, William Kristol, Richard Perle, Donald Rumsfeld, Paul Wolfowitz, and others sent a letter to President Clinton. "Dear Mr. President," they began, "we are writing you because we are convinced that current American policy toward Iraq is not succeeding, and that we may soon face a threat in the Middle East more serious than any we have known since the end of the Cold War. In your upcoming State of the Union Address, you have an opportunity to chart a clear and determined course for meeting this threat. We urge you to seize that opportunity, and to enunciate a new strategy that would secure the interests of the U.S. and our friends and allies around the world. That strategy should aim, above all, at the removal of Saddam Hussein's regime from power. We stand ready to offer our full support in this difficult but necessary endeavor."[18]

The Project never expected Clinton to accept its generous offer, but that wasn't the point. Just as its predecessor had attacked Carter in the hope of changing American leadership, so the Project's letter was looking to a Republican future. It warned that American allies can't be depended on to contain Saddam Hussein and that the United Nations will be unable to determine whether Iraq is making chemical, biological, or other weapons of mass destruction. But it didn't matter, for the Project was careful to have it both ways. "Even if full inspections were eventually to resume, which now seems highly unlikely, experience has shown that it is difficult if not impossible to monitor Iraq's chemical and biological weapons production." That means that "we will be unable to determine with any reasonable level of confidence whether Iraq does or does not possess such weapons." If inspections revealed the true nature of the Iraqi threat, the case for "regime change" would be easy to make. If inspections couldn't reveal the true nature of the Iraqi threat, the case for "regime change" would be even easier.

So the letter came to the obvious conclusion. In the end, it didn't matter whether Saddam Hussein was producing any weapons at all. It wasn't even important if the truth couldn't be known, even though "such uncertainty will, by itself, have a seriously destabilizing effect on the entire Middle East." In the absence of any evidence to support its claims about the Iraqi threat, the Project told Clinton that it would be prudent to assume the worst. Since Saddam either has or will be "almost certain" to acquire the capacity to deliver weapons of mass destruction if he stays in power, there's only one thing to do. The stakes were high, for "the security of the world in the first part of the 21st century will be determined largely by how we handle this threat." The letter called on Clinton to move past his crippling reliance on international law, multilateral institutions, and foreign allies.

> Given the magnitude of the threat, the current policy, which depends for its success upon the steadfastness of our coalition partners and upon the cooperation of Saddam Hussein, is dangerously inadequate. The only acceptable strategy is one that eliminates the possibility that Iraq will be able to use or threaten to use weapons of mass destruction. In the near term, this means a willingness to undertake military action as diplomacy is clearly failing. In the long term, it means removing Saddam Hussein and his regime from power. That now needs to become the aim of American foreign policy.

Saddam Hussein was a mortal threat to the United States if was pursuing weapons of mass destruction, and he was a mortal threat if he wasn't. Having it both ways was an added plus, for the Project was still pushing Vandenberg's basic story line. It was as easy to "scare hell" out of the country in conditions of unchallenged military supremacy as it was when the Soviet Union loomed as a mortal threat. And in both cases, the story meant that hopes for social progress and domestic welfare would be dashed. The Project's letter announced that militarism had acquired a logic and a momentum all its own.

It turned out that President Clinton wasn't interested in the Project's generous offer of help and four months later a follow-up letter was sent to the Republican Congressional leadership. The Honorable Newt Gingrich and The Honorable Trent Lott must have had some idea of what was coming, for the letter complained of Clinton's unwillingness to protect the country from the mortal danger emanating from Baghdad. "Instead of further, futile efforts to 'contain' Saddam, we argued that the only way to protect the United States and its allies from the threat of weapons of mass destruction was to put in place policies that would lead to the removal of Saddam and his regime from power. The administration has not only rejected this advice but, as we warned, has begun to abandon its own policy of containment." Once again, a Democratic administration's weakness, naiveté, and appeasement were leading the country to disaster. Signed by the same authors of the January overture to Clinton, it went on to say that "the American people need to be made aware of the consequences of this capitulation to Saddam." A loss of American credibility would allow Iraq to intimidate its neighbors and dominate the entire Middle East, make American troops in the area vulnerable to attack, and permit Saddam to control much of the world's oil. Looking toward the elections, the authors called on the Congressional leadership to assume its historic responsibilities and rescue the country from yet another "capitulating" Democratic President. "Now that the administration has failed to provide sound leadership, we believe it is imperative that Congress take what steps it can to correct U.S. policy toward Iraq. That responsibility is especially pressing when presidential leadership is lacking or when the administration is pursuing a policy fundamentally at odds with vital American security interests. That is now the case" and it is essential that American policy be dedicated to the overthrow of the Iraqi government. Since the appeasing and capitulationist Democrats couldn't be trusted, the Project looked to its real friends.

Most of the basic arguments the Bush administration used to justify the invasion of Iraq were in place well before September 11, 2001. So were the individuals making them, for the Project for the New American century is to George W. Bush what the Committee on the Present Danger was to Ronald Reagan. Its recommendations about Iraq, nurtured in the years when the neo-conservatives were out of power, were perfectly acceptable to an administration whose very first foreign policy steps were to dismiss the Kyoto Protocol, renounce arms control treaties with Russia, insult the United Nations, and refuse to recognize the International Criminal Court.

At first the Bush administration was having some trouble selling all this to the American people, who were not sufficiently convinced that Iraq represented a dangerous menace and were decidedly unenthusiastic about a war for "regime change" in Baghdad. But things can change very quickly—particularly if one is prepared to take advantage of opportunity. Ensconced in power well before the terrorist attacks of September 11, 2001, the neo-conservatives were ready, willing, and able to use national tragedy in service of an agenda that had been in place for years. They had started out as aggressive triumphalists in a world of nation-states, but now they knew that national catastrophe and a "war on terror" allowed them to apply Vandenberg's advice in a changed environment. Fusing Saddam Hussein's Iraq and Osama bin Laden's Al Qaeda, the administration began to insist that an attack on Iraq would provide safety and security in a world now teeming with murderous enemies and unreliable friends. Not much more was needed. The Project's early vagueness about the country's enemies had been replaced by George W. Bush's single, deadly certainty.

Worried about their safety and convinced of their country's innocent rectitude, many Americans were open to the argument that "the exercise of American power is key to maintaining what peace and order there is in the world today." If the first generation of neo-conservative thinkers had talked about the need to defend the country from external threat, the second is far more radical and aims at a revolutionary transformation of world politics. The Project for a New American Century wants to make it clear that every place on the planet is of strategic interest to the United States. "Imagine a world in which the U.S. didn't exercise this power," asks its Executive Director. "Who would handle a nuclear-armed North Korea? Who would prevent the one-party state of China from acting on its pledge to gather democratic Taiwan into its fold? Who would be left to hunt down Islamic terrorists increasingly interested in getting their hands on weapons of mass destruction? Who could have contained, let alone defeated, a tyrant like Hussein, preventing him from becoming the dominant power in the Middle East? Who can prevent the Balkans from slipping back into chaos? Who is going to confront regimes like those of Iran, Syria and Libya as they rush to get their own weapons of mass destruction? Given how little most of our allies and critics spend on defense, certainly not them."[19] Asia, Europe, the Middle East—just like its predecessor, the Project for the New American Century wants to be clear about what it means to be a world power. Nor is this a selfish matter of national pride or material interest. The exercise of American power is good for everyone, for the United States offers a beacon of hope to all mankind.

William Bennett, yet another PNC member and co-signatory of its letters, stepped forward to make the argument for "moral clarity and the war on terrorism." Trying to supply an answer to "why we fight," he fondly recalled the moment when vicious attack made possible a welcome distinction between good and evil. His hope that "moral clarity" can support a war to defend civilization is shared by other neo-conservative commentators and had supplied a set of easy certainties that have been endlessly repeated by the Bush administration and its supporters. A worldwide struggle against evil requires constant work on the domestic front, and Bennett was eager to rise to the challenge. One of the Project's original founders who had been agitating for an invasion of Iraq long before September 11, he knew that defending world civilization required firm American leadership. But years of moral relativism and claims of moral equivalence had weakened the country's moral fiber and eroded its ethical certainty. As always, a domestic enemy wasn't hard to find. "Weakening that consensus, sowing and reinforcing doubt about our purposes and our methods, was in fact the goal of the peace party. Its favored means: casting a shadow of moral doubt over our righteous and justified anger, promoting the idea that our tendency to jingoistic aggression could only be checked by a countercommitment to nonviolence."[20] His assertion that "we harbor no plans to conquer anyone" stood in some contradiction to the Project's letters that he had signed, but his desire to attack Iraq didn't change his intention "to place our response on an unassailable moral footing."[21] This meant a patriotic message of moral certainty and political authoritarianism leavened by nostalgic appeals to an upright past. "It used to be the case," he sighed nostalgically, "that a child in this country was brought up to revere its institutions and values, to identify with its customs and traditions, to take pride in its extraordinary achievements, to venerate its national symbols. What they taught along these lines in the home was reinforced in the community and the schools; what may have been wanting in the home was supplied by the community and the schools, and reinforced by public authority. The superior goodness of the American way of life, of American culture in the broad sense, was the spoken and unspoken message of this ongoing instruction in citizenship. If the message was sometimes overdone, or sometimes sugarcoated, it was a message backed by the record of history and by the evidence of even a child's senses. In the long saga of misery and inhumanity that is history . . . the American achievement is high and unique."[22]

Things were great when upstanding patriots were sure of their country's superior goodness, when reverence, identification, pride, and veneration were incubated in families, taught in schools, and "reinforced by public authority." But this simple historical morality has been sabotaged by an anti-American, morally degenerate cultural elite that insists on teaching the young something different. "Today the pyramid is inverted, the shoe is on the other foot. Whatever may or not be instilled at home, little schoolchildren in our country are routinely taught to believe that America represents but one of many cultures and in principle deserves no automatic preference, that there is no such thing as a better or worse society, that cultural values different from our own need to be understood and accepted in a spirit of sympathetic tolerance and that, all things considered, we ourselves have at least as much to answer for as to be proud of." Bennett wants to be clear about what's at stake when foreign assassins have domestic friends. Liberalism's misguided discomfort with patriotism, its conviction that all nations are part of a community of equals, and its insistence that none can be automatically held superior to others reflects a weak, unprincipled relativism that makes value judgment and moral action impossible. And the ability to make sharp and uncompromising distinctions between good and evil is precisely what's called for in the aftermath of terrorist attack. Like most other neo-conservatives, Bennett makes it clear that international law and multilateral institutions cannot be allowed to interfere with the exercise of American military power in service to moral superiority. This conviction serves as a guide to a whole generation of neo-conservative thinkers and policy-makers and supplies a ready answer to those who ask "why we fight." After all, Bennett asks at the end of his book, "how can we expect our children to meet tomorrow's hour of emergency as we would wish them to if we neglect to instruct them in civic devotion, and love of country, and in the certitude that the United States is one nation, indivisible?"[23] Leavened by Al Qaeda, neo-conservatism's hard-headed appeal to national interest had laid claim to American claims of moral rectitude and historical uniqueness.

> Our country *is* something to be proud of, something to celebrate. Why should we shrink from saying so? A sober, a sophisticated study of our history demonstrates beyond cavil that we have provided more freedom to more people than any nation in the history of mankind; that we have provided a greater degree of equality to more people than any nation in this history of mankind; that we have created more prosperity, and spread it more widely, than any nation in the history of mankind; that we have brought more justice to more people than any nation in the history of mankind; that our open, tolerant, prosperous, peaceable society is the marvel and envy of the ages.[24]

"Few things are more dangerous," the great historian Eric Hobsbawm recently observed, "than empires pursuing their own interest in the belief that they are doing humanity a favor."[25] Messianic revolutionaries can't reshape the world unless they can convince a lot of people to pay for it. The Project had warned against widespread hopes for a "peace dividend" long before September 11 because it knew that the "New American Century" will cost a lot of money. The Cold War had dominated a bipolar world but it turned out that the collapse of the Soviet Union hadn't changed much. The military's job had been to deter Soviet expansionism; today its task is to secure—and expand—the "zone of democratic peace," deter the rise of any new great-power competitor, defend key areas of Europe, the Middle East and East Asia, and take advantage of new technology in transforming the military. If anything, the Project warned that more money, greater political commitment, stronger national will, and deeper economic sacrifices would be required in a new world marked by fluidity and unpredictability than when the United States confronted a single armed, ruthless, and expansionist communist enemy.

The Project badly wants the country's strong, self-reliant, and morally certain citizens to avoid the siren call of "peace dividends" and economic justice. Appearances were deceiving and things are more dire than they seem. The new American preeminence means that more, not less, money has to be devoted to guns. The United States now faces a less predictable international environment that will require a wider and more expensive set of military capabilities. Since new challenges will come from a variety of sources, the military must be prepared to meet all of them. Specific threats may not be as great as that posed by the Soviet Union, but there will be more of them. And, reflecting the global terrain on which the Project saw American policy developing, it called for a new way of strategic thinking. The "two-war" strategy of the past decade has to be reconceptualized; now the standard is winning "multiple simultaneous large-scale wars."[26] More troops must be stationed overseas, the armed forces have to be reorganized and equipped to fight in new conditions of mobile and shifting war, the 1972 ABM Treaty with the USSR should be renounced so a space-based missile system can be built, the Army has to remain "the essential link in the chain that translates U.S. military supremacy into global American geopolitical preeminence," the Air Force must become a "global first-strike force," and the Navy has to be able to "dominate the open oceans."[27] American preeminence has imposed new, and more expensive, burdens. A changed environment requires accepting new realities, responding to new opportunities, and shouldering new burdens. Lest there be any doubt about the stakes involved or the sacrifices that will be demanded, the report made its priorities clear.

> Keeping the American peace requires the U.S. military to undertake a broad array of missions today and rise to very different challenges tomorrow, but there can be no retreat from these missions without compromising American leadership and the benevolent order it secures. This is the choice we face. It is not a choice between preeminence today and preeminence tomorrow. Global leadership is not something exercised at our leisure, when the mood strikes us or when our core national security interests are directly threatened; then it is already too late. Rather, it is a choice whether or not to maintain American military preeminence, to secure American geopolitical leadership, and to preserve the American peace.[28]

Remaking the world and organizing America's "benevolent order" won't be cheap. Years before the country embarked on its "war on terror," the Project was describing an endless struggle for world supremacy that would play out over many fronts for the indefinite future. Executive Director Gary Schmitt knows where the money to pay for all of this should come from. At a time when the United States spends more on armaments than the rest of the world combined, it's important to be clear about what's important. This should not be a problem if the country is willing to come to its senses, get its priorities straight, and reach the appropriate conclusions about who should pay for all this. "During the 1950s," Schmitt observed, "the budget was balanced and large sums went to the military. What has changed, of course, is spending on domestic programs. Although the drop in defense spending is linked to the end of the Cold War, it is not the sole nor principal reason why the decline started in the mid-1980s and continues unabated. Rather, the DOD budget has been squeezed by the persistent increase in entitlements and other domestic programs." None of this is necessary. "The notion that the United States cannot afford to spend more on defense is . . . largely a political and not economic judgment."[29]

The Committee on the Present Danger had called for reorienting federal spending during the late 1970s because it claimed that the United States was in imminent danger from the Soviet drive for supremacy. Twenty years later, the Project for the New American Century called for more military spending because the United States enjoyed unchallenged supremacy. Only when a permanent war economy is the order of the day can this sort of logic be acceptable. September 11 "changed everything" and nothing, marking a real turning point because it made the country much more susceptible to old arguments. Schmitt knows that the process has acquired a logic and momentum of its own. "Justifying such a budget increase," he said before September 11, "requires moving beyond the idea that defense spending is tied simply to meeting specific threats. It means, instead, defending a large defense budget as a necessary but affordable means for taking advantage of the strategic opportunity the country has at hand. Finally, it means adoption by the United States of a grand strategy that is animated not by fear of some looming danger but, rather, pride in the confluence on the world stage of American power and principles at the close of the 20th century."[30]

The money for all this has to come from someplace, and neoconservatives have shed the illusions of the movement's founding generation. Long before September 11, they warned against losing time by irresponsibly chasing the phantom of a "peace dividend." Unwilling to educate the American people about the costs of world leadership, President Clinton had allowed threats to develop that threatened the world order so carefully established by Ronald Reagan. "Americans and their political leaders have spent the years since 1991 lavishing the gifts of an illusory 'peace dividend' upon themselves, and frittering away the opportunity to strengthen and extend an international order uniquely favorable to the United States."[31] There can be no "return to normalcy"—even before September 11, key members of the

Project for the New American Century were saying that "the citizens of democracies must be willing to support the arsenals of democracy. We must be willing to maintain our defenses in a manner consistent with our role in the world and the threats posed against us. In the end, our survival and the survival of all we believe in and care most about—the defense of Western civilization and the nurture and protection of our children—will depend on whether we are vigilant and strong and committed in purpose."[32] Attacking entitlement programs and ending the illusions of a peace dividend make it pretty clear who's supposed to pay for ensuring "our" survival and the triumph of what "we" consider important.

This is no time to take a rest, the neo-conservatives warn. An historic opportunity has allowed the United States to press forward and begin to reorganize the world. Clearly mindful of how important ideas can be, the Project for a New American Century wanted to be sure that the country made the right choice. American preeminence cannot lead to a "strategic pause" that would increase spending on social programs, it argued. September 11 solved that problem in a particularly brutal way, but the position had been established before then. Project member Donald Kagan had made things clear a year earlier. "The chief problems facing American foreign policy today, as they have since the end of the Cold War, are how to maintain and strengthen a situation in the world that is unusually conducive to peace and to the goals and values of the United States, its allies and friends. This condition is not the result of historical happenstance; it was achieved mostly by a readiness on the part of the West to acquire and sustain predominant military force and the demonstrated willingness and capacity to use it when necessary. The collapse of the Soviet Union removed the main reason for an unprecedented commitment and sacrifice in peacetime on which the preservation of peace rested. Since then the U.S. has sharply reduced its military power, and its reactions to world events have raised serious questions about its readiness to continue in the role of chief keeper of the peace."[33] Reducing military spending in an irresponsible search for a "peace dividend" will sap the country's ability to press its international advantage and will distract citizens from the historic opportunities that lie open to the world's only superpower. Great nations must be ready to arm themselves and demonstrate that they are ready to use their arms. The only guarantee of peace and security is military strength, and organizing the American Peace will require a lot of it. "The twentieth century has repeatedly shown that for a great power, and especially for the world's leading power, there is no escape from the responsibility its position imposes," said Kagan. "Recent history has also demonstrated that the cost of these burdens is small compared with the costs of failure to bear them forthrightly; and in dealing with the issue of its power, a country like the U.S. is really dealing with its values and its security."[34]

Twenty-five years of right-wing ascendancy have set the conditions for a militarized and unilateral foreign policy backed up by continuous warnings of mortal danger. The Committee on the Present Danger has continued Vandenberg's work with a vengeance, saturating the current environment with constant talk of danger and threat. Color-coded alarms, warnings of vague plots, carefully-placed hints that elections will be postponed, and a host of other measures have become so much a part of national life that they have become background noise. "You've flown the flag," says the Department of Homeland Security in a full-page advertisement. "Now what?" And, between a large picture of the Stars and Stripes and the Great Seal of the United States, the very office that was born in fear and danger offers official reassurance to a population that it has worked very hard to frighten.[35]

In the months since September 11, 2001, we have all witnessed a powerful resurgence of the American spirit. But now, in a climate of new threats, it's clear that patriotism alone is not enough. We must also learn to protect ourselves and our families against future terrorist attacks.

There are three steps toward readiness. These steps are fairly simple and straightforward. And they work.

Make an Emergency Supply Kit

In a sturdy container like a plastic trash can or duffel bag, pack the items you and your family may need in an emergency and set them aside.

Your kit should contain 72-hours' worth of supplies: A gallon of water per person, per day. A three-day supply of non-perishable food. A first-aid kit. Clothes, sleeping bags and toilet articles. Flashlight, extra batteries, scissors, plastic sheeting, duct tape. Also, a battery-powered radio is essential. Be sure to write down the frequencies of radio stations in your area that will broadcast emergency information.

It's also helpful to have a second, smaller kit with a few essential items, something you can grab in a hurry in case you're asked to leave your house for a few days.

Make a Family Communications Plan

If your family knows where to go and what to do in an emergency, they'll save time and remain calm. Here's what your plan should contain: The name and phone number of out-of-state relatives to contact. (Long-distance calling may be easier than local calling). A family meeting place near your home and another one away from the neighborhood. An evacuation plan using alternative routes. A designated room in your house in case authorities instruct you to "shelter-in-place."

Be Informed

If there is a terrorist attack on your city, local authorities will broadcast information as quickly as possible concerning the nature of the emergency and what you should do next. Be sure to keep listening for updates. What can you do right now? Get information, educate yourself and your family. For more details on emergency preparedness, visit our website at www.ready.gov. Or get a free brochure by calling **1-800-BE-READY (1-800-237-3239)**.

Neo-conservatism is only one branch of the contemporary American Right, but it has been particularly influential in George W. Bush's administration and has worked hard to establish the contours within which American foreign policy operates. Buttressed by a healthy dose of moral authoritarianism, its message has been remarkably consistent for a quarter of a century: economic equality and social justice must yield to the requirements of the military. Particular assessments of the international environment have changed over the years, but there's a remarkable unity to this endlessly-repeated core position. Unlike other right-wing tendencies, neo-conservatism wants an active, strong, centralized, and militarized state to defend "national security," spread democracy, and organize the "New American Century"—three goals that had become one before Osama bin Laden and George W. Bush plunged the United States into an endless "war on terror." September 11 only accelerated its radicalization, yielding Bennett's overheated moralizing authoritarianism and a belligerent agenda for American foreign policy from David Frum and Richard Perle: "Support the overthrow of the terrorist mullahs of Iran, end the terrorist regime of Syria, regard Saudi Arabia and France not as friends but as rivals—maybe enemies, withdraw support from the United Nations if it does not reform, tighten immigration and security here at home, radically reorganize the CIA and the FBI, squeeze China and blockade North Korea to press that member of the axis of evil to abandon its nuclear program, and abandon the illusion that a Palestinian state will contribute in any important way to U.S. security."[36]

Even an endless "war on terror" fought by God's favorite country is not immune to the lessons of history. Americans would do well to remember that for every empire that's born, a republic has to die. Dwight Eisenhower, of all people, seems to have understood this. Since the country's thirty-fourth President had actually seen war firsthand, he had a good idea of the price it exacted. He understood how easily militarism could become the grim partner of diminished expectations of social justice and historic levels of inequality at home. Perhaps that's why he warned the country that "every gun that is made, every warship launched, every rocket fired, signifies in the final sense a theft from those who hunger and are not fed, those who are cold and not clothed. The world in arms is not spending money alone. It is spending the sweat of its laborers, the genius of its scientists, the hopes of its children."[37]

Fear and threat can be powerful tools in the hands of determined leaders. When effectively used, they can quickly mobilize support for contested policies, rescue the careers of unpopular figures, and dramatically change the terms of political debate. From Machiavelli to Karl Rove, skilled political tacticians have known that scaring people can help advance a disputed program. No less an expert than Hermann Goering knew that "of course the people don't want war. Why would some poor slob on a farm risk his life in a war when the best that he can get out of it is to come back to his farm in one piece? Naturally, the common people don't want war; neither in Russia nor in England nor in America, nor for that matter in Germany. That is understood. But after all, it is the leaders of the country who determine the policy, and it is always a simple thing to drag the people along, whether it is a democracy, or a fascist dictatorship, or a parliament, or a communist dictatorship." When asked how Nazi Germany's leadership managed the task and mobilized widespread support for war, Hitler's confidant had a ready answer. "Voice or no voice," he observed, "the people can always be brought to the bidding of its leaders. That is easy. All you have to do is tell them they are being attacked, and denounce the pacifists for lack of patriotism and exposing the country to danger. It works the same in any country."[38]

The American Right has ruthlessly taken advantage of Osama bin Laden's gift and used crisis and war to advance an agenda that would have had little support in an earlier period. George W. Bush was an illegitimate President and Rudolph Giuliani a failed mayor before September 11, but they've ridden the wave of insecurity, fear, and threat—a wave they've helped to create. They're not alone. The Right has aggressively used the undeniable reality of international terrorism to advance a political program that will magnify inequality and paralyze any future possibility of addressing it. This isn't what millions of anxious citizens who've worried about their personal safety or the future of their country had in mind, but it's what they got.

Notes

1. Norman Podhoretz, *The Present Danger: Do we have the will to reverse the decline of American power?* (New York: Simon & Schuster, 1980), pp. 58–60.

2. Jeane Kirkpatrick, "Dictatorships and Double Standards" in *Dictatorships and Double Standards: Rationalism & Reason in Politics* (New York: Simon & Schuster, 1982), p. 23.

3. *Ibid.*, p. 32.

4. *Ibid.*, p. 53.

5. Max Kampelman, introduction to *Alerting America: The Papers of the Committee on the Present Danger* (Washington: Pergamon-Brassey's International Defense Publishers, 1984), pp. xv–xvi.

6. "Common Sense and the Common Danger," *ibid.*, p. 3.

7. "What is the Soviet Union up To?," *ibid.*, p. 11.

8. *Ibid.*, p. 4.

9. "Is America Becoming Number 2? Current Trends in the U.S.-Soviet Military Balance," *ibid.*, p. 42.

10. Paul Nitze, "Is SALT II a Fair Deal?" *ibid.*, p. 160.

11. "What is the Soviet Union Up To?" p. 14. The emphasis is Kampelman's.

12. *Ibid.*

13. *The Present Danger*, p. 86.

14. *Ibid.*

15. "Common Sense and the Common Danger," *ibid.*, p. 5. See also "Is America Becoming Number 2? Current Trends in the U.S.-Soviet Military Balance," *ibid.*, p. 87.

16. See the website at http://www.newamericancentury.org/.

17. See http://www.newamericancentury.org/defensenationalsecurity.htm.

18. See http://www.newamericancentury.org/iraqclintonletter.htm.

19. See http://www.newamericancentury.org/global-032303.htm.

20. *Why We Fight: Moral Clarity and the War on Terrorism* (New York: Doubleday, 2002), p. 20.

21. *Ibid.*, pp. 45–46.

22. *Ibid.*, p. 47.

23. *Ibid.*, p. 155.

24. *Ibid.*, pp. 150–151. His emphasis.

25. *Le Monde Diplomatique*, June 2003. http://MondeDiplo.com/2003/06/02/hobsbawm.

26. "Rebuilding America's Defenses: Strategies, Forces and Resources for a New Century," p. 6.

27. *Ibid.*, pp. 30, 49.

28. *Ibid.*, pp. 75–76.

29. "American primacy and the Defense Spending Crisis," *Joint Forces Quarterly*, Spring 1998, pp. 55–56.

30. *Ibid.*, p. 56.

31. Robert Kagan and William Kristol, introduction to *Present Dangers: Crisis and Opportunity in American Foreign and Defense Policy* (San Francisco: Encounter Books, 2000), p. 4.

32. William Bennett, "Morality, Character and American Foreign Policy," *ibid.*, p. 295.

33. Donald Kagan, "Strength and Will: A Historical Perspective," *ibid.*, p. 339.

34. *Ibid.*, p. 362.

35. *The New York Times*, September 15, 2004. The same advertisement appeared in many other newspapers and was repeated in *The New York Times* on December 23, 2004.

36. David Frum and Richard Perle, *An End to Evil: How to Win the War on Terror* (New York: Random House, 2003).

37. President Dwight D. Eisenhower, Speech to the American Association of Newspaper Editors, April 16, 1953, http://www.eisenhower.archives.gov/avaudio.htm.

38. From Gustave Gilbert, *Nuremberg Diary* (New York: Farrar Straus and Company, 1947), pp. 178–79. Http://blog,case.edu/mxs24/2005/06/29/politics_and_the_fear_factor3.

CHAPTER THREE

Authority

Neo-conservatism took shape during the late-70s as the muscular antidote to alleged liberal weakness in foreign affairs, but it never limited itself to the Cold War. Its claim that more guns would mean less butter quickly drove its first generation toward domestic affairs—and toward the right. Scarcity required difficult choices, and the neo-conservatives were sure that it was high time for the country to get its priorities straight. Trying to convince political leaders wouldn't be enough; gearing up for a more belligerent foreign policy would require an intense domestic campaign to end the confusion of the late 1960s and 70s. Such arguments were not new and had been made by a broad swath of conservative spokesmen for years. Both Richard Nixon and George Wallace had organized their presidential campaigns around calls for conformity and normalcy, but it was the neo-conservatives who connected domestic authoritarianism to overseas aggressiveness. A widespread feeling that the country was spinning out of control and that it was time to impose "law and order" helped shape an environment in which the relationship between authority and freedom could be reconfigured. If the period's social movements had proven that democracy is nourished by political activity and social protest, the Right was ready to serve notice that it now required peace and quiet.

The Democratic "Distemper"

Samuel Huntington was one of the first to argue that it was time to abandon unrealistic dreams and recognize the limits of what was possible. Fresh from his notorious suggestion that American strategic bombing would help "modernize" South Vietnam by driving its population into cities and strategic

49

hamlets, the Harvard professor urgently called for the restoration of authority at home. B-52s were his preferred response to Vietnam's "governability crisis," but he also wanted to remind the advanced countries that liberty and responsibility were connected. Things were getting out of hand. It was time to set them right.

Nor were these problems limited to the United States; Huntington joined others in noting that democratic upheaval had become a feature of many societies all over the world. In 1975, he contributed to a famous collection of essays written for the Trilateral Commission that examined general problems of "democratic governance" in Europe, the United States, and Japan. Commission Director Zbigniew Brzezinski identified three areas of concern that had emerged in the Trilateral areas: the rise of a left-wing "adversarial" intelligentsia, a shift away from work-oriented and public-spirited values toward private satisfaction and individual fulfillment, and—perhaps most importantly—contradictions that were inherent to democratic politics everywhere. Although the specifics might differ from area to area, "the operations of the democratic process do indeed appear to have generated a breakdown of traditional means of social control, a delegitimation of political and other forms of authority, and an overload of demands on government, exceeding its capacity to respond."[1] Businessmen weren't the only ones worrying about the future. Brzezinski worried that these three challenges to democracy had come together to create a general crisis:

> The current pessimism about the viability of democratic government stems in large part from the extent to which contextual threats, societal trends, and intrinsic challenges have simultaneously manifested themselves in recent years. A democratic system that was not racked by intrinsic weaknesses stemming from its own performance as a democracy could much more easily deal with contextual policy challenges. A system which did not have such significant demands imposed upon it by its external environment might be able to correct the deficiencies which arose out of its own operations. It is, however, the conjunction of the policy problems arising from the contextual challenges, the decay in the social base of democracy manifested in the rise of oppositionist intellectuals and privatistic youth, and the imbalances stemming from the actual operations of democracy itself which make the governability of democracy a vital and, indeed, an urgent issue for the Trilateral societies.[2]

The Sixties had stretched things to the breaking point. "The demands on democratic government grow, while the capacity of democratic government stagnates. This, it would appear, is the central dilemma of the governability of democracy which has manifested itself in Europe, North America, and Japan in the 1970s," said Jimmy Carter's future National Security Advisor.[3] Since it believed that the immediate future was likely to be marked by inten-sifying pressures for political democracy and social justice, the Trilateral Commission thought it important to probe some of the era's motive forces. Such was the task to which Huntington addressed himself as he examined the United States.

He was especially troubled by two features of the democratic upsurge that had begun with the Civil Rights Movement. For one thing, higher levels of political activity announced the entry of new groups that had been absent or inactive for a long time. Taken by itself, this would have been enough of a challenge. But there was more, precisely because of *who* was involved. The political system had been predictable and stable for decades because its parti-cipants had been predictable and stable. Organized around the economic requirements of the country's large white middle class, American democracy had also rested on the voluntary non-participation and forcible exclusion of millions of citizens. Voting rates had been relatively high during the 1950s and early 60s, but the period's moderation meant that high levels of partici-pation had not been terribly destabilizing. But dramatically higher levels of activity associated with the new social movements had begun to threaten core institutions. Something had changed. Quite apart from the challenge posed by higher numbers, there were also questions of content—and one of them loomed particularly large. Increased participation by blacks, young people, workers, and women carried with it an important reassertion of egali-tarian and redistributionist social policies.

Neo-conservatives had been warning that the happy days of guns and but-ter were over, and Huntington gave an unpleasant argument the contextual analysis it needed. The period had raised a set of egalitarian demands that posed broad challenges to the political system. One disturbing possibility suggested itself. The erosion of state legitimacy and governmental authority made it more difficult to satisfy new demands at precisely the same time that doing so had become a precondition for stability and order. "The basic point," Huntington said, "is this: *The vitality of democracy in the United States in the 1960s produced a substantial increase in governmental activity and a sub-stantial decrease in governmental authority.*"[4] Higher levels of participation and more democratic movements had simultaneously demanded more govern-mental activity and had limited its authority. Huntington wasn't sure if the system could—or should—try to satisfy all the new actors. He *was* sure, though, that there was entirely too much democracy in the air and suggested that "the democratic surge of the 1960s raised once again in dramatic fashion the issue of whether the pendulum had swung too far in one direction."[5]

Huntington wasn't troubled by the period's heightened levels of governmental activity; like most neo-conservatives, he was a statist. It was the erosion of central authority that bothered him. The trajectory of governmental activity in the United States, measured in terms of size and content, had gone through two phases since the end of World War II. The first, which Huntington called the "Defense Shift," initiated the Cold War and resulted in a larger and more vigorous peacetime federal government. The second, the "Welfare Shift," was a direct response to the democratic surge of the 1960s and 70s and also expanded state activity. The first was largely the product of elite leadership and mass response; the second occurred because of mass demand and elite response. If the first had "scared hell" out of the people, the second had done the same to the politicians. It made sense for Huntington to worry about the "Welfare Shift," since increases in social spending had come about because of the activity of domestic groups rather than because of elite determination of broad national purpose. The "Defense Shift" had required more governmental spending for arms and the conduct of foreign affairs, but it had reached its natural limits and stabilized after an initial expansion. Huntington worried that democracy might drive the Welfare Shift along a different trajectory that would be far more disruptive. Demands for social justice and economic equality might raise more burdensome issues than the system could address. The "Welfare Shift" was so dangerous precisely because it had not originated with the country's leadership and because it had no natural limits.

"The essence of the democratic surge of the 1960s was a general challenge to existing systems of authority, public and private," Huntington said.[6] The challenge was everywhere—in the family, in school, in business, in popular music, in high culture, in bus stations, and in polling booths. People simply did not feel the same compulsion to obey those whom they had previously considered their social superiors and political leaders. New groups demanded social rights, political participation, and cultural recognition that they had never sought before. And, if skepticism about received wisdom and established hierarchies was roiling every institution, it had become particularly disruptive in politics. "The questioning of authority pervaded society. In politics, it manifested itself in a decline of public confidence and trust in political leaders and institutions, a reduction in the power and effectiveness of political institutions such as the political parties and presidency, a new importance for the 'adversary' media and 'critical' intelligentsia in public affairs, and a weakening of the coherence, purpose, and self-confidence of political leadership."[7]

Huntington worried that core political institutions were cracking under the pressure of the period's democratic movements. More demands led to less confidence, and he was convinced that the country faced a deepening crisis of legitimacy. Large sections of the population were developing a more focused approach to politics, were acquiring considerable political experience, were no longer easily put off, and were more suspicious of the state even as they felt emboldened to demand more from it. The Presidency had been weakened while Congress and the media, institutions generally associated with the opposition, had significantly increased their power. Political parties were decaying as more voters registered as independents, split their tickets, and voted according to issues instead of party identification. The political system as a whole seemed to be buckling under the accumulated weight of popular demands it could not meet. Huntington coined a wonderfully appropriate term to describe what was happening. "The vigor of democracy in the United States in the 1960s," he announced, "contributed to a democratic distemper, involving the expansion of governmental activity, on the one hand, and the reduction of governmental authority, on the other."[8]

American history had seen earlier periods of "democratic distemper" that had disturbed settled political arrangements, assumptions, and institutions. Marked by heightened participation, deeper political knowledge, and strengthened drives toward equality, they often challenged authority and heralded important periods of political and economic reform. Huntington understood the importance of changing with the times. Formerly marginalized groups had been energized and the clock probably couldn't be turned back. But no political system can survive for very long with too much activity from below. Blacks, women, the young, workers, and others—particularly blacks—had to understand that democracy can be threatened when it undermines the legitimacy of core institutions by overloading the system's ability to respond. This was already happening, Huntington warned. There was too much democracy in the air. It was time to reassert the authority of experience, seniority, and expertise.

Americans had to learn to understand that nothing was free. Restoring stability in a period of intense activity required lower expectations and reduced demands. This was the price that everyone would have to pay for heightened levels of participation. "Less marginality on the part of some groups," Huntington announced, "needs to be replaced by more self-restraint on the part of all groups."[9] If democracy was to be broadened, then everyone had to ask for less. "A value which is normally good in itself is not necessarily optimized when it is maximized. We have come to recognize that there are potentially desirable limits to economic growth. There are also potentially desirable limits to the indefinite extension of political democracy. Democracy will have a longer life if it has a more balanced existence."[10] Too much participation would shake the foundations of postwar American democracy. "Al Smith once remarked that 'the only cure for the evils of democracy is more democracy.' Our analysis suggests that applying that cure at the present time could well be adding fuel to the flames. Instead, some of the problems of governance in the United States today stem from an excess of democracy," he said. "Needed, instead, is a greater degree of moderation in democracy."[11]

Huntington's essay marked an early step toward the Right's message of moral authoritarianism, political restoration, and social peace. It captured something that was in the air. People were starting to get tired of all the chaos. Elite concerns about disruptive social movements soon began to resonate with an insecure, confused, and threatened population. An early foundation for Huntington's warning had been established when Nixon and Wallace had posed as the authentic representatives of "average" white Americans. Fanning popular resentment of federal spending programs, the urban counter-culture, and the black poor, they paved the way for the Right's later attacks on equality and redistribution. Huntington's important claim that the country's governability crisis developed because people were demanding too much had acquired a certain pedigree years before it was formally articulated. All he did was give it a name. Demands for equality and redistribution had become a malady, a "distemper." Social health and political coherence demanded that they be controlled.

Huntington proved remarkably prescient. As a well-funded network of right-wing organizations began to take shape, a conservative revitalization movement centered in the South began to explain defeat in Vietnam, economic crisis, social disorder, and cultural change by talking about "values." A broad reaction quickly gained traction among a threatened and insecure white population. Pat Robertson and his Christian Coalition, Jerry Falwell and his Moral Majority, the Traditional Values Coalition, and others began to articulate a conservative, pious, and middle-class populism that would defend hard-working, godly Americans from the bureaucratic state and its amoral, anti-Christian elites. Religious revivals weren't new in American history and had often accompanied periods of dramatic economic and social change. What was new about this most recent Great Awakening was its sharp political edge. When it was joined by the secular cultural warriors, a powerful right-wing authoritarianism began to articulate a narrative of diligent toil, moral piety, and self-governing communities—an important reason why the Republican Party would bridge class gaps it had been unable to cross since the Great Depression. As millions of wage earners began to define themselves as whites, men, consumers, and property-owners before anything else, they mobilized around a program of moral restoration, tax cuts, militarism, gender supremacy, and racial privilege. The fight over the Equal Rights Amendment and *Roe v. Wade* fused with demands that the state enforce a set of moral lessons on an irresponsible, dangerous, and parasitical black underclass. Arguments that stressed personal rectitude mobilized an increasing constituency of socially conservative voters behind a program of "values" that undermined solidarity, denied any sort of social compact, substituted individual responsibility for state programs, and fortified later attacks on democracy, equality, and solidarity.

Black "militancy" was particularly threatening. But explicit and coded appeals to racism were only the tip of the iceberg—though it was a powerful tip indeed. The Right's chief target was a liberalism that could not reverse the country's decline because it had caused it. A degenerate elite that was overtly cowardly and secretly treasonous pandered to female hysterics and black extortionists because it was unable to protect traditional limits and institutions. Animated by a fervent belief that civilization was under attack, right-wing spokesmen demanded that authority and tradition be defended. And there was a lot to worry about. Rising divorce rates, teen-age pregnancy, newly assertive gays and lesbians, apologies for crime and excuses for bad behavior, drug use, abortions—everything was coming undone. "Middle Americans," convinced that their morality, "values," and choices were under attack from the new barbarians and their political enablers, were increasingly open to cultural authoritarianism, nostalgia, and a fight against upper-class liberalism and its social programs. The more whites of modest means became convinced that they were being unfairly required to foot the bill for years of social chaos and the country's diseased racial history, the more they turned against the welfare state. Once liberalism's staunch defenders, they concluded that it had betrayed them by undermining their values and hobbling their struggles for self-reliance.

Many American families were profoundly troubled by what appeared to be a general breakdown of social and moral order. When lashed by persistent economic stress and framed by a decidedly conservative religious revival, their protest movement rapidly embraced an authoritarian social and ideological program. It was able to do so, in large part, because the Right was not afraid to provide arguments that were out of reach for the Democrats. As millions of whites began to feel besieged and put-upon, their desire to protect what they had looked to an earlier, more "decent" period when women were content and blacks were quiet. A tide of permissiveness in family life, jurisprudence, school curricula, patriotic observance, sexual relations, and religious matters offended and frightened many hard-working traditionalists. Braless women, anti-war veterans, communal living, blacks with afros, guns, and sunglasses, flagrant homosexuality, open drug use, the disrespectful and androgynous hair of the hippies, the American flag customized with peace decals—all these things were unacceptable signs of anarchy. The entire society seemed to be collapsing, its most basic institutions under attack from those without any discipline or respect. People looked to assign blame, and it wasn't long before the Right began to get some traction by calling liberalism a pandering doctrine that made the satisfaction of appetites easy, legitimate, and cheap.

Widespread resentment had begun to feed a rebellion against the welfare state just when Huntington told Americans that it was time to ask for less, not more. It wasn't long before a broad desire to hold the fort against permissiveness and chaos become an explicit call for more authority and an urgent demand for order. There was a lot more to all this than simple-minded nostalgia. While cultural reaction was critical in creating a populist conservatism, it was always clear that the Right was aiming to further its political and economic program. Opposition to the social movements of the 1960s and 70s fueled its growth, but attacks on the welfare state always loomed in the background. Keynesianism had been the coin of America's bipartisan realm for decades, but the period's economic difficulties enabled conservatives to draw a link between the "irresponsible" demands of the social movements and a parasitical welfarist "culture of dependence." Others soon joined Wallace and Nixon in using the coded language of race. The developing Christian Right took aim at the "secular humanism" that had been behind the assault on America's godly civilization and its "traditional values." As it became easier to identify the Democratic Party with blacks, women, and the "rights revolution," conservatives began to harness a general sense of resentment and a specific list of grievances to begin an attack on social welfare.

The Christian Warrior

In 1980, a little-known Jerry Falwell shouted *Listen, America!* at a sinful and ungodly country after organizing the Moral Majority to help Ronald Reagan win the presidential election. The Reverend's remedy was a religious version of Huntington's: restore the authority of the state, of the male-headed household, and of revealed religion. Subtitled "the conservative blueprint for America's moral rebirth," Falwell's book repeatedly and urgently proclaimed that a deep crisis was at hand.[12] "America, our beloved country, is indeed sick. Our people must be made aware of that fact and be called together to turn this country around before it is too late," he warned. "It is time that we come together and rise up against the tide of permissiveness and moral decay that is crushing in on our society from every side."[13]

His religious terminology notwithstanding, Falwell's project was a political one from first to last. The country sits poised on the knife-edge of disaster, but it's not too late to bring America back to God. In the end, it's a matter of will; like the rest of the Right, Falwell was afraid that liberals had made the United States lose its nerve. Turning things around, restoring God's law, and reclaiming national greatness will require discipline, authority, and moral certainty. But the hour is late and defeat looms. "We are not committed to victory," he complained. "We are not committed to greatness. We have lost the will to stay strong and therefore have not won any wars we have fought since 1945."[14] He was sure that the main problem was ideological, for "America can only be turned around as her people make godly, moral choices." Falwell's God wanted a strong America that could win its wars.

Godless communism, government regulation, economic redistribution, and personal pleasure were useful foils for Falwell's authoritarianism. Religious piety strengthened an avowedly political project and patriotism fused seamlessly with God's will, male supremacy, and the familiar political program of the Right. Urgent calls for godly, brave leaders who will save the country from spiritual rot and moral decline punctuated his repeated calls for the restoration of national strength and the election of conservative politicians. An intensely right-wing political content lurked underneath all the apocalyptic warnings of impending doom and calls for moral correction. Falwell's God opposes state welfare activities, but the Old and New Testaments tell us how much he loves capitalism, property, and wealth. "The free-enterprise system is clearly outlined in the Book of Proverbs in the Bible. Jesus Christ made it clear that the work ethic was part of His plan for man. Ownership of property is biblical. Competition in business is biblical. Ambitious and successful business management is clearly outlined as a part of God's plan for His people." Falwell supplied no proof of this, but he didn't have to. Having stated God's love for the rich, he turned his attention closer to home. Restoring the United States to the path of godliness, military power, money, and theocracy requires strengthening male authority in society, politics, and the family. "We need in America today powerful, dynamic, and godly leadership. Male leadership in our families is affecting male leadership in our churches, and it is affecting male leadership in our society. As we look across our nation today we find a tremendous vacuum of godly men who are willing to be the kind of spiritual leaders who are necessary not only to change a nation, but also to change the churches within our nation and the basic units of our entire society, our families."[15]

A seamless web of religious authority would knit the country together, provide integrity to all her institutions, and guide her people on the path of righteousness. An uncompromising hostility to the Equal Rights Amendment expressed Falwell's fear that it would reverse the natural, God-ordained mandate that "the husband is the head of the wife, even as Christ is the head of the church."[16] Like other opponents of gender equality, he raised the Right's alarmist warning that it would destroy the army, the family, locker rooms, bathrooms, and the psychological future of the nation's children. It was all because people no longer knew their place. Feminism originates in boredom, unhappiness, and sinful self-indulgence. It nurses an unhealthy spirit of rebellion, undermines families, weakens nations, and sets the stage for social collapse. As dangerous as reckless women were, though, abortion and homosexuality were worse. "History proves that homosexuality reaches a pandemic level in societies in crisis or in a state of collapse" and sexual deviancy is destructive of masculine strength.[17]

All this insecure, angry talk about "families" was a way to rescue the natural order of things. And, since God loves stability, he was a political conservative. Day care, health insurance, housing, poverty, education—these weren't "family" issues. God loves authority, male supremacy, property, deferential women, church schools, righteous leaders, and rich people. Restoring authority was the first step in the long journey back to national salvation, but Falwell was a political actor above all else. "Through the ballot box Americans must provide for strong moral leadership at every level. If our country will get back on the track in sensibility and moral sanity, the crises that I have herein mentioned will work out in the course of time with God's blessings. It is now time to take a stand on certain moral issues, and we can only stand if we have leaders. We must stand against the Equal Rights Amendment, the feminist revolution, and the homosexual revolution. We must have a revival in this country."[18]

Falwell repeatedly talked about strengthening national defense, fighting communism everywhere, cutting back on state welfare and regulatory activity, and defeating "secular humanism," the devil's instrument. A weak and self-indulgent civilian leadership cannot rescue American society because it does not understand that "moral decay always precedes political turmoil, economic instability, and military weakness in a country."[19] Falwell opposed governmental activity when it came to economic equality, regulation and redistribution but had no problem when it served moral authoritarianism:

> The bearing of the sword by the government is correct and proper. Nowhere in the Bible is there a rebuke for the bearing of armaments. A political leader, as a minister of God, is a revenger to execute wrath upon those who do evil. Our government has the right to use its armaments to bring wrath upon those who would do evil by hurting other people. Good citizens show their subjection to governmental powers by paying taxes and showing honor to those in high places because those 'ministers of God' attend continually to providing them safety; that is, they should be continually providing them safety. Thus we see that the role of government is to minister justice and to protect the rights of its citizens by being a terror to evildoers within and without the nation.[20]

So a political leader is a "revenger," a stern, fatherly, and powerful minister of God who protects his people and brings terror to "evildoers" everywhere. Good Christian citizens obey righteous leaders and their godly state. Samuel Huntington didn't phrase things in quite the same way, but he and Falwell supplied mutually reinforcing secular and religious arguments that more authority was needed throughout society. Weakening the state's welfare function would clear the way for a militant anti-communist foreign policy, increased defense spending, sexual repression, and a godly campaign against sin of all kinds. But years of corruption and weakness had taken their toll. Falwell knew that if they are to combat Satan and restore America to godliness, Christians must mobilize, vote, write letters to the editor, raise money, and talk to their friends. "I am convinced that we need a spiritual and moral revival in America if America is to survive the twentieth century. The time for action is now; we dare not wait for someone else to take up the banner of righteousness in our generation. We have already waited too long. Now is the time to begin calling America back to God, back to the Bible, back to morality!"[21]

The same social transformations that precipitated the contemporary Right prompted a twenty-five-year religious Great Awakening, but there's no particular reason why evangelical and fundamentalist Protestantism should have been so conservative. And there was certainly nothing new about its power in the South. What was special was the way it became so politicized just when the South was flexing its muscle. It was the evangelicals, after all, who had been in the forefront of the abolitionist and temperance movements, and there is a strong social-justice streak in all varieties of Christianity. But the modern Christian Right descends from the Southern churches that defended slavery, organized post-World War I nativism, and supported Jim Crow, not from the Northern ones that opposed them. Southern-based evangelical Protestantism played a major role in the revival of the Ku Klux Klan during the 1920s and helped it become a national organization that was as concerned with moral regulation, male power, and immigration restriction as with enforcing racial supremacy. Like other nativists, the Klan fused moral contamination with racial pollution. Supported by a wide network of Protestant churches in the South and Midwest, it helped spark a dramatic change in the country's immigration policy in 1921 and 1924. Sharply reducing southern and eastern European immigration served its larger purpose of establishing a claim that the United States was a country of white Protestants. American politics has always been influenced by the nation's intense religiosity, and it stands to reason that religious excitement would often have a sharp political edge. In contemporary conditions, that edge's right-wing quality veered from calls for aggressive and godly state activity to demands for protection from a hostile secularism whose permissiveness threatened individual piety and apologized for moral cowardice. When federal and state governments presumed to intervene in areas that conservative Christians saw as private matters, they determined to stand and fight for cherished beliefs that they believed were under attack. Male supremacy was particularly important, but so were cherished cultural symbols, sexual propriety, and racial hierarchy. From the Supreme Court's 1954 *Brown* decision down to the present, judicial protection of free speech and governmental intervention on the side of racial equality shook the South and its fundamentalist Protestantism. Since its sons and daughters had carried their religion with them to the Southwest and to Southern California, the conditions for a new electoral alignment came into focus around issues of race, gender, "family values," and public welfare. A whole generation of Christian warriors began to march against too much individual freedom, too much self-gratification, and too much concern with the affairs of man.

Moral Certainty

It was a measure of the times that the mid-1980s saw Allan Bloom's *The Closing of the American Mind* become a minor cultural phenomenon.[22] At first

sight the book was an erudite and elitist attack on American higher education's egalitarianism and near-universal belief in the relativity of truth. But
Bloom was really aiming at bigger prey, and widespread disaffection with liberalism helped him become something of a celebrity. Anxious to protect civilization from the ravages of the Sixties, he made it clear that toleration and
open-mindedness weren't enough to guide people in troubled times. The
good life requires adherence to ethical principles and moral values, and it is
a disservice to truth to pretend otherwise. Bloom knew full well that he was
standing against the prevailing orthodoxy. "Openness—and the relativism
that makes it the only plausible stance in the face of various claims to truth
and various ways of life and kinds of human beings—is the great insight of
our times," he complained. "The true believer is the real danger. The study
of history and of culture teaches that all the world was mad in the past; men
always thought they were right, and that led to wars, persecutions, slavery,
xenophobia, racism, and chauvinism. The point is not to correct the mistakes and really be right; rather it is not to think you are right at all."[23]

Bloom's goal was a frankly political one: to demolish the intellectual foundations of the Sixties' great democratic upsurge. Updating ancient criticisms
of democracy that had been articulated by his teacher Leo Strauss, he
insisted that privileging tolerance and equality over eternal moral truths can
only make the search for the good life impossible or, worse, dangerous.
Strauss had indicted modernity in general, and Machiavelli in particular, for
substituting institutions, politics, and reason for "values" or "character" in
the formation of people, groups, and civilizations. He insisted that a great
gulf separated Greece, Rome, and the Middle Ages from the modern world,
and many of his students wanted to provide a bridge between the former's
wisdom and the latter's emptiness. The ancients sought virtue rather than
freedom, tried to understand how people ought to live instead of how they
do live, looked for the fixed core of human nature rather than the malleable
circumstances of history and culture, exalted the life of the seeker of wisdom
in contrast to the impermanence of the material world, and judged regimes
on the basis of transcendent truths instead of their necessary compromises.
But modernity places degraded man at the center of its ethics, puts its faith
in institutions, elevates instrumental reason above all else, reduces life to
worldly success and material improvements, and values effectiveness more
than truth. A great deal had been lost in the transition from heroism and
glory to security and predictability.

Strauss's aristocratic critique of modernity informed Bloom's attack on the
alleged corruption of the university. He began with the claim that open-

mindedness and its bastard child, cultural relativism, make it impossible to search for excellence and act on ethical choices. It was true that American students were notoriously ignorant of history, knew little geography, and didn't have much interest in anyone else, but well-meaning college diversity requirements would fail if they tried "to force students to recognize that there are other ways of thinking and that Western ways are not better. It is again not the content that counts but the lesson that is to be drawn. Such requirements are part of the effort to establish a world community and train its members—the person devoid of prejudice. But if the student were really to learn something of the minds of any of these non-Western cultures—which they do not—they would find that each and every one of these cultures is ethnocentric."[24] Under the circumstances, the best course of action is to embrace the West's claims with no apologies. Frankly evaluating different cultures according to a single invariant standard of good and evil will lead to the inescapable conclusion that some are better than others.

> Cultural relativism succeeds in destroying the West's universal or intellectually imperialistic claims, leaving it to be just another culture. So there is equality in the republic of cultures. Unfortunately the West is defined by its need for justification of its ways or values, by its need for discovery of nature, by its need for philosophy and science. This is its cultural imperative. Deprived of that, it will collapse. The United States is one of the highest and most extreme achievements of the rational quest for the good life according to nature. What makes its political structure possible is the use of the rational principles of natural right to found a people, thus uniting the good with one's own. Or, to put it otherwise, the regime established here promised untrammeled freedom to reason—not to everything indiscriminately, but to reason, the essential freedom that justifies other freedoms, and on the basis of which, and for the sake of which, much deviance is also tolerated.[25]

Bloom was disappointed that he was condemned to live in a society whose members knew little—and cared even less—about history, the life of the mind, or Great Ideas. An open, democratic, and multicultural society values decency, permissiveness, self-realization, tolerance, and freedom. These are important values in their place, but he was convinced that history had driven up the price for service to unprincipled liberal flexibility. The universities were failing in their responsibility to inject some nobility into a young, uneducated, and superficial country. Educating the masses is difficult enough in the best of conditions, but it would be impossible if the academy voluntarily gave up the enterprise. And so it had. Having yielded to mob rule and the tyranny of self-righteous destructiveness, American universities no longer offered the refuge that Strauss and his disciples sought. Instead, it had come to embody all the problems that the aristocratic search for excellence encounters in a democratic social order.

Like his teacher, Bloom had never gotten over the student movement. He believed that a deliberate and purposeful attack had been launched against the only institution capable of defending and transmitting civilized values in a time of dramatic change and fevered politics. Traumatized by the politicization of college campuses and deathly afraid that their indispensable neutrality had been sacrificed to short-run partisanship and cheap passions, Strauss, Bloom, and others were certain that a destructive nihilism had become the order of the day. Civilization was under assault from ruthless communist enemies abroad and arrogant liberal elites at home. The challenge from the Soviet Union was clear enough. The challenge from the student left, the counter-culture, and their "adversarial" intelligentsia had to be defeated.

Bloom supplied the educated, secular version of Falwell's apocalyptic warnings that an angry God was about to smite a short-sighted and self-indulgent country. Besotted by the search for individual "happiness," corrupted by wealth, and drugged by "needs," Americans have forgotten about the holy and the mysterious. Their restless search for fulfillment is that of ignorant, self-absorbed children. Everything has gotten so easy that life's difficult questions can be ignored or neutered by affable shallowness and easy tolerance. "Conflict is the evil we most want to avoid, among nations, among individuals and within ourselves. Nietzsche sought with his value philosophy to restore the harsh conflicts for which men were willing to die, to restore the tragic sense of life, at a moment when nature had been domesticated and men had become tame. That value philosophy was used in America for exactly the opposite purpose—to promote conflict-resolution, bargaining, and harmony. If it is only a difference in values, then conciliation is possible. We must respect values, but they must not get in the way of peace."[26]

Bloom's attack on the Sixties flowed from an acute sense of betrayal and failure. Insulating the university from "the world outside" proved impossible in the highly ideological atmosphere of the times. He wanted to protect society from the lethal combination of historical ignorance, ethical shortsightedness, and the willingness to sacrifice intellectual integrity to the claims of higher truth offered by the period's political crusades. It sounded so attractive that there was little reason for moderation. It was to be expected that students would act like the young barbarians they were, but the worst offenders were their servile professors and cowardly administrators. Having capitulated to the claim that education should foster commitment to social change instead of training in the dispassionate use of reason, they had given savages the power to define what civilization meant. This reversal of the natural order of things was catastrophic. Once matters of values were turned over to an ignorant democratic majority—or, even worse, those claiming to represent the views of a democratic majority—the game was up. "Whether it be Nuremberg or Woodstock, the principle is the same," warned Bloom. "As Hegel was said to have died in Germany in 1933, Enlightenment in America came close to breathing its last during the sixties."[27] If social movements possessed a truth higher than that of the university, then commitment trumped science, passion was more important than reason, history meant more than nature, victimhood carried moral superiority, and the young knew more than the old. It was one thing when ignorant and indignant children became convinced of their own importance and genius. It was ruinous when those who knew better surrendered to such nonsense. "The professors, the repositories of our best traditions and highest intellectual aspirations, were fawning over what was nothing better than a rabble; publicly confessing their guilt and apologizing for not having understood the most important moral issues, the proper response to which they were learning from the mob; expressing their willingness to change the university's goals and the content of what they taught."[28] Openness led to neutrality and a refusal to take sides. Having embraced relativism, the universities had become complicit in the inevitable slide toward nihilism.

Bloom's disappointment was tempered by genuine intelligence and a measure of reflection. For the most part, his attack on the Sixties was limited to the university and its combination of youthful narcissism and adult cowardice. When he talked about the corrupting trends that had been set loose in the larger society, he limited himself to warning about liberal relativism and egalitarianism. He was convinced that the West's deep spiritual and ideological crisis could be resolved only if classical education was deployed to train society's natural elites about the important issues of public life. This was certainly not true of Robert Bork, whose infuriated *Slouching Towards Gomorrah* identified its real target in the subtitle of *Modern Liberalism and American Decline*.[29] If Bloom was inconsolable about what had happened to his beloved universities, Bork was an angry Old Testament prophet. If Bloom was nervous about the future, Bork was convinced that American culture had deteriorated past the point of no return. If Bloom was worried about the health of the academy, Bork claimed that liberalism had ruined the whole society. If Bloom sought to rescue intellectual integrity from youthful barbarians, Bork said that rebellious women and blacks were actively trying to destroy Western civilization. If Bloom looked to the authority of the noble past, Bork embraced that of the profane state.

The theme of American decline haunts Bork's book. Just when many on the right, left, and center took the end of the Cold War and a booming economy to be signs of the country's strength, he saw only decline and corruption—the final victory of the Sixties, the "vertical invasion of the barbarians." Since the economy was sound, the military strong, and foreign affairs in order, Bork turned to "culture," that dependable reservoir of right-wing rage. He dragged out a familiar laundry list. Rap songs that glorify cop killings, "coercive left-wing indoctrination at a prestigious university," the collapse of the criminal justice system, illegitimate births, rampant sexuality, feminism, homosexuality, environmentalism—all this was proof positive of a deeply destructive process of cultural decay. "This situation is thoroughly perverse," Bork announced. "Underclass values become increasingly acceptable to the middle class, especially their young, and middle-class values become increasingly acceptable to the cultural elites."[30] Bork would clear up any lingering confusion about the skin color of the diseased "underclass" that was polluting American culture soon enough, but for the moment he remained on the high road of ideas. Wedded to an ethic of social reconstruction and personal well-being and ready to use the state to redistribute wealth, liberalism is powered by two pernicious ideas that have come together in decay and coercion.

Egalitarianism and individualism, twinned lodestars of mindless protest and self-serving rebellion, had driven the country into a ditch. Communism had collapsed and the economy was roaring ahead, but Bork saw only disaster. Liberals were succeeding where the Soviet Union had failed. Having taken over the destructive legacy of the Sixties, they were now the carriers of corruption, decay, and disease. Their egalitarianism thrust them toward collectivism and commitment to individual happiness drive them toward hedonism and corruption. Unless they are stopped, the result can only be "one or another variety of statism presiding over a degenerate society."[31] Bork had no doubt about how important his struggle was. An all-powerful liberalism has enlisted a treasonous cultural elite and corrupted Hollywood, the universities, churches, the press, the foundations, both political parties, the judiciary, and just about every other institution in the land. The culture war was in full swing, and he donned the armor of its secular standard-bearers to sally forth against civilization's degenerate internal enemy.

The Vietnam War, Jim Crow, male supremacy—those were just excuses. The real problem was simpler: there were too many young people and they had overwhelmed the institutions responsible for turning them into civilized human beings. Driven by a reckless ignorance of the limits of human nature, destructive and nihilistic to its core, totalitarian and wildly contemptuous of ordinary people, committed to remaking human nature and willing to use violence in pursuit of its utopian ends, the Sixties was the logical end-point of modern liberalism. Having cut their teeth in a barbaric attack on Western civilization and sharpened them as they determined to bring the United States to its knees, the radicals had migrated into the institutions that specialize in molding popular opinion. Safely inhabiting the universities, media, entertainment, and foundations, they have traded their revolutionary rhetoric and embrace of redemptive violence for the steady corruption of the culture and an attack on the country's foundations.

> Unlike any previous decade in American experience, the Sixties combined domestic disruption and violence with an explosion of drug use and sexual promiscuity; it was a decade of hedonism and narcissism; it was a decade in which popular culture reached new lows of vulgarity. The Sixties generation combined moral relativism with political absolutism. And it was the decade in which the Establishment not only collapsed but began to endorse the most outrageous behavior and indictments of America by young radicals. It was the decade that saw victories for the civil rights movement, but it was also the decade in which much of America's best educated and most pampered youth refused to serve the country in war, disguising self-indulgence and hatred of the United States as idealism. What W. H. Auden said of the 1930s was even more true of the 1960s: it was a 'low, dishonest decade.'[32]

Too much liberty has culminated in liberalism's embrace of whining white women and predatory black thugs. Neither can be tolerated by a civilized society, and there is no ethical warrant for going beyond equality before the law. Since no one is rich because another is poor, redistribution is out. The rich deserve their wealth and the only thing that can explain widespread objections to unprecedented inequality is an enfeebled, corrupt, and hedonistic culture that "distorts incentives by increasingly rejecting personal achievement as the criterion for the distribution of rewards."[33] As angry as he was when it came to "culture," Bork was most fed up with calls for social justice. Liberalism is responsible for all the moral failings of contemporary society, but none of them are so grievous as nurturing the politics of envy. "The usual strategy of coping with the discomfort of knowing that others are superior in some way is to reduce the inequalities by bringing the more fortunate down or by preventing him from being more fortunate."[34] The rage for equality attacks excellence, achievement and merit, undermines authority, has a pernicious leveling feel to it, is inherently authoritarian and statist, reeks of the intelligentsia's impatient utopianism, reflects its love of violence and its embrace of romantic brutality, and would institutionalize envy as the law of the land. Bork was particularly sure that liberalism's commitment to regulation and redistribution in the name of more economic equality makes it an active enemy of achievement and accomplishment. But even that attack on civilization pales before the liberal attack on authority. One of the most important influences on the "originalist" jurisprudence of Antonin Scalia and William Rehnquist, the former Solicitor General and Acting Attorney General of the United States was sure that things had gone too far. "There has to be a limit somewhere to what a culture can tolerate and still retain not just creative choice but a vestige of decency," he warned ominously. "That limit is now beyond us."[35]

Bork was particularly incensed by two of the most powerful movements that democratized modern American life. "Radical feminism," he announced, "is the most destructive and fanatical movement to come down to us from the Sixties. This is a revolutionary, not a reformist, movement, and it is meeting with considerable success. Totalitarian in spirit, it is deeply antagonistic to traditional Western culture and proposes the complete restructuring of society, morality, and human nature."[36] References to a "ranting" Bella Abzug and an "icy" Gloria Steinem" illustrated Bork's belief that "it would be better, I think, to drop the word 'feminism' altogether since the movement no longer has a constructive role to play; its work is done. There are no artificial barriers to women's achievement."[37] Since there is no legally mandated gender superiority, women face no real problems and should stop complaining. Incited by embittered, neurotic, and irrational leaders, they are being cynically used to serve "radical" feminism's hostility to the family, capitalism, religion, and the intellect. Deeply false and dangerously totalitarian, feminism invades the private sphere, politicizes the culture, denies the individual any sanctuary, insists on controlling all spheres of thought and action. Just as this variant of female insanity originated in Sixties radicalism and has been perpetuated by liberalism since then, so do black irresponsibility, paranoia, opportunism, ignorance, and low expectations. Like feminism, racism had been eliminated by the Civil Rights Act, and it's also time for blacks to stop complaining.[38]

The primary cancer had originated in the universities. It has spread rapidly, metastasizing to other institutions and coarsening society's moral fabric in the name of a whining, sniveling ideology of self-serving victimhood. Sexism and racism have "utterly evaporated," but that doesn't stop Bork's extortionists. Reason and rationality have been thrown overboard by hysterical women and thuggish blacks who are being aided and abetted by their anti-American liberal allies. Afraid to compete on equal terms, they have become experts at demanding something for nothing. And there is precious little in the culture that can resist them. The problem cannot be approached with halfway measures. The Sixties committed many sins, one of the most important of which was its war on religion and its secularization of life. Liberal egalitarianism and individualism deny the source of the first principles that alone can make for a decent society. Like Falwell, Bork fell back on a simple authoritarianism that embraced the truth of revealed religion and demanded unquestioning deference to received wisdom. Obedience is the undivided source of morality. "Only religion can accomplish for a modern society what tradition, reason, and empirical observation cannot. Christianity and Judaism provide the major premises of moral reasoning by revelation and by the stories in the Bible. There is no need to attempt the impossible task of reasoning your way to first principles. Those principles are accepted as given by God."[39]

Like others on the Right, Bork's authoritarian politics led him to an authoritarian God. It's been a long journey, moving him from his starting point in New Deal liberalism through the University of Chicago and Leo Strauss, then to Yale Law School, the Nixon administration, and a starring role in Watergate's "Saturday Night Massacre." A founding member of the Federalist Society and long-time Senior Fellow at the American Enterprise Institute, Bork had been on the United States Court of Appeals for the District of Columbia from 1982 to 1988 when he was nominated by President Ronald Reagan to the Supreme Court in 1987. His extreme views certainly contributed to his famous and well-deserved defeat, but he's not a crank. A central player in the rise of the contemporary Right, his initial concern with "values" quickly developed into a standard call for authoritarian moral restoration and the use of political power in the service of wealth.

Carried forward by a long, powerful, and conservative religious Great Awakening, the Right has successfully cast itself as the spokesman of hard-working, law-abiding citizens whose modest desire to be left alone has been systematically betrayed by crazed feminists, criminal blacks, and a weak-willed and corrupt liberal elite. Just as it first appeared as the tough-minded defender of the national interest in a threatening international environment, so it responded to broad domestic crisis, general social breakdown, and liberal paralysis with calls for an authoritarian moral restoration. It had a lot to work with. Widespread fears that things had gone too far and that it was time to stop the slide into anarchy rested on the lived experiences of millions of Americans. From the late 1960s on, many middle- and working-class families sought refuge in a stronger and more coercive state to protect them, their families, and their possessions from criminal violence. The population decisively rejected "soft" strategies for dealing with anti-social behavior and liberals took a well-deserved beating around the country for their unwillingness to respond to the real fears and insecurities of city-dwellers and suburbanites alike. As many urban working-class neighborhoods became war zones and whole cities descended into violence and criminality during the 1980s, it seemed that only tough-minded conservatives were willing to look the problem in the eye and design effective strategies for ensuring safety and restoring civilized behavior.[40] The seeming failure of core instruments of the liberal welfare state to make a dent in the cycle of drive-by shootings, menacing street thugs, and general anarchy set the conditions for an embrace of the Right by reliably Democratic constituencies. When conservatives warned that no society could survive a general breakdown of order and indicted liberals for their inability to provide safety and security, millions of people were ready to listen.

Under the circumstances, it seemed that liberalism's defense of economic equality and social justice had degenerated into reflexive apologies for crime and irresponsible attempts to blame society for individual and family pathology. Since carrots had failed to stop the murders, robberies, and rapes, alarmed and fed-up Americans searched for sticks to do the job. The last twenty-five years have seen the Right periodically trot out variations on the same dependable theme, even though millions of blacks and women have benefited from the long-overdue collapse of its beloved "traditional values." Bork's claims that the Sixties had begun a slide into chaos have been echoed in Newt Gingrich's 1994 announcement that the Right's goal was to rid the country of President Clinton and the remnants of the "countercultural McGoverniks" he represented.

Just as in foreign relations, though, the Right's solution to breakdown was a betrayal and a dead end. As successful as it's been as a political slogan and as deeply as it expressed very real anxieties, "the breakdown of family values" is a singularly unhelpful way of understanding social crisis. Policing sexual activity, enforcing conformity, and demanding good behavior may have gone down well with a population that was tired of all the disorder, but obedient women, deferential blacks, and being "right with God" won't solve anything if abortions, illegitimacy, crime, and unemployment are treated as private failings. So long as inequality, health care, stagnant wages, homelessness, lost pensions, and the West's longest workweek are not seen as moral issues, then Americans will be unable to understand how the wealthiest 20% of the population increased its share of the country's income from 44% to 50% between 1973 and 2002. Two-thirds of President George W. Bush's tax cuts have gone to families that average $203,740 per year, yet failure to treat this as a moral problem makes it hard to address the long, successful drive to channel wealth to the top.[41] Thirteen million American children live below the poverty line, but the Right's "family values" talk only about abortion and same-sex marriages. If Bork is right and the rich are rich because they're better, then the "crisis of the family" will seem to be as good an explanation of poverty, divorce, welfare, unwed motherhood, drug abuse, family stress, and unemployment as any other. But restricting moral judgment to individual behavior is a false promise and a cynical betrayal. It's profoundly true that liberals failed to enforce codes of decent behavior and didn't care about the daily fear and insecurity that millions of decent Americans were feeling. But it's no less true that the Right manipulated the desire for peace and quiet to serve its wider project of protecting wealth. Every answer it proposed intensified the very problems it claimed to solve. If social welfare programs were part of the problem, then restoring authority was the answer. Why waste money on more teachers when we all know that kids don't learn because their families don't care about them? Why spend money on efforts to relieve poverty when we all know that it comes from the bad behavior of irresponsible women? Why bother with public housing when we all know that they'll quickly become pig sties? Why try to reform the prison system when we know that crime is caused by absent fathers? Why supply birth control and family planning when illegitimacy is caused by sexy movies, hip-hop music, and teen-age promiscuity? Why waste money on welfare when the poor will just spend it on drugs and sneakers?

Millions of hard-working Americans wanted an end to social crisis and the restoration of peace and civility. The Right took their legitimate concerns, dressed them up in the authoritarian language of law and order, and used them to attack the Great Society, social welfare, shared responsibility, and the very idea of equality itself. In the absence of a credible alternative, these arguments carried the day. This is not what people who worried about their kids' education, the safety of their neighborhoods, or the welfare of their country wanted, but once again it's what they got.

Notes

1. Introductory Note to *The Crisis of Democracy: Report on the Governability of Democracies to the Trilateral Commission* (New York: New York University Press, 1975), p. 8.

2. *Ibid.*, pp. 8–9.

3. *Ibid.*, p. 9.

4. "The United States," *ibid.*, p. 64. His emphasis.

5. *Ibid.*, pp. 63–64.

6. *Ibid.*, p. 74.

7. *Ibid.*

8. *Ibid.*, p. 102.

9. *Ibid.*, p. 114.

10. *Ibid.*, p. 115.

11. *Ibid.*, p. 113.

12. Jerry Falwell,. *Listen, America!* (New York: Doubleday, 1980).

13. *Ibid.*, p. 6.

14. *Ibid.*, p. 5.

15. *Ibid.*

16. *Ibid.*, p. 131.

17. *Ibid.*, p. 157.

18. *Ibid.*, p. 17.

19. *Ibid.*, p. 89.

20. *Ibid.*, p. 85.

21. *Ibid.*, p. 232.

22. Allan Bloom, *The Closing of the American Mind* (New York: Simon & Schuster, 1987).

23. *Ibid.*, p. 26.

24. *Ibid.*, p. 36.

25. *Ibid.*, p. 39.

26. *Ibid.*, p. 228.

27. *Ibid.*, p. 314.

28. *Ibid.*, p. 313.

29. Robert Bork, *Slouching Towards Gomorrah: Modern Liberalism and American Decline* (New York: HarperCollins, 1996).

30. *Ibid.*, p. 4.

31. *Ibid.*, p. 7.

32. *Ibid.*, pp. 50–51.

33. *Ibid.*, p. 2.

34. *Ibid.*, p. 75.

35. *Ibid.*, p. 132.

36. *Ibid.*, p. 193.

37. *Ibid.*, p. 194.

38. *Ibid.*, pp. 229–230.

39. *Ibid.*, p. 278.

40. Edward Banfield's *The Unheavenly City* (Boston: Little, Brown, 1970) and James Q. Wilson, *Thinking About Crime* (New York: Basic Books, 1975) are two early examples.

41. *The New York Times*, August 13 and 16, 2004.

CHAPTER FOUR

Racial Fear

Insistent calls for discipline and authority found millions of willing listeners as the Right began to articulate a strategy of national strength and moral rebirth. Things had seemed bad enough when American diplomats were held hostage in Teheran, when the Soviet Union appeared to be advancing everywhere, and when national politics had apparently fallen into institutional deadlock and permanent instability. But one particular area of public life trumped everything else during the late 1970s. Nowhere was social crisis more acute, nowhere were its effects so visible, and nowhere was the Right's ability to exploit it more effective than when Americans turned their attention to the catastrophe engulfing the nation's black population.

As black working-class neighborhoods were battered by a series of ruinous plagues, the Right learned how to deploy images of crime, violence, and social pathology to assist its larger political project. Skillfully adapting key elements of the nation's poisoned racial history, it constructed a new attack on equality and the welfare state that suddenly found a mass audience. As deindustrialization destroyed hundreds of thousands of jobs and disinvestment shattered prospects for recovery from riots and civil disorders, conservative solutions gained traction in conditions of chronic unemployment, a paralyzing heroin epidemic, a dramatic increase in violent crime, white flight, a cycle of arson and abandonment, the virtual disappearance of the two-parent family, the collapse of basic institutions like public housing and schools, and—most important—liberal silence.

Working-class and lower-middle class whites could not easily insulate themselves from these developments and their political attitudes were inevitably shaped in response to them. None of this was particularly new, but the late 1970s brought their anxieties and insecurities to a head and drove many of them to the right. Lurid descriptions of chaotic, dangerous, and disorderly black neighborhoods had played important roles in the anti-busing crusades of the 1960s, in George Wallace's 1964 presidential bid, in the mayoral campaigns of "backlash" candidates like Frank Rizzo in Philadelphia, Anthony Imperiale in Newark, Louise Day Hicks in Boston, and Mario Procaccino in New York, and in the evolution of neo-conservatives like Norman Podhoretz and his *Commentary* magazine. Scary descriptions of urban crisis allowed the Right to mobilize white hopelessness, resentment, and anger against an ostensibly selfish and demanding black population that had proven unwilling to respect the new rules that came with the victories of the civil rights movement. As blacks insisted on squandering their hard-won equality, conservatives claimed, they became increasingly parasitical on hard-working and productive taxpayers. It wasn't long before a picture of an ungrateful, demanding, and undeserving people began to serve the Right's more general project of attacking social welfare. Its core position was easy to make, all the more so because it seemed obviously true that a entire large stratum had become dependent on a welfare state that did little but transfer resources from the hard-working, talented, and overburdened to the lazy, incompetent, and undeserving. A popular narrative suggested that blacks systematically undermined the normal rules of social progress through acts of individual and collective violence, public expressions of contempt for middle-class morality, and excessive demands on others. It fed a racial discourse that began to blame an allegedly self-destructive and irresponsible population for its own failure to advance. The "grass roots" sentiment that stood behind this was framed by conservative analysts who claimed that blacks' disorganized families, lack of respect for civility in public spaces, dependence on the state for direct income and benefits, and constant demands for special treatment signaled how different their mores and behaviors were from those of earlier immigrants and hard-working, "normal" citizens.

Right-wing spokesmen claimed that city life was being undermined by the bad habits of black residents who rejected the norms of past generations of the urban poor. It wasn't long before they were seconded by polemics against the "affirmative" steps that had addressed black poverty, unemployment, and social isolation. Although there were significant differences between some of these early commentators, they all agreed on one thing: the most important threats to social peace, political stability, and democratic institutions came from below. The black poor were acting in ways that no other large group of recent urban migrants had ever dared, and the reckless demands of their extortionist leaders could no longer be accommodated within the moral framework of elementary fairness. Later arguments claiming that misguided liberal welfare policies had actively contributed to the destruction of inner city communities supplemented the discovery of a pathological "culture" of the black underclass that constantly destabilized and endangered the larger society. Inner-city troubles, it was said, came from destructive values and bad behavior. By the mid-80s, blacks had become symbols for everything that was wrong with the country and were systematically presented as greedy welfare mothers, wilding young people who saw every white person as an opportunity to launch a personal crime spree, opportunistic leaders who cried racism at the drop of a hat, cold-eyed predatory drug dealers, vicious rapists, hyper-sexualized irresponsible women, and the country's newest crybabies who were always ready to deflect attention from their own failures by blaming others for a predicament that they had only brought on themselves. Discrimination can no longer explain poverty and degradation, a unified right-wing chorus maintained, and the black community must cure its own profound moral deficits if it wants to win popular white support for its efforts to advance. In the 90s, the argument was taken to new heights by public claims that blacks act badly because of their biological inferiority and by a formal position that they had become so impossible to live with that they should be permanently segregated or sterilized.

These claims were profoundly attractive—and deeply destructive. As anxious whites sought peace and safety, they became increasingly willing to sacrifice many of their own claims for social welfare and began to move toward a right-wing political leadership that was openly prepared to discipline unruly blacks. The pain and anguish on both sides of the racial divide generated a set of arguments that exploited both the distress of the black poor and the anxiety of the white working and lower middle classes. All were hurt by the policies that followed. In the end, American history held the trump cards. The Right's calls for renewed militarism and the restoration of authority were powerful enough, but they paled in comparison to the historic force that lay behind its ability to take advantage of racial politics. As liberalism, equality, and social reform became the point of attack, Irving Kristol's famous *bon mot* that "a neoconservative is just a liberal who got mugged by reality" anticipated more explicit racial barbs.

Black crime, illegitimacy, rudeness, and welfare were effective images for the Right's attack on social equality because they were real problems. When drugs, protests, pornography, violence, abortion, and obnoxious behavior threatened to overwhelm "middle America," the claim that the country had lost its moral underpinnings was an easy sell. As liberals proved unsympathetic to their fears, vulnerable whites fled to racial backlash in the belief that it would help them safeguard their hard-won and vulnerable position. Convinced by the Right that they were being squeezed between the unprincipled demands of the minority poor from below and the contemptuous disdain of the liberal elite from above, millions of whites of modest means were ready to abandon the welfare state from which they had gained so much. Kevin Phillips expressed it best:

> The principal force which broke up the Democratic (New Deal) coalition is the Negro socioeconomic revolution and liberal Democratic ideological inability to cope with it. Democratic 'Great Society' programs aligned that party with many Negro demands, but the party was unable to defuse the racial tension sundering the nation. The South, the West and the Catholic sidewalks of New York were the focal points of conservative opposition to the welfare liberalism of the federal government; however, the general opposition which deposed the Democratic Party came in large part from prospering Democrats who objected to Washington dissipating their tax dollars on programs which did them no good. The Democratic Party fell victim to the ideological impetus of a liberalism which had carried it beyond taxing the few for the benefit of the many (the New Deal) to programs taxing the many on behalf of the few (the Great Society).[1]

Old-fashioned conservatives had long been skeptical of popular government, were often explicitly anti-democratic, and tended to embrace the "excellence" that came with tradition, blood, and wealth. But the late-1970s combination of a broad religious revival, middle-class tax revolt, cultural conservatism, and racial backlash helped fuel a right-wing populism that went far beyond glorifying the past or defending the status quo. As it became a forward-looking political movement, the Right developed a defense of hardworking, ordinary Americans against the effete cosmopolitanism of the urban liberal "elite." Tired of welfare, hostile to higher taxes, frightened by rising crime, worried about their children, and suspicious of social engineering, important elements of the New Deal coalition became ripe for the picking.[2] As it fanned resentment of disruptive social movements, demanding women, the youthful counter-culture, and the black poor, the Right tied racial fatigue and a desire for peace and quiet to an attack on the broad social programs that had built the welfare state. As more and more whites lost their faith in public programs and felt put-upon, misunderstood, and ignored, right-wing spokesmen blamed an unholy alliance between a rapacious black underclass and the country's liberal elite for policies that were endangering their children and threatening their property. Convinced that they were being used and complaining that they just wanted to be left alone, millions of whites decided they were overtaxed, overregulated, and underappreciated. The politics of danger and dispossession announced the beginning of retrenchment, fed by a near-universal sense that uncivilized blacks had to be brought under control before they ruined the country. The country announced that it had had enough.

Left to itself, racial anxiety can't fully explain what happened in the late 1970s. In alliance with the period's other forces, it proved to be exceptionally powerful. As liberals refused to deal with a broad desire that welfare be curbed, that deliberately offensive behavior be stopped, and that crime be punished, millions of whites abandoned them. They embraced the Right's claim that "culture" explained systematic black failure. The disappearance of explicit racial discrimination only made the argument more attractive. If crime, welfare dependency, unemployment, drug abuse, offensive music, illegitimacy and all the rest can no longer be laid at the door of the racist institutions of white America, said the Right, then the explanation must lie in black individuals and their communities. Hostility to all broad, comprehensive social efforts generated dozens of books, articles, and pronouncements claiming that any state action is bound to fail if its target population is not prepared to live in a cooperative and productive fashion. Self-serving and opportunistic civil rights leaders continue to find malign intent and conscious discrimination where there isn't any, said the Right, and public programs that had failed to eliminate poverty demonstrated the power of "values" and the importance of individual responsibility. Liberal love of state activity is actively counter-productive, since it blinds people to the true source of failure and perpetuates a culture of dependence that does no one any good. The urban poor choose to remain chained by their own history, are unable to take advantage of opportunity, and end up fleeing the responsibilities that come with equality. Blacks will never overcome poverty and dependence, it was said, until they drop their demands for "quotas," "reverse discrimination," and "preferential treatment." It's time to administer a healthy dose of tough love, take them off the dole, set them loose, and let them sink or swim.

Equality Before the Law

Nathan Glazer's influential 1975 argument against affirmative action was organized around a simple claim: in their eagerness to create an egalitarian and integrated society, liberal policy-makers were actually tearing it apart. Insisting that rights are carried by individuals and that the whole idea of group rights is an anti-democratic fiction, *Affirmative Discrimination* claimed that the federal government was recreating the same harmful environment it wanted to end. In their haste to stop punishing individuals for being black, affirmative action programs proposed to reward individuals for being black. The conditions might be different, but the results were bound to be the same. Even if busing, affirmative action, and other positive interventions had brought some benefit to their intended recipients, said Glazer, they ended up doing more damage than any tolerant and diverse society could accept. They violated a long-established American commitment to equal treatment, demanded an unacceptable price from those who were not responsible for the problem in the first place, generated an angry reaction that would inevitably undermine white support for racial equality, and centralized power in unaccountable federal bureaucracies and judges. We are well on the way, Glazer warned repeatedly, to a situation in which race and ethnic group identification will determine individual prospects—the very last thing that racial justice requires. The goals of the civil rights movement were being endangered by the bad uses to which its self-appointed guardians were putting its victories.

All government regulations and court decisions that require employment, promotion, and school assignment by race are suspect, said Glazer. To begin with, they fly in the face of a basic American proposition about citizenship and fair play. The core American project is the public attempt to broaden individual horizons while treating identity as a private matter. Equality and achievement, the country's two most important values, are inherently opposed to all claims of ethnic and racial privilege. More inclusiveness, not less, should be the guiding principle of social policy. The Civil Rights Act of 1964 had established a powerful federal commitment to support individual rights, but Glazer worried that the period's broad consensus was being destroyed by an insistent civil rights establishment's habit of demanding special treatment on the basis of race. Two different notions of equality were at war, and the idea of group rights was paving the way for quotas, affirmative action, and other intrusive federal programs. Glazer wanted to be careful. An individualistic notion of rights will generally stop at equality of opportunity. A commitment to group rights, on the contrary, will tend to go further and embrace a theory of equal outcomes. Once equality is defined in terms of results rather than of opportunity, the road is open to the claim that *any* racial imbalance must be due to discrimination. Consciousness no longer matters. Once intent is taken out of the picture, it's only a short step to requirements that demand certain results regardless of circumstances. A slippery slope guarantees that equal opportunity will become statistical parity as the horizons of acceptable conduct narrow and the opportunity for bureaucratic and judicial meddling expand.

> 'Affirmative action' originally meant that one should not only not discriminate, but inform people one did not discriminate; not only treat those who applied for jobs without discrimination, but seek out those who might not apply. This is what it apparently meant when first used in executive orders. In the Civil Rights Act of 1964, it was used to mean something else—the remedies a court could impose when some employer was found guilty of discrimination, and they could be severe. The new concept of 'affirmative action' that has since emerged and has been enforced with ever greater vigor combines both elements: It assumes that everyone is guilty of discrimination; it then imposes on every employer the remedies which in the Civil Rights Act of 1964 could only be imposed on those guilty of discrimination.[3]

The result of all this, says Glazer, can only be an entirely new system of racial preference in hiring, pay, promotion, and other areas of the American job market. This is an enormous job in such a diverse society and will require drawing an ever-more complicated map of the country's ethnic and racial groups. All suffered different levels of historic deprivation, require different levels of support, and will benefit from different remedies. This is a road to disaster, he warned. All such efforts to end discrimination, no matter how laudable their intent, will end up with professionals trying to organize and impose policy. An unavoidable tendency to draft mandates will pull integration away from public opinion and democratic accountability. Measures that appear perfectly sensible and just to those who organize them will be widely perceived as unfair and will always create more problems than they solve. This is the last thing that public policy should be doing. "New lines of conflict are created, by government action. New resentments are created; new turfs are to be protected; new angers arise; and one sees them on both sides of the line that divides protected and affected from nonprotected and unaffected."[4]

Glazer did not want to be misunderstood. He supported integration and was glad to see it moving ahead. But he doubted that "forced" busing or "coercive" affirmative action would do much to advance equality and equal treatment. Justice requires moderation about ends and patience about means. It was important that individual whites and their communities not be held responsible for crimes they didn't commit. Class will trump race sooner or later anyway, and Glazer believed that the economics of the race problem would blunt the hard edge of animosity and ease white concern about black criminality and social pathology.

> The integration of blacks proceeds, and at a pace related to their rise in incomes and occupation level. The segregation of other minority groups is based more on income and occupation than on racial and ethnic discrimination and will decline with rising incomes and related changes in occupation and culture. The integration of the poor is quite another matter, and is hardly likely to be much advanced whatever measures of public policy we adopt. The poor are constrained in their movements by limited income, are resisted by the middle classes because of the social problems they bring, and further, it is not at all clear that the poor will be better off if distributed through an active public policy—even if it were possible—among the middle classes.[5]

Whites needn't worry about integration, Glazer implied. Economics will marginalize the black poor in a way that should protect the white middle class. But working-class whites might have more to fear—and Glazer worried about how they would respond to threat. This is what convinced him that the modest gains made possible by affirmative action programs—gains that probably would have come in any event—were just not worth the cost. Driven forward by integrationist enthusiasm and bureaucratic inertia, policies designed to remedy discrimination had gone far beyond what was initially intended, what constitutional law permitted, or what was really necessary. Originally intended to prepare members of minority groups for jobs and educational opportunities, they had become programs for filling numerical quotas by recruiting those who might not be qualified in the first place. Then they morphed into imposing abstract statistical requirements on employers and educational institutions, all of whom were presumed to have discriminated in the absence of numerical proof to the contrary.

Slowly but surely, Glazer warned, the country was abandoning its commitment to individual rights and replacing them with measures to redress the wrongs done to politically-defined racial and ethnic groups. This could only lead to trouble. "Compensation for the past is a dangerous principle. It can be extended indefinitely and make for endless trouble. Who is to determine what is proper compensation for the American Indian, the black, the Mexican American, the Chinese or Japanese American? When it is established that the full status of equality is extended to every individual, regardless of race, color, or national origin, and that special opportunity is also available to any individual on the basis of individual need, again regardless of race, color, or national origin, one has done all that justice and equity call for and that is consistent with a harmonious multigroup society."[6]

Glazer's critique of affirmative action was organized around a single claim that would come to have great traction when taken up by analysts who were much more conservative than he: it is always wrong to attach benefits and penalties to individuals on the basis of their membership in this or that racial or ethnic group. Individual interests are the only dependable lodestar for public policy. The state should clear away overt discrimination and then get out of the way. Anything more is politically destructive, ethically indefensible, and pragmatically dangerous. "The implications of the new course," he said, "are an increasing consciousness of the significance of group membership, an increasing divisiveness on the basis of race, color, and national origin, and a spreading resentment among the disfavored groups against the favored groups. If the individual is the measure, however, our public concern is with the individual's capacity to work out an individual fate by means of education, work, and self-realization in the various spheres of life."[7] *Affirmative Discrimination* established the Right's central argument about policies that were designed to make up for past discrimination.

On the face of it, Glazer's appeal for strict racial neutrality sounded sensible enough. Once official, state-sanctioned discrimination has been eliminated, then political authorities are responsible to ensure that skin color plays no role in public life. Equal opportunity requires that everyone be treated the same—no more and no less. If group rights are a recipe for disaster and if "compensation for the past is a dangerous principle," then racial peace requires that blacks shoulder their own responsibilities, look ahead, stop thinking of themselves as members of an aggrieved group, and model their behavior on that of other minorities. The argument was a comforting one, for it seemed to be grounded in a time-honored American ethic of individual accomplishment and hostility to unearned outside help.

But the problem is that it's not based on the country's real history, runs counter to logic, and provides little help in understanding how official race blindness has often intensified poverty, isolation, and inequality. Legislating a "level playing field" and mandating official neutrality in matters of race were certainly big steps forward, and the Civil Rights Act of 1964 and Voting Rights Act of the next year brought racial democracy that much closer. But they haven't been enough, and not just because they've been weakly applied. The problem lies deeper: in an environment of deeply rooted, historically formed injustice, formal equality before the law often makes things worse.

Ira Katznelson's *When Affirmative Action Was White* traces the roots of

President Johnson's programs to the seemingly race-neutral federal legislation that began thirty years before the civil rights movement.[8] It finds that the federal government's official neutrality has often widened racial disparities and reinforced white privilege. Social Security, unemployment compensation, and the minimum wage—all these ambitious and seemingly egalitarian programs, organized as they were on the basis of official color-blindedness, actually turned out to be instruments of inequality. Deferring to the demands of Southern Congressional leaders that white supremacy be maintained, these federal programs did not cover agricultural and domestic workers and thus denied protection to most black laborers. The GI Bill—the period's other major "color-blind" advance—was also shaped by the politics of race. As the price of congressional passage, the Southern political barons invoked the "democratic" virtues of decentralization and demanded that the GI Bill be administered by local—and Jim Crow—political office-holders, businessmen, college administrators, and bankers rather than by "bureaucrats' from Washington. This concession guaranteed the continued exclusion of black veterans from the law's opportunities for educational advancement, job training, home mortgages, and business loans.

Just as many Southern states had organized Jim Crow by pretending that black disenfranchisement rested on color-blind residency requirements, poll taxes, and interpretations of state constitutions, so post–World War II white supremacy was reinforced by official federal color-blindedness. Government programs that were officially neutral were consciously designed to maintain white supremacy throughout the South and in the country as a whole. The result was to be expected: black veterans who were formally eligible for federal assistance failed to advance as rapidly as their white counterparts. Under the circumstances, it was easy for the Right to say that the federal government was wasting its time on a black population that was congenitally unable to take advantage of opportunities for home ownership, job retraining, college education, and economic advancement.

"Culture"

Glazer's critique provided the foundation for the Right's attack on affirmative action, but a broader appeal to racial anxiety rested on a stronger foundation. If special privilege offended justice and fair play, it was important to assign responsibility for black failure where it belonged. There had to be more at work to explain persistent isolation and pathology, and the Right moved quickly to blame a "culture" that was proving as harmful in conditions of freedom as the law had been in conditions of segregation. Like Glazer, Thomas Sowell painted a picture of gradual black progress in an improving environment that really didn't need much governmental tinkering.[9] For the most part, he said, the United States has been pretty successful at assimilating different racial and ethnic groups. Geographic space and economic expansion proved more powerful than past grievances or memories of oppression. Sowell knew that black history is unlike that of immigrant and ethnic groups, but he was cautiously optimistic that there was nothing inherent in the larger culture that stood in the way of progress and assimilation.

The answer had to be internal. Sowell was one of the first conservative analysts to focus on culture—particularly what he called "human capital"—to explain the persistent difficulties faced by blacks even after formal barriers to progress had been dismantled. "Whether in an ethnic context or among peoples and nations in general, much depends on the whole constellation of values, attitudes, skills, and contacts that many call a culture and that economists call 'human capital,'" he observed.[10] The Chinese, Japanese, and Jewish success stories featured high levels of social cohesion and social capital, and this had enabled them to succeed in the face of bitter resistance, hostility, and violence. But American blacks had come to this country in different circumstances, constituted an easily identifiable race instead of an ethnic group, and had been a dependent population far longer than the others. Their relative lack of helpful "values, attitudes, skills, and contacts" can be explained in different ways, but Sowell was sure that black advancement was being systematically sabotaged by a culture that consigned them to failure when others had succeeded. His understanding of "culture" was very different from that of later right-wingers and focused on habits of solidarity, mutual assistance, community resources, and accumulated knowledge. In an environment where liberals wouldn't go near this issue for fear of offending one of their core constituencies and "blaming the victim," Sowell's focus on human capital was an early attempt to explain the persistent difficulties faced by black neighborhoods. After an appropriate metamorphosis, "culture" would provide the second leg of the Right's successful appeal to white racial anxiety. It seemed to make sense to a population whose deep attachment to fair play and self-reliance couldn't explain what was going on in black communities. Something terrible was happening to the nation's cities, and as the basic institutions of public order collapsed it began to seem that there was something internally wrong as well. Family breakdown, disappearing community organizations, persistent unemployment, decaying physical infrastructure—black neighborhoods seemed trapped in an endless cycle of disorder that defied remedy. For people who were desperately trying to create social spaces with some measure of security, "culture" seemed as credible an explanation of everyday mayhem as any.

Sowell's was an intelligent and thoughtful analysis of issues that went beyond liberal pieties, but the Right had other plans. In 1978, William Simon and Irving Kristol had organized the Institute for Educational Affairs with start-up grants from the right-wing Olin, Scaife, and Smith Richardson Foundations. Coca Cola, Dow Chemical, Ford Motor Company, General Electric, K-Mart, Mobil, and Nestle made substantial contributions to enable the IEA to "seek out promising Ph.D. candidates and undergraduate leaders, help them establish themselves through grants and fellowships and then help them get jobs with activist organizations, research projects, student publications, federal agencies or leading periodicals." The Institute began to construct a network of conservative college magazines, and a year after its formation the *Dartmouth Review* appeared. Its attacks on affirmative action, gay students, and women's groups, promoted as expressions of free speech and reactions to liberal conformity, conferred immediate national recognition—and deserved notoriety—on the paper and its editor, an undergraduate named Dinesh D'Souza. After graduation, D'Souza went to work for the Reagan White House. Making the rounds of the American Enterprise Institute, the Hoover Institution, and kindred safe havens, he has published a series of books on such subjects as "What's so Great About America" and became something of a young conservative celebrity. Like other right-wingers who appeal to racial anxiety, he does not want to be misunderstood. *The End of Racism* begins with the claim that the author is a friend of blacks, supports civil rights, understands multiculturalism, and believes in equality. But new conditions demand new thinking.[11]

D'Souza starts with what's wrong. The primary explanation for black failure in the United States, he tells us, is "a culture that was an adaptation to historical oppression but is, in several important respects, dysfunctional today." Neither genetic, psychological, nor historical explanations can account for the persistent black failure that sets African-Americans apart from all other groups. Neither multiculturalism nor targeted programs incorporating proportional representation will cure it. No, "black failure to meet merit standards of academic achievement and economic performance" must be met head on and confronted with honesty, bravery, and compassion. The United States has succeeded in eliminating official racism, so the Right's cultural argument explains that blacks are responsible for creating their own problems—and for overcoming them.

Black rage, white backlash, and liberal helplessness have made a toxic brew of festering problems and inadequate solutions. Togther, says D'Souza, they are the legacy of an anti-racism that has been inadequate for years and is now collapsing under the weight of its own failure. Old nostrums won't do. It's imperative to start at the beginning, and D'Souza is not afraid to name names. Black cultural deficiency, not racism, disinvestment, or economic structure, is responsible for failure and explains why equality before the law has not led to substantial progress. Simple-minded multicultural tolerance won't help. It's time to break with the illusion that all cultures are equally worthy of respect and frankly recognize that some are better than others. A "civilizational crisis" that afflicts the black underclass above all was D'Souza's chosen point of attack, buttressed by the unstated but clear implication that the failure of all blacks comes from the same poisoned source: "excessive reliance on government, conspiratorial paranoia about racism, a resistance to academic achievement as 'acting white,' a celebration of the criminal and outlaw as authentically black, and the normalization of illegitimacy and dependency. These group patterns arose as a response to past oppression, but they are now dysfunctional and must be modified."[12]

D'Souza doesn't explain how these pathologies once worked for blacks, but that's not the point. It's important to understand what needs to be done and who needs to do it. The civil rights movement had gone as far as it could and had succeeded in eliminating official racial supremacy, so it makes no sense to talk about racism any more. Blacks are being childish, self-indulgent, and dishonest if they cling to the misguided notion that they live in a hostile society, and they will make no progress until they change their irrational ideas and their consequent bad behavior. Until they do so, they will deserve what they're getting: white indifference and hostility. Their social pathologies, criminality, and violence legitimize what D'Souza winningly calls "rational discrimination"—the sort of behavior that leads a white woman to cross the street when a group of young black men are on the same sidewalk or that encourages a store clerk to follow a browsing black customer around. Unfair treatment does exist in American life, but it's not racism. It's "rational discrimination."

White perceptions that blacks are lazy, loud, violent, irresponsible, sexually promiscuous, and disposed to crime have a "rational" basis that is built on white observation of black behavior.[13] After all, said D'Souza, blacks *do* commit more crimes, *are* more dependent on welfare, *act* more obnoxious in public, *have* more illegitimate children, and *make* more noise than whites. Predictive generalizations like these don't arise out of thin air, he reassures his reader. There's a rational basis, built on observation and experience, for claims that blacks know how to dance. There's a rational basis, built on observation and experience, for the high arrest rates of young black men. There's a rational basis, built on observation and experience, for cabbies' refusal to pick up black fares. There's a rational basis, built on observation and experience, for regarding young black women as sexually irresponsible. There's a rational basis, built on observation and experience, for the high rates of black incarceration. But none of this is racism, for we have equality before the law. It's "rational discrimination," and it's triggered by bad black behavior. It might be ethically wrong in some instances, but the responsibility for eliminating it falls on those whose behavior elicits it in the first place. Until then, rational discrimination is a perfectly understandable and defensible strategy for coping with a difficult, dangerous, and uncivilized population.[14] Racial backlash isn't a monopoly of urban white working-class neighborhoods. D'Souza's is its soft, published, considered voice, substituting the language of fairness and worried concern for that of rage and threat:

> The last few decades have witnessed nothing less than a breakdown of civilization within the African American community. This breakdown is characterized by extremely high rates of criminal activity, by the normalization of illegitimacy, by the predominance of single-parent families, by high levels of addiction to alcohol and drugs, by a parasitic reliance on government provision, by hostility to academic achievement, and by a scarcity of independent enterprises. Civilizing institutions such as the small business, the church, and the family are now greatly weakened and in some areas they are on the verge of breaking down altogether. The next generation of young blacks is especially vulnerable.[15]

The disappearance of stable blue-collar jobs, capital flight from the country's cities, attacks on organized labor, politically-supported residential segregation, racial profiling, conscious state policies that shortchange urban public schools, a generation of cutbacks in social programs—none of this figures in D'Souza's world. Neither does the Great Society's undeniable success in prying open broad sections of the economy, tamping down urban disorder, helping to integrate higher education, expanding the black middle class, and denting the hard edge of persistent poverty. No, a pathological and dependent black "culture" has metastasized past the ghetto and now threatens American society. All blacks are afflicted with this diseased culture, all are responsible for its continuing strength, and the larger society will remain reluctant to help until they deal with it. "The civilizational crisis of the black community is not the result of genes and it is not the result of racism," says D'Souza. "The conspicuous pathologies of blacks are the result of cata-strophic cultural change that poses a threat both to the African American community and to society as a whole."[16] The black underclass has become dangerous to everyone. Racism might still exist in society's nooks and cran-nies, but it's vestigial and can no longer explain or justify black failure. The only time it matters is when the black underclass elicits it—and then it's deserved.

White America had done quite enough. Racial anxiety and profiling had turned out to be rational and white suspicion that blacks were responsible for their own misery had been accurate all along. Consistent black failure is a sure sign that white generosity has gone unrecognized and unrewarded. A disorganized, ungrateful, and pathological population cannot make full use of American citizenship because it has been morally unprepared to do so. The future is up to blacks; if they "can show that they are capable of perform-ing competitively in schools and the work force, and exercising both the rights and the responsibilities of American citizenship, then racism will be deprived of its foundation in experience. If blacks can close the civilization gap, the race problem in this country is likely to become insignificant."[17]

Since official discrimination has ended, it's an article of faith for the con-temporary Right that the remaining difficulties facing blacks are their own responsibility. If only blacks worked as hard as whites, saved as much as whites, studied as hard as whites, trusted American institutions as much as whites, played soccer as much as whites, bought homes as much as whites, went to college as much as whites, supervised homework as much as whites, and read for pleasure as much as whites, then the country's residual racial issues would fade away. A generation of right-wing propaganda seized upon evidence of pathology to blame black communities for continuing inequality and failure. Under the circumstances, many whites were open to the argu-ment that the country's collective obligation had come to an end with legal equality. It wasn't long before the Right extended this position and used it to support a broad assault on social equality and the welfare state. Among others, the influential Harvard team of Stephan and Abigail Thernstrom agrees that blacks are largely responsible for their own situation, that affirm-ative action and other programs have done nothing for their intended bene-ficiaries, and that the best thing is to adopt race-neutral standards and try to stop thinking about race altogether.[18] It's time to abandon distorted thinking and reject all preferential programs. Blacks have to start at home. Their future is in their hands, and it's time to grow up.

The Right has been demanding for years that American society stop rewarding blacks for their allegedly destructive behavior and unwillingness to compete. All its arguments make the same basic claims that were pioneered by Nathan Glazer: the country would be closer to a color-blind meritocracy if it weren't for affirmative action. Political, bureaucratic, and judicial policies are legitimate only if they accord the maximum degree of freedom to the pursuit of individual interests. Strict color-blindness is the only way life can be organized in a complex and diverse social order. Any system of racial discrimination or preference, it says, is indelibly unjust because the individual will always disappear and be replaced by the attribute.

The Right has built a powerful case by repeatedly affirming these bedrock positions. It claims that affirmative action is undemocratic, makes fair competition impossible, must lead to reverse discrimination, imposes undeserved burdens on the innocent, and substitutes an artificial guarantee of equal results for the time-honored standard of equal opportunity. A democratic government guarantees self-determination, equal treatment, the rule of law, and the dignity of the individual. Nothing more is called for. A "land of opportunity" conveys the promise that achievement will reflect talent and industry. Affirmative action makes this impossible, says the Right. Affirmative action in college admissions, race-conscious employment practices, business set-asides, court-ordered busing, and legislative redistricting are equally offensive.

There are many kinds of affirmative action and preferential treatment, and it's no accident that the Right has organized against only one. Veterans routinely receive a bonus on civil service tests, and their family members often benefit as well. The elderly get discounted seats on mass transit. The handicapped receive special preferences and expensive construction projects to guarantee them access to public space and accommodations. The government protects farmers with a variety of powerful and popular programs. College admissions offices routinely discriminate in favor of athletes and the children of alumni. Women often receive special consideration in receiving government contracts or in hiring practices. Private-sector nepotism in hiring and promotion is routine and untouched by law. These policies have enjoyed wide support for many years, and none has been particularly controversial.

Only affirmative action programs that provide advantages to blacks are at issue, and it's not because all such programs are inherently offensive. It's because they benefit blacks. The preferences that flow to farmers, veterans, the handicapped, athletes, and others reflect a calculation of moral desert that is withheld from blacks. Having agreed to sacrifice for us all, the veteran is morally worthy of preference. The elderly have lived most of their lives and made contributions to society for a long time, and they are worthy of preference. Farmers work hard to feed us, and they are worthy of preference. The handicapped should not be treated any differently from other sectors of the population, and if that requires spending lots of money to buy new buses, build ramps, and provide elevators, then simple equity requires a measure of preference. Nepotism, athletic scholarships, legacy admissions, and the like do offend the principle of achievement, but they are not seen as deeply unjust and provoke no widespread opposition. This contradictory set of attitudes reflect a history that is supportive of equal opportunity, most of the time, and of inclusion, for the most part.

But not always. The Right's opposition to affirmative action pivots on the concrete question of race in America, not on abstract claims about merit or equal opportunity. Its position is simple: blacks do not deserve any more preferential treatment. The country has done enough. Equality before the law is the end point of legitimate governmental action. Anything more has to come at someone's expense, and blacks don't deserve it just because they're black. They finally have a level playing field and shouldn't demean themselves any further by asking for more favors. At its worst, says the Right, affirmative action caters to the cowardice of a population that can't compete and wants to be protected from the consequences of its own failure. The lofty goals of the civil rights movement have been betrayed by its leadership's willingness to indulge in the corrupt logic of group rights and special privileges.

But affirmative action originated as a bipartisan tool of crisis management, not from some misguided alliance between a rapacious black leadership and a fawning liberal establishment. Civil rights groups were not campaigning for them, and their root was not official segregation but black poverty and unemployment in conditions of formal equality.[19] Even as they originated "when affirmative action was white," they were an immediate response to the urban riots of the 1960s. Dozens of Northern cities that had not experienced slavery or Jim Crow were shaken by overwhelming evidence that racial justice was a long way off. Like the riots themselves, all the social programs that characterized the period developed from an unavoidable truth that is still difficult to accept. The foundational premise of the civil rights movement—the assumption that equality before the law would soon lead to equality of outcome—turned out to have been naive. By the mid-1970s it had become clear that official racial supremacy wasn't the entire problem and that the United States hadn't become a full racial democracy with the passage of the Civil Rights and Voting Rights Acts. Indeed, legal equality

sometimes helped establish a racially segmented workforce, segregated neighborhoods and schools, and an impoverished—if legally free—black population clustered at the bottom of the social ladder. Racial democracy clearly
meant more than legal equality. The economic destitution, massive disinvestment, chronic unemployment, and persistent poverty afflicting black
communities was every bit as destructive of democracy as Jim Crow in the
South and informal segregation in the North.

It was this realization, and not some mixture of blackmail and cowardice,
that led to affirmative action. The Right's claim that urban riots were nothing more than criminal shopping sprees contained a bizarre kernel of truth
and it was soon obvious that black communities all over the country
wouldn't quiet down or begin to heal themselves without systematic programs of economic development. Race-targeted programs that centered on
employment and job training became a means of defusing racial tension,
averting more catastrophic urban riots, protecting American foreign policy
during the Cold War, strengthening Washington's ability to speak of human
rights, creating a stable black middle class, and injecting some purchasing
power into inner-city communities. It was governmental and business elites
who organized affirmative action and anti-poverty programs so they could
manage an explosive crisis. Many of them were very successful.

Americans usually agree that the government should step in to assist the
victims of natural disasters, protect the family farm, provide assistance to
public schools, build highways, subsidize prescriptions for the elderly, and
retrain unemployed workers. No aversion to "big government" or evocations
of a benign natural order intrude when it's a matter of aiding those who
deserve it. But affirmative action directed at blacks is different, for resistance
is rooted in the particular meaning of race in America. As the Right hitched
its wagon to the beneficial politics of racial backlash, it learned to defend a
"color-blind" vision of formal equality that has been perfectly consistent
with substantive racial inequality. Its opposition to public programs of racial
preference does not rest on some sort of principled commitment to equal
opportunity or to a defense of merit. It rests on a clear-eyed understanding
of how white anxiety could be used to support its core economic project of
tax cuts for the rich, deregulation, and privatization.

Attacks on affirmative action resonated widely in a troubled economic
environment marked by widespread white anxiety that their kids might find
it harder than they had expected to get into the colleges they thought they
deserved, to find the jobs for which they thought they were qualified, to
secure the promotions which they thought they earned, and to get the con-

tracts for which they bid. All of this has continued to strengthen the Right and has become part of the received wisdom about affirmative action. But middle-class anxiety was only part of the story. As powerful as right-wing attacks on affirmative action have been, they paled in comparison to the useful discoveries of the "underclass," the enduring problem of black "culture," and the seeming permanence of black poverty. These discoveries proved to be no less of a gold mine for the Right as was affirmative action, enabling it to appeal to the anxieties of millions of whites who lived near black neighborhoods, whose children went to integrated schools, and who encountered racially-charged danger every day. Here is where economic redistribution, social egalitarianism, and the welfare state could be directly blamed for a set of attitudes and behaviors that supposedly harmed the black poor and threatened American civilization at the same time.

Making Things Clear

Two enormously influential books led the way. Published in 1981, George Gilder's best-selling *Wealth and Poverty* was followed three years later by Charles Murray's equally popular *Losing Ground*. Their argument that the welfare state both caused black poverty and paralyzed efforts to eliminate it has defined almost all subsequent positions—starting at the top with those of Presidents Reagan, Clinton, and both Bushes. Aiming their fire directly at Johnson's Great Society, Gilder and Murray claimed that the most ambitious redistributive effort in modern American history had made poverty worse and demanded that all programs aiming at economic equality be abandoned before they fatally damaged the work ethic, family structure, popular expectations, race relations, and the prospects of their intended beneficiaries. Building on Irving Kristol's earlier claim that the War on Poverty had been "one of the great reform disasters of our age," they went far beyond his lament that Johnson had done little more than throw money at the black poor.[20]

Kristol had set the basic terms of the right-wing attack on contemporary social welfare; Gilder and Murray simply broadened its reach, explicitly organized it around race, and extended it to indict the welfare state as such. Kristol liked the New Deal and supported universal programs like public education, national health insurance, Social Security, children's allowances, unemployment insurance, and Medicare because they appealed to wide constituencies, brought diverse interests together, and provided an important measure of social cohesion. But he was uncomfortable with Johnson's desire to target a particular population with special programs that could only come at the expense of others. He was equally unhappy about particular features of the Great Society, arguing that they tended to trap the poor in a "poverty trap" by punishing productive and useful activity. Nervous about big, intrusive bureaucracies, Kristol preferred market-based solutions to problems like inadequate housing, arguing that vouchers would be more effective than public housing programs. He feared that state-organized measures to create social welfare always tend to grow, lose their initial orientation, and become impossibly ambitious, expensive, intrusive, and disruptive. The steady expansion of what Americans understood a "great society" to mean served as Kristol's case in point. Driven by an outsized ambition to eliminate all social ills and abolish all pain, Johnson had started with a "war on poverty" but went on to develop policies about mental health, pollution, urban revitalization, and the environment. It was bound to fail, for making governmental bureaucracies the main agents of social change was both futile and dangerous. In the end, Kristol repeated many times, the only reliable anti-poverty program was economic growth, for it made more resources available to those who needed them and—best of all—did not come at others' expense. The bureaucrats and politicians who designed welfare policies didn't understand this. "Egalitarianism may be motivated by a sincere desire to eliminate poverty, but it is one of the most efficient poverty-creating ideologies of our century," he warned.[21] Since there was no connection between the wealth of the rich and the poverty of the poor, the former could rest easy in the knowledge that helping the latter wouldn't have to cost them anything.

For all his criticisms of the Great Society and his faith in the market, Kristol did believe that a "modest" welfare state could alleviate some of the most crippling effects of poverty and inequality. But Gilder and Murray were radically different, and the sea-change they articulated found early support in Reagan's popular claim that welfare was the cause of poverty rather than its solution. The President's first economic report rejected "paternalism" in social policy, suggested that anti-poverty programs only aggravated the problems of the poor by trapping them in a cycle of poverty and dependence, and began to develop a broad ideological attack on the welfare state that enjoyed sustained support at the highest levels for the first time. It's common knowledge that Reagan didn't follow through on his early proclamations, but he was an important part of the Right's long effort to change public expectations about social welfare. So were Gilder and Murray, whose books helped shape a new, and decidedly more narrow, American consensus about equality.

Long before George W. Bush started talking about "compassionate conservatism," Gilder and Murray were arguing against social welfare in the name of the poor and talking about race without talking about it. *Wealth and Poverty* was written to address "the devastating impact of the programs of liberalism on the poor," said Gilder, and from the very beginning the book argued that the welfare state was harmful to its intended beneficiaries and that ending it would be good for all concerned.[22] As they defended established wealth and inequality, Gilder and Murray developed an argument against all political programs that aimed at economic redistribution. The idea was to take equality off the table entirely, and the best way of doing so was to blame liberalism for making poverty worse. It would be a short jump from there to the claim that any public program that encourages economic equality was immoral and doomed to fail.

Like D'Souza, Gilder started off on the high road, talking morality, announcing that he wanted to end poverty, and inventing a "golden rule of capitalism." Pursuing one's own interest isn't inherently selfish, he assured his readers, for every individual gain requires that someone be satisfied. Capitalism originates in giving and can be sustained only through sharing. Its moral core "consists of providing first and getting later," every market transaction forcing rational actors to give up something they have before they can get something they want.[23] Gilder's market was a moral network that linked self-serving and generous actors in a matrix of mutual support. Economic redistribution will make moral life impossible because "its deeper effect is to challenge the golden rule of capitalism, to pervert the relations between rich and poor, and to depict the system as 'a zero-sum game' in which every gain for someone implies a loss for someone else, and wealth is seen once again to create poverty."[24] Before Gilder identified the moral relationship between wealth and poverty that is "perverted" by too much concern about inequality, he decided to reveal the real cause of poverty.

Gilder started at the beginning: poverty is not the fault of the rich. And he named a much more substantial villain than D'Souza's favorite, but vague, "culture." It's the welfare state that causes poverty. If the past few years have taught us anything, he said, it is that the Great Society was an unmitigated catastrophe *for the poor*. The fault lay in the inherent logic of all public programs. Johnson's "war on poverty" was really a disguised war against wealth that had perversely worsened the lives of the poor. It discouraged work, penalized marriage, encouraged men to drop out of the labor force, and made it easy for unmarried women to have children. Gilder saw a general lesson here. Keynesian-inspired social welfare programs that redistributed wealth and sought to create purchasing power put the cart before the horse, and the results were always catastrophic for their intended beneficiaries. They promoted sluggishness, penalized risk-taking, depressed productivity, and rewarded personal failure—exactly the opposite of what they should be doing.

Gilder's "supply-side" attack on Keynesian social welfare policy played a central role in the developing right-wing assault on the welfare state. It claimed to have uncovered the reason why high-minded projects of social reform ended up solidifying exactly what they intended to uproot. Keynes had it wrong, Gilder announced; supply calls forth demand, not the other way around. A sensible anti-poverty program requires stimulating production first and foremost, and this means that the interests of the poor are best served by helping the rich accumulate, invest, and make big profits. Tax cuts, deregulation, and privatization are good for the poor. The state can't organize an orderly and successful project of social reform. Keynes just didn't understand how the golden rule operates.

Gilder's "theology" of capitalism is simple: the rich can help the poor by investing and getting even richer. Accumulated wealth provides the neutral, unencumbered cash that can be devoted to the economic expansion that will help everybody. The wealthy are always ready to invest because they have more wealth than they can consume, but they require fiscal and monetary policies that will encourage them to help others and become the benevolent agents of capitalism's golden rule. Cutting their income taxes, eliminating their estate taxes, lowering their capital gains taxes, reducing their corporate taxes, privatizing Social Security, and deregulating as much as possible is not just good economic policy for society as a whole. Now it's the height of morality. One must give in order to get, but first it will be necessary to change misguided liberal economic policy. For the moment, morality and good economic policy mean that the rich need to receive so they can give.

American blacks have fared worse than other generations of the poor, and it's not their fault. It's because they've been treated differently from everyone else, and the results have been catastrophic for them and for American society as well. As long as politicians insist that black poverty is the outcome of racism, technological change, corporate greed, globalization, or capital's need for surplus labor, they will continue to design social and governmental programs that are certain to fail. And, worst of all, they will not pay the price for their failure. That price will be borne by the black poor, for government programs cannot help but institutionalize and reward their failure. The dead end of liberalism, said Gilder, is that poverty cannot be cured or even ameliorated by redistributionist schemes, no matter how laudable their moral intent. If one wants to lift the incomes of the poor, "it will be necessary to increase the rates of investment, which in turn will tend to enlarge the wealth, if not the consumption, of the rich." Liberalism's failure to eliminate poverty was inevitable because it doesn't understand that "an effort to take income from the rich, thus diminishing their investment, and give it to the poor, thus reducing their work incentives, is sure to cut American productivity, limit job opportunities, and perpetuate poverty."[25]

American blacks need more work, family, and faith. This is why their culture is so destructive, irrational, and counter-productive. But it's not their fault. Prevented from working by liberal social policies, discouraged from forming stable families by welfare, and suffering from a misplaced faith in social engineering, they will never prosper until they discard the ideology and the social programs that perpetuate their difficulties. Poverty isn't caused by capital, the rich don't oppress the poor, and liberalism's "war against wealth" has so distorted people's thinking that they can't understand that "what causes poverty is the widespread belief that wealth does."[26] Gilder had revealed his priorities—and those of the Right as well. He was never all that interested in poverty. It was wealth that turned him on.

Only in the Age of Reagan could Gilder have gotten away with painting his defense of the rich as an anti-elitist populism. Liberalism's hostility to wealth, he said repeatedly, characterizes a snobbish, aristocratic, and morally degenerate elite whose influence had to be eliminated if the poor were to advance. Irving Kristol had been one of the first right-wing ideologues to argue that liberalism's romantic infatuation with equality was the flip side of its contempt for the acquisitive commercialism that was the only dependable path of upward mobility. Gilder took this argument one step better; now defending the rich helps the poor, inequality is populism, markets express the most elevated principles of social morality, and the wealth of the few helps everyone. "There is something, evidently, in the human mind, even when carefully honed at Oxford or the Sorbonne, that hesitates to believe in capitalism: in the enriching mysteries of inequality, the inexhaustible mines of the division of labor, the multiplying miracles of market economies, the compounding gains from trade and prosperity."[27] The "enriching mysteries of inequality" add a level of religiosity to Gilder's repeated assertions that the market is the way out of poverty. It is in the economy, not in the protected enclaves of state bureaucracies or in their permanent welfare rolls, that people can learn the skills that will make them successful. Liberalism perpetuates poverty because its welfare state can go no further than make-work and charity. It might not be possible to learn this at Oxford or the Sorbonne, but the home-grown truth is there for all to see. "The "dead end of egalitarianism," Gilder assured his many readers, is that "to help the poor and middle classes, one must cut the tax rates of the rich."[28]

Gilder's book was so popular because it captured the mood of the Reagan presidency and summed up the developing right-wing assault on equality. Best-selling author, White House advisor, influential columnist, and Reagan's most-quoted source, he was just the man to argue that morality and social health demanded rewarding the rich. There was nothing particularly new in any of this. The unprecedented concentration of wealth that has characterized the past twenty-five years has been accompanied by all sorts of reminders of the Roaring Twenties—which, with the Gilded Age, is the only historic period in modern American history that comes close to contemporary levels of inequality. It's easy to argue that the moral thing to do is to make the rich even richer if others can be convinced that the concentration of wealth is good for everybody—and particularly for those at the bottom. Ideas about economic equality and social welfare are things of the past, obsolete vestiges of an earlier period that will harm those who need help the most. It's time to break with the old and embrace the new. Enlightened and forward-looking social policy requires that the state unapologetically protect and encourage wealth.

Charles Murray shared Gilder's deep concern for the poor. As clear-eyed as Gilder about the importance of accommodating the rich, *Losing Ground* was relentless in its attack on equality and the welfare state. Where Gilder had invested his approach with a thin veneer of moralizing concern, Murray articulated a frank Social Darwinism that identified a generation of liberal social policy as the worst enemy of the poor. But it was always the black poor he was talking about, and when *Losing Ground* talked about poverty it was really talking about race. Murray wanted to help, he assured his readers, but he was put off by the frustrating tendency of government programs to reproduce what they intended to eliminate. Thus it was that busing programs produced more white flight and more segregation in public schools, welfare payments produced more dependency, the burden of affirmative action fell hardest on working-class white males, and all these programs ended up creating more poverty. Seeking to understand why all this happened, Murray made a dramatic and far-reaching claim: any state attempt to organize social reform will be undermined by "the law of unintended consequences." Since all government welfare programs end up exacerbating that which they are designed to ameliorate, almost all should be abolished—for the sake of the poor, of course. The Great Society had failed to eliminate poverty—and not because it hadn't been given a chance. On the contrary, the problem was that it had been tried at all. Seemingly endless prosperity, the discovery that poverty cannot be automatically removed by economic growth, and the understanding that the country's racial problems are not confined to the South had enabled liberals to say that poverty originates in something more substantial than individual failure. The claim that it was embedded in the social system justified state redistributive and regulatory activity. When the urban riots erupted, white America stood ready to make good its historic debt to blacks and manage an acute social crisis at the same time. The Great Society's community action programs, direct income transfers, manpower development projects, and job training encouraged hope that poverty could be licked once and for all.

But they all failed, said Murray, and he continued that "it soon became clear that large numbers of the American poor were not going to be moved off the welfare rolls by urban development schemes or by training programs."[29] But even the failure of federal anti-poverty programs didn't shake the prevailing orthodoxy about race and poverty—not yet. Despite the fact that experts, politicians, and bureaucrats knew better, said Murray, the structural approach to poverty encouraged the poor to believe that poverty wasn't their fault. Something more insidious and powerful than personal shortcomings must be at work if the War on Poverty had failed so miserably. And so, said Murray, liberals found their answer. "It was the system's fault. It was history's fault."[30] And, if "the system" would spontaneously produce injustice and inequality, then it had to be prevented from doing so. Interventionist, proactive, and statist interventions would prevent it from doing what it was naturally disposed to do.

None of this was necessary, Murray assured his readers. Black poverty—the only kind of poverty he was interested in—had been getting better before the Great Society had ever occurred to President Johnson and the elitist axis that Irving Kristol and George Gilder had identified. The 1950s and early 60s saw improvements for blacks across the board in matters of poverty, employment, education, wages, crime, and family structure, he said. But all that changed once the government got involved. The federal programs designed to compensate for failure were actually responsible for accelerating the deterioration of the black poor. As the 1960s faded into the 70s, it became clear that the old ways of thinking about poverty, race, crime, and the like were no longer adequate. Things were getting worse, not better, for the black poor despite historic levels of federal commitment and activity. It would have been better to have done nothing.

The number of poor rose during these years in stubborn defiance of the enormous amount of money being spent. Murray was sure of the reason: large numbers of black men had left the workforce and there was an accompanying increase in the number of female-headed black families. Like Falwell and Gilder, he insisted that restoring male authority in the family was essential to civic health and economic betterment. But liberalism was unable to design programs that would protect two-parent households, and the core insights of the popular wisdom that elected Ronald Reagan in 1980 signaled the beginnings of a new approach to a problem that was getting dangerous. "The popular wisdom," he said, "is characterized by hostility toward welfare (it makes people lazy), toward lenient judges (they encourage crime), and toward socially conscious schools (too busy busing kids to teach them how to read). The popular wisdom disapproves of favoritism for blacks and of too many written-in rights for minorities of all sorts. It says that the government is meddling far too much in things that are none of its business."[31] He acknowledged that much of this "popular wisdom" was mean-spirited, even racist, at its core. But there was something to its basic claim that social policy had to be aimed at civilizing and moralizing the uncivilized and amoral black poor. It was time to change liberalism's mix of rewards and punishments so people could be held accountable for their actions and others were not forced to pay the price for their failure.

The failure of liberal social policy, Murray went on, lay in its systematic failure to pay attention to these elementary requirements. Because they were unwilling to get tough with the poor, liberals undermined the link between present behavior and future outcomes and made destructive action rational. If "the system" was responsible for failure, then self-sufficiency was devalued. If an attack on middle-class norms of work and sobriety legitimized poverty, then welfare became a right and self-sufficiency was no longer a goal.

The net effect of all this has been a disaster, he said. Its core message to the black poor was that, since they are not responsible for their poverty, they were not responsible for ending it. This message took away all the incentives to work, to save, to invest, to defer gratification, to marry and plan for the future that have been the essential conditions of upward mobility for generations of the immigrant poor. When the lazy are rewarded and students who don't study are passed along with those who do, then working is for chumps and studying is for fools. If the way to get anything from the welfare state is to be a failure, then it doesn't pay to be a success. If all are victims of "the system," then no one is responsible for his or her own failure. Society can't work this way, said Murray. It must distinguish between the deserving and the undeserving poor so it can identify those who should be helped and those who shouldn't. But liberals can't do this. Their weakness and pandering have created a monster that can be tamed only with a new mix of punishment and laissez-faire.

Murray was sure that the welfare state was rewarding what was wrong and punishing what was good. Poverty should not come with entitlements, incapacity should not be valued, and self-reliance should not be discouraged. Simply throwing money at people who are in a difficult position will do nothing to help them better their condition. Liberalism harmed the poor and damaged the wider society, since it "demanded an extraordinary range of transfers from the most capable poor to the least capable, from the most law-abiding to the least law-abiding, and from the most responsible to the least responsible. In return, we gave little to these most deserving persons except easier access to welfare for themselves—the one thing they found hardest to put to 'good use.'"[32] Unable to develop a morally defensible case for redistribution, liberalism has failed to solve the very problems that constitute its *raison d'etre* and has saddled the entire society with unjustified entitlements, misplaced rewards, counter-productive messages, and a chaotic bundle of contradictory policies.

Murray's critique of liberal failure touched a nerve, but his central target wasn't poverty, race, or even the Great Society. He was going after all public programs that aimed at economic redistribution and social equality. His central claim—that no defensible moral position can ever justify transferring resources from the rich to the poor—rests at the heart of the Right's long attack on the welfare state. Murray claimed that he was trying to distinguish between the deserving and the undeserving, but it was always the interests of the rich that he had in mind. Confident that the lives of the poor will be improved if they're cut loose, he ends with a simple slogan that eloquently expresses the right's defense of wealth and its hostility to social welfare and economic equality. "Billions for equal opportunity," he proclaims, but "not one cent for equal outcome."[33]

It's not surprising that Murray came to earth thirteen years later with an explicitly racist explanation of black failure. Co-authored with Richard Herrnstein, *The Bell Curve* went far beyond his earlier indictment of liberalism. Murray warned that neither abolishing official racism nor changing liberalism's backward system of rewards and punishments nor the law of unanticipated consequences could explain why blacks still failed so consistently. So he proposed to examine the rise of a new "cognitive elite" in the hopes that he would get better results. Intellectual ability, as measured by IQ tests, is unevenly distributed among different groups in American society, Murray and Herrnstein announced. Stratification used to be organized along the lines of heredity and birth, but *The Bell Curve* provided "scientific" support for Bork's assurance that people with power and privilege deserve what they have because they're more capable than everyone else. IQ is importantly related to employment, job performance, productivity, and all-round social usefulness. This is why smart people have higher earnings and greater power. And the same is true in reverse: if the cognitive elite are those with wealth and power, then the "cognitively impaired" occupy the bottom of the social hierarchy. A simple and familiar conclusion flows from all this: it makes no sense to organize public policy on the basis of an egalitarian ethos that is directly contradicted by nature. Murray's earlier arguments against social welfare had rested on inefficiency, moral weakness, and unanticipated consequences, but he had now discovered the bedrock justification for inequality. Intelligence is just not distributed equally. Ignoring this simple fact in the name of social justice—or, worse, pretending that differences in intelligence don't matter—will waste enormous sums of money on useless governmental interventions that will only intensify the problems they propose to solve. The reformist impulse is doomed to failure in any event, for even its successes will perversely prove that social stratification is a pretty accurate reflection of natural hierarchies. "Meanwhile, high cognitive ability means, more than ever before, that the chances of success in life are good and getting better all the time. Putting it all together, success and failure in the American economy, and all that goes with it, are increasingly a matter of the genes that people inherit."[34] One can only expect this pattern to intensify. Since intelligence is one of the most important factors shaping mating habits, high-IQ people will tend to produce high-IQ children, with the pattern getting stronger over time. An hereditary aristocracy of brain-power is forming.

The same is true for those at the bottom of the ladder. Murray and Herrnstein announced that intelligence—now established as largely genetic in origin—is highly correlated with the country's most pressing social problems. Low cognitive ability is a better predictor of poverty than is socioeconomic status. It's also powerfully predictive of dropping out of school, being unemployed or disabled, becoming a criminal, having illegitimate children, marrying, and being faithful to one's spouse. Political knowledge and activity, voting, and other indices of civility and citizenship are equally connected to IQ. The bad habits of the poor might be mediated by culture and worsened by governmental programs, but there's an invariant genetic foundation to the concentration of wealth in America. "High cognitive ability," *The Bell Curve* informs its readers, "is generally associated with socially desirable behaviors, low cognitive ability with socially undesirable ones."[35] If an aristocracy of superior intelligence is developing at one social pole, then a peonage of inferiority is taking shape at the other.

The final piece of the argument is an overtly racist one. East Asians score higher than whites on IQ tests and blacks have scored consistently lower than whites for some time. Individuals and groups who are socially useful and productive have high cognitive ability. It's time to recognize this and formulate appropriate policies before it's too late. Focusing on the threat of the "underclass," Herrnstein and Murray warned that "a new kind of conservatism is becoming the dominant ideology of the affluent—not in the social tradition of an Edmund Burke or in the economic tradition of an Adam Smith but 'conservatism' along Latin American lines, where to be conservative has often meant doing whatever is necessary to preserve the mansions on the hills from the menace of the slums below. In the case of the United States, the threat comes from an underclass that has been with American society for some years but has been the subject of unrealistic analysis and ineffectual, often counter-productive policy. The new coalition is already afraid of the underclass. In the next few decades, it is going to have a lot more to be afraid of."[36] As a permanent black underclass of the cognitively inferior continues to threaten social peace and prosperity with its crime, unemployment, illegitimacy, and generally bad behavior, the reaction from the "cognitive elite" is likely to become more harsh and punitive. Fear of crime, more intrusive and dangerous police powers, bigger prisons, and a more authoritarian government will arise to supplement the country's large urban reservations. If the black poor can't be contained, they'll have to be punished.

Anticipating the furious reaction that greeted their racially-driven Social Darwinism, Murray and Herrnstein made it clear that they wanted to be known as democratic thinkers. After all, they had warned about the consequences of too much cognitive inequality. People might be unequal by nature, but everyone is entitled to equal treatment by the state. No matter how unequally cognitive ability may be distributed among racial groups, every individual has an equal right to advance his or her own interest. But genetics won't permit a government-led effort to reduce social or economic inequality. Freedom is measured by the ability to act, not by the outcomes of action; equality of rights is crucial to democracy, but equality of outcomes is not. Diversity and democracy now require a frank embrace of inequality and a warm assurance that external things don't matter. It's what inside that counts.

> Inequality of endowments, including intelligence, is a reality. Trying to pretend that inequality does not really exist has led to disaster. Trying to eradicate inequality with artificially manufactured outcomes has led to disaster. It is time for America once again to try living with inequality, as life is lived: understanding that each human being has strengths and weaknesses, qualities we admire and qualities we do not admire, competencies and incompetencies, assets and debits; that the success of each human life is not measured externally but internally; that of all the rewards we can confer on each other, the most precious is a place as a valued fellow citizen.[37]

The Bell Curve's racist core was a little too much for many, and its appearance provoked an immediate, fierce, knowledgeable, and effective set of counter-arguments—much of it from the right and center.[38] Even so, the best-selling book has to be seen as part of the Right's political and ideological argument. It was one thing to argue that the black poor can't be helped because they are imprisoned by a self-defeating and pathological culture. It was yet another to claim that the state would inevitably ruin anything it tried to accomplish. Herrnstein and Murray carried right-wing arguments to a new level. So, although their book's toxic blend of crank science and outright racism did offend many on the Right, it continued the basic argument that equality is a waste of time and money—and leads to undesirable social outcomes to boot. If one can find a "scientific" basis for failure, then equality of opportunity will not threaten privilege. Blacks are too "cognitively impaired" to be a real threat, and the state will be ready to defend the deserved privileges of society's "cognitive elite" if things get out of hand.

On another level, The Bell Curve continued a long Social Darwinist tradition of explaining why equality of opportunity hadn't ushered in the Golden Age of peace and prosperity for all. A free market and equality before the law only meant that the genetically inferior precipitated down the social ladder until they naturally came to rest at the bottom. Perhaps it was this reassuring message that explains why such an overtly racist book became a bestseller. The Bell Curve provided its own gloss for the same set of right-wing arguments about race: that attacking welfare, ending affirmative action, cutting back on most anti-poverty programs, and pretending to be "color-blind" made a lot more sense than trying to fight nature with arbitrary plans of redistribution and equality. It makes no sense to try to improve the cognitive functioning of those at the bottom of the social ladder and would be far more sensible to acclimate them to the roles they are "naturally" disposed to occupy.

Whether they were the product of a pathological culture, liberal weakness, or the immutable laws of nature, the black "underclass" served as a particularly potent reinforcing image for right-wing attacks on equality. An unchanging picture of predatory youth, drug-addled men, and slovenly women described a parasitical and dangerous population that dominated the way the Right talked to white Americans about the country's concentrations of black poverty. Its very presence was a constant rejection of the nuclear family, bourgeois morality, the work ethic, and the most elementary obligations of citizenship. The image was so powerful because it was oddly comforting to discover a mass of black desperation. Anxious whites could veer from pity to disgust in a heartbeat, secure in the Right's assurances that intractable black poverty was due to moral deficits, governmental inefficiency, and genetics. One needn't bother with equality, since many blacks are beyond hope and can't be helped.

The right-wing racial narrative of culture, unintended consequences, and genetics was never about poverty. There's a reason why its focus on "values" was largely reserved for the black poor and why it has studiously ignored the real question of unemployment and social isolation.[39] Riding the wave of a white backlash that it encouraged and from which it has benefited for years, the Right positioned itself as the authentic spokesman of "average" white Americans besieged by greedy blacks and put-upon by arrogant liberals. It constructed a discourse about affirmative action, poverty, welfare, and race that drew on both halves of that backlash and allowed it to zero in on equality and the welfare state. Its "cultural" argument blamed the black poor for being dependent and poor, and its Social Darwinism blamed the welfare state for keeping them dependent and poor. It constructed a perfect self-reinforcing frame of reference. It could accuse the black poor of abusing the welfare state, then turn around and accuse the welfare state of abusing the black poor. Both arguments resonated deeply with a white population that had grown tired of feeling guilty. Both were widely available and could be adapted to any given situation—as could a second, related ideological scissors that the Right constructed. If the situation of black Americans was improving before the Great Society, then that proved that governmental programs were unnecessary. But if the situation of blacks had worsened since then, then that proved that government programs didn't work. Many ingredients formed the period's arguments about race and welfare. However it was sliced, the Right had its cake and ate it too.

Its real aim was never the color-blind meritocracy of its official position. Like its apologies for militarism and its call for order and authority, the Right's appeal to racial fear aimed at paralyzing the welfare state, legitimizing inequality, and taking economic redistribution off the table. Distinguishing between the poor who deserved help and those who didn't attached moral judgments of merit and worth to success and failure. Welfare and "reverse discrimination" now explained economic stagnation and moral decay. Low wages, union-busting, restricted opportunities for women, unemployment, deindustrialization, capital flight, an insufficient minimum wage, and the virtual absence of child care couldn't explain black poverty. Liberalism was at fault.

Economic justice and political democracy soon fell off the country's racial radar screen. Now "culture" explained why people were poor and why they remained so. Misguided social programs—particularly affirmative action and the Great Society's efforts at redistribution—only made matters worse. The welfare state hurt the poor by demoralizing them and encouraging a poisonous "culture of dependence." If one wanted to help the poor, the best thing to do was cut their benefits, send them back to work, put them in jail when necessary, shovel more money to the rich, and let the market work its magic. Everyone will benefit from the concentration of wealth. Making the rich even richer was the best way to help the poor.

The right was never really interested in the debate about poverty, but it was virtually alone in talking about important issues that were agitating millions of Americans. Something terrible was happening to the country's black population, and liberals were silent. The Right seized on the fear, resentment and anxiety provoked by crime, litter, graffiti, welfare, and decay. Liberals didn't want to go anywhere near these matters, and in the absence of any credible alternative the Right's account soon became the standard model. It didn't have to be that way, but liberals were unwilling to make a strong defense of social welfare and clearly assign blame where it belonged. Medicaid and Medicare, AFDC, food stamps, Supplemental Social Security, and indexing Social Security payments to the rate of inflation were significant accomplishments that succeeded in virtually eliminating poverty among the elderly and alleviating the difficulties of millions of others, but the Right had opposed them all. Even Nixon's surprising proposal for a guaranteed minimum income for families had been unacceptable. Federal housing programs, Head Start, Upward Bound, college loans and grants, Legal Services, the Job Corps—all these highly successful programs had demonstrated the ability of government to act as an agent of change. That's why they elicited such violent opposition. The Right has always opposed programs like them because they demonstrated that public power can be effectively used to advance economic equality and social justice. If the welfare state is the cause of disorder, crime, and isolation among the poor, then countries like Canada, England, and France should have more crime, worse slums, and deeper despair than the United States. They don't of course, but cutting back on social programs is only a means to the Right's larger end. Everyone knows that big government is inevitable in an advanced economy like that of the United States. The Right's project is to make sure that it works to the advantage of the wealthy.

A paradox rests at the heart of how the Right used racial fear and anxiety. The past twenty-five years have witnessed the substantial enlargement of the black middle class. There's no doubt that it enjoys substantially broader opportunities than ever. Racial politics don't play as large a role in national affairs as they used to, and the Right hasn't had to fan white fear and position itself as the guardian of racial supremacy for some time. As important as racial appeals were to its consolidation and early growth, they've become less important with the advance of its economic program. But there's no denying the role they played, if only because it would be simple to dust off the old arguments in times of stress. This is what allowed William Bennett, former Chairman of the National Endowment for the Humanities, Secretary of Education, "drug czar," compulsive gambler, and self-appointed moral guide to the country, to offer a time-honored solution to the crime problem—even when it wasn't a problem. Addressing a caller to his syndicated radio show on September 28, 2005, he cut right to the chase. "If you wanted to reduce crime, you could—if that were your sole purpose—you could abort every black baby in this country and your crime rate would go down."[40] As shocking as this sounded, Bennett was simply reverting to form, demonstrating how easy it would be to trot out the coded words that would stimulate racial anxiety and fear. It was one thing to demand that liberals stop making excuses when cities were burning, children were being shot, public spaces were being defaced, and urban life had become dangerous and unpleasant. It was quite another to use racial anxiety in a cynical and conscious project of channeling wealth upward. Once again, the Right betrayed those for whom it claimed to speak. A comprehensive assault on social welfare isn't what the whites who resisted busing, demanded stronger policing, and grumbled about affirmative action had in mind, but it's what they got.

Notes

1. Kevin Phillips, *The Emerging Republican Majority* (New York: Anchor, 1970), p. 37.

2. See Jonathan Rieder, *Canarsie: The Jews and Italians of Brooklyn Against Liberalism* (Cambridge: Harvard University Press, 1985).

3. Nathan Glazer, *Affirmative Discrimination: Ethnic Inequality and Public Policy* (New York: Basic Books, 1975), p. 58.

4. *Ibid.*, pp. 75–76.

5. *Ibid.*, pp. 166–67.

6. *Ibid.*, p. 201.

7. *Ibid.*, p. 220.

8. Ira Katznelson, *When Affirmative Action Was White: An Untold History of Racial Inequality* (New York: Norton, 2005)

9. *Ethnic America: A History* (New York: Basic Books, 1981).

10. *Ibid.*, pp. 282.

11. Dinesh D'Souza, *The End of Racism* (New York: Free Press, 1995), p. ix.

12. *Ibid.*, p. 24.

13. *Ibid.*, pp. 259ff.

14. *Ibid.*, p. 287.

15. *Ibid.*, p. 477.

16. *Ibid.*, p. 478.

17. *Ibid.*, p. 527.

18. See Stephan and Abigail Thernstrom, *America in Black and White: One Nation, Indivisible* (New York: Simon & Schuster, 1997).

19. See John David Skrentny, *The Ironies of Affirmative Action* (Chicago: University of Chicago Press, 1996).

20. Irving Kristol, *Two Cheers for Capitalism* (New York: Basic Books, 1978), p. 235.

21. *Ibid.*, p. 243.

22. George Gilder, *Wealth and Poverty* (New York: Basic Books, 1981), p. ix.

23. *Ibid.*, p. 23.

24. *Ibid.*, p. 10.

25. *Ibid.*, p. 67.

26. *Ibid.*, p. 99.

27. *Ibid.*, pp. 96–97.

28. *Ibid.*, p. 188.

29. Charles Murray, *Losing Ground: American Social Policy, 1950–1980* (New York: Basic Books, 1984), p. 39.

30. *Ibid.*

31. *Ibid.*, p. 146.

32. *Ibid.*, p. 201.

33. *Ibid.*, p. 233.

34. Charles Murray and Richard Herrnstein, *The Bell Curve: Intelligence and Class Structure in American Life* (New York: Free Press, 1994), p. 91.

35. *Ibid.*, p. 117.

36. *Ibid.*, p. 518.

37. *Ibid.*, pp. 551–52.

38. See, for example, Steven Fraser ed., *The Bell Curve Wars: Race, Intelligence, and the Future of America* (New York: Basic Books, 1995).

39. See Michael B. Katz, *The Undeserving Poor: From the War on Poverty to the War on Welfare* (New York: Pantheon, 1989) and William Julius Wilson, *The Declining Significance of Race* (Chicago: University of Chicago Press, 1980), *The Truly Disadvantaged: The Inner City, the Underclass, and Public Policy* (Chicago: University of Chicago Press, 1990) and *When Work Disappears: The World of the New Urban Poor* (New York: Vintage, 1997).

40. http://www.cnn.com/2005/POLITICS/09/30/bennett/comments/.

CHAPTER FIVE

⁓

Attacking the Welfare State

Millions of Americans moved toward the Right during the late 1970s because they wanted an end to social disorder, and it wasn't long before Democratic paralysis and indecision yielded to backlash and retreat. The country seemed to be falling apart and liberal silence left the door open to authoritarian calls for order and obedience. Sensing an historic opportunity, conservative spokesmen rushed to capitalize on widespread anxiety and fatigue. Opposition to affirmative action and welfare amplified their earlier calls for militarism and the restoration of authority, but more was on the way. As politicians and ideologues drew the line at equality of opportunity, they developed a general assault on social justice that built on earlier arguments. The Right's short-run assurances were trumped by long-term betrayal, but few saw it coming and even fewer seem to have cared. A twenty-five-year project of channeling wealth and power upward was made immeasurably easier by a set of arguments against the welfare state.

The standard conservative complaints about social programs had been in place for some time, but they suddenly acquired a legitimacy they hadn't had in decades. They were fed by three different sources: the classical *laissez-faire* free marketeers, who feared that federal initiatives would distort the economy and encourage further social disorder; the neo-conservatives, who attacked the Great Society in the name of rearmament and a more aggressive foreign policy; and a new breed of "supply-side" economists and propagandists, who warned that taxation was discouraging investment and paralyzing economic growth. They were nourished by the period's "southernization" of national politics, but the region's growing importance in national affairs also illustrated the self-serving inconsistencies of those who argued that the government would always mess things up. Fed by billions of dollars of direct federal expenditures and enormous indirect transfers of wealth, the South increased its population by 40% between 1970 and 1990, double the national rate. Aggressively pro-business, anti-union, and pro-military, it attracted half of all foreign investment during the same period. None of this would have been possible without massive and continuous federal help. The Interstate Highway System, farm subsidies, the oil depletion allowance, the Taft-Hartley Act, Social Security, defense spending, the space program, the Tennessee Valley Authority, subsidized airport construction, and a host of other federal initiatives had opened the most isolated and backward region of the country to industry and commerce. The most anti-governmental region in the country owes its growth and domination of national politics to the very same government it has spent so much time attacking. As they learned how to milk both sides of this particular cow, Sunbelt politicians captured the Republican Party, drove American politics to the right, laid the foundation for a new kind of "populist" conservatism, weakened federal redistributive and egalitarian social programs, organized the Right's ideological assault on the welfare state, fanned the tax revolt, and fortified its core project of serving wealth.[1]

The assault on the welfare state began with a campaign to depress public expectations about what Washington could do. Even as they argued for a more aggressive foreign policy and increased spending on arms, Samuel Huntington, Norman Podhoretz, Irving Kristol and others worked to blunt popular expectations that the national government could ensure economic security. Arguments that the state was inherently tyrannical and terminally incompetent served the purpose well. These older right-wing claims were fortified by a more frankly Social Darwinist explanation of social stratification and inequality. Popular suspicion that liberal "social engineering" would erode family, faith, community, and work was encouraged by right-wing arguments that went beyond attacking the means and went after the end. Not only was the government to be avoided at all costs. Now equality was morally suspect and economically disastrous. As expansion was replaced by stagflation and optimism yielded to austerity, the Right was able to find popular support for old arguments that an earlier generation had dismissed. The welfare state, it said, was the first step down a slippery slope that led to tyranny and poverty.

Appeals to a powerful tradition of American anti-statism rested on repeated claims that the country was overtaxed and overregulated. It took the shape of a *faux* populist charge that the Great Society was created by anti-market elitists whose programs perpetuated poverty and increased the tax burden on the suffering middle and working classes. Friedrich Hayek,

William Simon, Ronald Reagan, and others claimed repeatedly that the inner logic of state activity was inherently despotic. It might once have been an instrument of social progress, but those days are over. Given the state's propensity to produce exactly the opposite of what it intended, said Charles Murray, it should get out of social reform altogether. The sudden appearance of "supply-side" economics and its "Laffer Curve" provided a pseudo-scientific theory of growth that explained how everyone would benefit by cutting taxes on the rich. All of these arguments built on a foundation of long-established conservative thought and adapted them to new conditions. The old Right had opposed the welfare state by declaiming about the virtues of individualism, property rights, and business entitlements, but these earlier arguments always had the faint whiff of self-interest about them. By arguing that lowering taxes on the rich and deregulating the economy would be good for everyone, the new right-wing populists managed to blunt the old charge that business and the rich were just being selfish. Now they were wealth creators, employers, and the guardians of a prosperous and free future.

The United States has long been an outlier among the world's advanced countries in its support for social welfare. Americans tend to be more individualistic, more supportive of meritocratic ideals, and more willing to tolerate inequality than their contemporaries in similar societies.[2] The quintessential American is the self-made man, and the Right's argument that artificial barriers blocking individual advancement should be demolished and that Washington should do as little "positive" social engineering as possible had deep historical roots. A widespread belief that equality of opportunity and personal achievement are better than anything the state can do has long supported a willingness to accept inequality of condition so long as the same rules are applied to all, the formal principles of equality are respected, and everyone has an equal chance to get ahead. The Right has skillfully mined this deep cultural attachment to mobility and fairness, even if its material roots harken back to the vanished world of yeoman farmers and Jeffersonian political economy. It has used the language of "liberty" and "freedom" to support the claim that the United States has always been suspicious of government and that society would regulate itself if the intrusive, disruptive, and incompetent state would just leave it alone.

There have been four periods of state-building in modern American history: the Civil War and the abolition of slavery, industrialization, immigration, and urbanization at the end of the Nineteenth Century, and the New Deal and Great Society programs during the Twentieth. It's no coincidence that each was closely connected to the spread of democracy, equality, and freedom. From the struggle to transform the South to the rights of women and workers, from public education to protecting public land, from efforts to control the trusts to the protection of small business, from the minimum wage to Social Security, it's the federal government that has usually nurtured democratic renewal and fostered public oversight of the economy. It has never happened automatically, and the country's history is full of as many examples of federal sabotage as it is of federal assistance. Nevertheless, American democracy has usually advanced because of pressure that the national community brought to bear on local centers of inequality. As modern democratic politics developed, people who were not white male property-owners looked to the state to help them overcome entrenched political power and economic privilege. This hasn't changed much; for all their individualism and anti-statism and even after twenty-five years of relentless right-wing propaganda, Americans still think that Washington should take the lead in reducing inequality, cushioning the impact of unemployment, supporting the needy, protecting the environment, and seeing to the economic well-being of its citizens.[3] Henry Steele Commager was right when he observed that "those who declaim against Big Government as the enemy of liberty are ignorant of America's history. The most elementary and overshadowing fact of that history is that there has been a causal connection between the enlargement and deepening of liberty in America and the growth of a strong national government."[4]

None of this prevented Reagan from endlessly repeating the old right-wing canard that the "sovereign states" are more important than the federal government because they preceded and formed it. His celebration of the local and the intimate, repeated hundreds of times in reverential homages to family, community, and faith, touched on a central element in American mythology. Reagan may have really believed the media's hype that he personified authentic American values, but the fact is that these questions have been contested throughout the country's history. As ideology, though, his rhetorical anti-statism summarized the Right's claim that national renewal, economic growth, and individual initiative required cutting back federal power. Reducing the size and scope of the national government, lowering taxes, deregulating the economy, devolving power back to the states—all of this was advertised as returning "power to the people" and restoring "their" money that had been unjustly confiscated by the hated IRS.

The Right has learned how to build a populist conservatism around the long anti-democratic record of states' rights, low taxes, and limited government. Even though the United States provides less social welfare and taxes its citizens less than comparable societies, the Right feeds the myth of an overtaxed population. Even though the United States provides less economic oversight and relies on lawsuits rather than an effective regulatory apparatus to safeguard its population, the Right feeds the myth of greedy trial lawyers, suffering businessmen, and an overregulated economy. Even though the United States is marked by higher levels of economic and social inequality than comparable societies and does less in its tax and transfer policy to mitigate the effects of both, the Right feeds the myth of an extortionist state that takes money from the industrious and gives it to the lazy. Even though the country's modern consumer economy was built by a long collaboration between industry and the state that enriched and empowered business more than in comparable societies, the Right feeds the myth of a state that arbitrarily interferes with consumer choice, systematically distorts the market, and makes life difficult for entrepreneurs.

Two interlocking arguments about the state allowed the Right to reinvent itself as the forward-looking, innovative midwife to the future. Each drew on a self-serving reading of American history, and earlier versions of each had been made many times before. It was the combination of the two, in an environment conditioned by accelerating inequality, the crisis of Keynesianism, and a determined political offensive by business and the rich, which created the opportunity to portray the welfare state as the backward and inefficient defender of "special interests." The first claim was a political one: the welfare state is a reactionary and despotic enemy of freedom and liberty. The second claim was an economic one: the welfare state is an obsolete, arbitrary, and inefficient enemy of investment, innovation, productivity, and growth. As unacceptable as these claims had been to an earlier generation, they acquired considerable traction in the country's new environment.

The Enemy of Freedom

In his 1994 inaugural speech as the newly-elected Speaker of the House, Georgia Congressman Newt Gingrich suggested that his fellow countrymen read three things: Alexis de Tocqueville's *Democracy in America*, the Constitution, and Friedrich Hayek's *The Road to Serfdom*. Written during the height of World War II, Hayek's book had addressed "the socialists of all countries" with dark warnings that "fascism and communism are merely variants of the same totalitarianism which central control of all economic activity tends to produce."[5] An erudite piece of political argumentation, *The Road to Serfdom* had been regarded for years as the overheated work of an isolated European reactionary. Its journey from the margins of academia to the well of the House was a measure of how far the country's center of gravity had shifted.

Hayek was an ideologist first and foremost, and he worried that leaders of the postwar West would be tempted to organize far-reaching programs of social welfare. The classical social democracies, he warned, were poised to accelerate the economic planning and redistribution that would inevitably lead them toward Nazi Germany and the Soviet Union. Public ownership, central planning, and redistributive economic policies were the pillars of the postwar welfare state, but Hayek was never really concerned about the Europeans. He was talking to Americans, and he wanted them to understand that "socialism has come to mean chiefly the extensive redistribution of incomes through taxation and the institutions of the welfare state." His famous analysis of information overload was designed to convince them that central planning for economic equality would never work. He didn't doubt the good intentions of those who wanted more social justice and general security but claimed that the holders of political power could never have enough information to make decisions that would be good for everyone. Those choices had to be left to individuals, and the market was the only coordinating agency that could summarize the isolated decisions of self-serving actors in a way that would serve both social welfare and political freedom. "The question," he observed, "is whether it is better that the holder of coercive power should confine himself in general to creating conditions under which the knowledge and initiative of individuals are given the best scope so that *they* can plan most successfully; or whether a rational utilization of our resources requires *central* direction and organization of all our activities according to some consciously constructed 'blueprint.'"[6] Hayek was describing a straw man here, since no American postwar leader has ever talked about "blueprints" that could organize "all" human activities, but he was less concerned with the motives of the "socialists" than he was to make sure his readers understood the virtue of markets. Free economic competition is the best way to coordinate individual efforts, he said repeatedly, and any attempt to impose central direction on a process that functions best when it functions spontaneously will only lead to disaster.

This was not a *laissez faire* argument, for Hayek wanted the state to actively defend market society with law and coercion. But he insisted on maintaining classical liberalism's strict separation between the state and society in order to argue against all politically driven supervision of market processes. Planning is inherently coercive, he announced, because it substitutes an arbitrary notion of the "common good" for the market's summation of countless individual calculations. The only way to keep the state in its place is to limit it through the rule of law, for "this means that government in all its actions is bound by rules fixed and announced beforehand—rules which make it possible to foresee with fair certainty how the authority will use its coercive powers in given circumstances and to plan one's individual affairs on the basis of this knowledge."⁷ Political power that is self-constrained will permit free individuals to pursue their personal ends and desires without outside intrusion, interference, or direction.

Because it is impersonal in scope and effect, the rule of law applies in a universal way to unknown individuals and to their future decisions. It has to be indifferent to the ends that individuals choose for themselves and, since Hayek was immediately suspicious of any suggestion that a free society could be organized around the pursuit of a "common good," he steadfastly held that political direction of economic processes could never serve freedom. He knew that this would produce inequality of condition but it seemed like a small price to pay. So long as inequality was unintentional and was not embedded in law, the state wasn't responsible.

> A necessary, and only apparently paradoxical, result of this is that formal equality before the law is in conflict, and in fact incompatible, with any activity of the government deliberately aiming at material or substantive equality of different people, and that any policy aiming directly at a substantive ideal of distributive justice must lead to the destruction of the Rule of Law. To produce the same result for different people, it is necessary to treat them differently. To give different people the same objective opportunities is not to give them the same subjective chance. It cannot be denied that the Rule of Law produces economic inequality—all that can be claimed for it is that this inequality is not designed to affect particular people in a particular way.⁸

Hayek assumed that market processes are non-discriminatory in intent and fair in outcome—a claim that anticipated the right's argument that gender neutrality had eliminated sexism and that official "color-blindness" had eliminated racism. Each individual is presumed to enter into market transactions on a basis of legal equality with every other individual. Justice is served so long as political power protects the integrity of these exchanges and does not try to affect their outcome. If a choice is to be made between a system in which a few people decide who is to get what and one in which the ability and enterprise of those concerned determine the outcomes, Hayek knew where he stood. And if "the rule of law" came at the expense of substantive equality, it was better to be free and insecure than unfree and secure. Hayek was perfectly prepared to tolerate substantial inequality of outcome. "The fact that the opportunities open to the poor in a competitive society are much more restricted than those open to the rich does not make it less true that in such a society the poor are much more free than a person commanding much greater material comfort in a different type of society."[9]

He was unimpressed by good intentions. Markets and societies are inherently difficult to organize centrally, and intervention and redistribution are difficult to stop. The lesson of the interwar period, Hayek said repeatedly, is that the planner is always tempted to plan some more and the organizer is always tempted to organize some more. Even if they are countered by other centers of power, state bureaucracies, offices, and experts are always striving to distribute more equally, regulate more fairly, organize more efficiently. A series of tiny steps, each of them apparently inconsequential in and of itself, begins the long slide toward the totalitarian attempt to control all of social life. The risk is too great, he announced. The freedom that comes from consciously taking sides is far more dangerous than any degree of unintentional inequality. It's better to submit to the blindness of the market than to trust the generosity and good intentions of those with power. "Inequality is undoubtedly more readily borne, and affects the dignity of the person much less, if it is determined by impersonal forces than when it is due to design," Hayek assured his readers.[10]

This idea didn't play very well outside right-wing circles at first, but Hayek's position was a seductive one: any system of thought or mode of social organization that puts the imagined interests of the group ahead of the concrete interests of the individual is a step toward slavery and despotism. Social democracy, nazism, and communism are different variants of the same general phenomenon. Hayek knew that he was living in a time of grand dreams and big projects. He warned Americans to be modest, get their hopes under control, and tread carefully, for "the only alternative to submission to the impersonal and seemingly irrational forces of the market is submission to an equally uncontrollable and therefore arbitrary power of other men. In his anxiety to escape the irksome restraints which he now feels, man does not realize that the new authoritarian restraints which will have to be deliberately imposed in their stead will be even more painful."[11]

Hayek penned his pessimistic warning just as victory in World War II ushered in the Golden Age of twentieth-century Keynesianism, but few were listening. A broad consensus in favor of planning and equality was built on widespread hopes for social progress, a sober assessment of the price that unregulated capitalism had inflicted on the world during the interwar period, and a determination to avoid a repetition of the carnage. All over the world, democratic governments, labor parties, independence movements, and popular organizations pressed for ambitious state programs of reform and redistribution. Hardly anyone outside a discredited and powerless Right complained. This was particularly true in Europe and North America, where a very broad consensus identified economic anarchy and inequality as unacceptable threats to social order. Hayek's warnings seemed so extreme and overwrought that hardly anyone outside the small circle of established enemies of the welfare state paid him much mind. Like other critics of equality, he remained on the margins of legitimate intellectual life until changed conditions led him to Newt Gingrich and the halls of Congress.

Irving Kristol certainly helped. As American neo-conservatives began to attack liberals for being insufficiently anti-communist in foreign affairs, they drifted rightward in domestic matters as well. Almost all of the movement's first generation had started out as New Dealers, but the austerity of the late 70s and their preference for guns over butter soon drove them against the period's social movements and the Great Society. Kristol made a shrewd calculation that allowed him to Americanize Hayek. When *Two Cheers for Capitalism* called on business to organize itself and "think politically," it suggested that a long American emphasis on freedom might be used to good advantage. Kristol drew a sharp distinction between liberty and equality and suggested that the former might be made the centerpiece of a new conservative critique of the latter. He went on to elaborate three traditional principles that he thought might serve as the foundation of a new right-wing attack on the welfare state. Taken together, they would summarize—and, more important, they would modernize—the old conservative fears about being too ambitious that had characterized the anti-modern Right since Edmund Burke had attacked the French Revolution. Kristol's contribution was to attack planning in the name of fairness, call it arbitrary and unjust, and say that democracy required that the claims of liberty supersede those of equality. In doing so, he pointed the way for an attack on the welfare state that helped the Right reinvent itself as the party of the future.

First, Kristol said, "there is no rational method which permits us to determine, *in the abstract*, which principle of distribution is superior."[12] It's always easier to develop ideas about a perfect society than to apply them, but in the end all plans for dramatic social reform must fall back on the arbitrary selection of justifying principles. The problem comes when reformers actually try to do something, for such principles almost always drive toward implementation. Sooner or later power-holders will be forced to attack a reality that is more resistant to dramatic change than they expected. Kristol shared Hayek's conviction that this is where the slippery slope began.

Even if a conception of the "common good" or the "public interest" could be developed, he said, it would require a powerful consensus about the nature of that "good." But freedom requires that people be allowed to entertain and act on different notions of all "goods." No matter what one believes, no one can really know the "common good" with any certainty, and public authorities must be discouraged from trying to define it in any but the broadest terms. There is something important about respecting the limits of a society with a "weak consensus" about aims and purposes, Kristol said. He knew that it wasn't a very heroic vision, but it did have the virtue of moderation and common sense.

There's really only one justifiable principle of distribution, he said, and it comes from the sphere of economics rather than from politics. No ethical principle permits us to privilege any free individual's choice over that of any other individual. Freedom requires wide toleration of all "capitalist transactions between consenting adults because such transactions are for mutual advantage, and the sum of such transactions is to everyone's material advantage. And, consequently, a liberal society will think it reasonable and 'fair' that income should, on the whole, be distributed according to one's productive input into the economy, as this is measured by the marketplace and the transactions which occur there."[13] If the rule of law provides equality of opportunity, then one can be pretty sure that distribution is a faithful measure of social worth. Fairness requires that the market be left alone to register the quality of individual contributions to the general good. Any effort to interfere with its principle of distribution threatens freedom and is incompatible with democracy.

Like Hayek, Kristol called himself a "liberal" in the Lockean sense of preferring private transactions, property, and freedom to public goods, welfare, and equality. Justice requires that conflicts between liberty and equality be resolved in favor of the former. This was Kristol's signature contribution to business's ability to "think politically." A lot of right-wing money and a determination to undo the postwar political order certainly helped, but Kristol had adapted Hayek to American conditions and made an important ideological contribution to later attacks on equality and the welfare state. He wanted to make it clear that, if freedom and liberty were to be the talismans of a new Right that was "thinking politically," then it had to draw sharp distinctions with a Left whose worldview pivoted on equality. None of this was new. It was the environment that had changed, and by the end of the

1970s he wasn't alone. Many right-wingers wanted to swing the pendulum away from the welfare state and toward the market, and it seemed that juxtaposing freedom to equality might help construct a new conservative populism. Kristol adroitly used public fatigue with liberal social engineering to make a wider point. Once again, the old McCarthyite tactic of saying that liberals were closet Stalinists found new life. Kristol explained how their shared preference for equality over liberty and their tendency to rely on state-organized programs of social reform explained the deep affinity between American liberalism, European Social Democracy, and international communism. "It is precisely because they define 'social justice' and 'fairness' in terms of equality that so many liberal thinkers find it so difficult genuinely to detest left-wing (i.e., egalitarian) authoritarian or totalitarian regimes. And, similarly, it is precisely because they are true believers in justice-as-equality that they dislike a free society, with all its inevitable inequalities."[14] He was on to something, for equality has always been particularly dear to those with progressive politics. The trick was to claim that liberty would be fatally damaged by anything that went beyond equality of opportunity. A newly emboldened Right would use Americans' individualism and reflexive embrace of freedom as a ram with which to batter equality of outcome and the welfare state. Like Hayek, Kristol assured his readers that the overt tyranny of planners and their egalitarian state was far more dangerous than the unseen indignities of inequality and the justice of the market.

As important as Hayek and Kristol were, it was really Milton Friedman, the 1976 Nobel Laureate in Economics, who provided the broad foundation for all contemporary attacks on the welfare state. Written with his wife Rose in 1980, *Free to Choose* quickly became an important manifesto of an increasingly powerful and coherent Right. Intended for a popular audience and supplemented by a successful television series, the book's central claim was that the state would always violate freedom because it always drives toward monopoly. By the time it was published, the Friedmans were well on their way toward identifying the state as the stultifying, dead hand of the past and the market as the creative, dynamic force of the future.

Prosperity requires freedom of choice, they said, and this requires limiting the state's ability to intervene in the economy. Winning support for this argument had been difficult while Keynesianism was expanding the horizons of millions, but the Friedmans were convinced that the United States was turning from collectivism and the state toward individualism and the market. Their argument rested on a series of simple claims, the most basic of which was that "we know of no society that has ever achieved prosperity and freedom unless voluntary exchange has been its dominant principle of organization."[15] Like Hayek and Kristol, they regarded the market's pricing mechanism as the uniquely sensitive and accurate source of information required for rational individual decision and effective social coordination in conditions of freedom. But it was threatened by a state that had moved far beyond maintaining peace, enforcing the rule of law, providing for those public goods that are beyond the scope of the market, and protecting members of the community who cannot function.

If the market is an Eden of freedom and prosperity, the state is a hellish sphere of coercion organized by bureaucratized planning and command. The despotic core of governmental activity had become particularly pronounced with the rise of the contemporary welfare state, said the Friedmans. But there was more. Not only was the state inherently despotic—it was also incompetent. The law of unanticipated consequences helped explain why. More federal control of education distorts market incentives and produces dumber students; more public housing means less housing for the poor; more governmental regulation raises medical costs; more environmental rules and stronger labor unions mean higher consumer prices that hurt the poor most of all. Like Gilder and Murray, the Friedmans were able to package an attack on liberalism as a defense of the poor. But all of their theoretical distinctions between liberty and equality were beside the point. The Friedmans were interested in limiting the state because they were interested in protecting wealth and justifying inequality. Certainly they knew that equality of condition doesn't necessarily threaten freedom; a glance at the European social democracies would have demonstrated that substantial levels of economic equality and a great deal of personal liberty are perfectly compatible. More libertarian than other elements of the contemporary Right, their genuine hostility to the government and their suspicion of politicians has to been seen in light of their broader desire to protect wealth.

A society that puts equality—in the sense of equality of outcome—ahead of freedom will end up with neither equality nor freedom. The use of force to achieve equality will destroy freedom, and the force, introduced for good purposes, will end up in the hands of people who use it to promote their own interests.

On the other hand, a society that puts freedom first will, as a happy by-product, end up with both greater freedom and greater equality. Though a by-product of freedom, greater equality is not an accident. A free society releases the energies and abilities of people to pursue their own objectives. It prevents some people from

arbitrarily suppressing others. It does not prevent some people from achieving positions of privilege, but so long as freedom is maintained, it prevents those positions
of privilege from becoming institutionalized; they are subject to continued attack
by other able, ambitious people. Freedom means diversity but also mobility. It pre-
serves the opportunity for today's disadvantaged to become tomorrow's privileged
and, in the process, enables almost everyone, from top to bottom, to enjoy a richer
and fuller life.[16]

So equality of outcome leads to tyranny and inequality means freedom.
Ever the political ideologues, the Friedmans wanted to reverse the view that
had been dominant since the Twenties inaugurated a move "away from a
belief in individual responsibility and reliance on the market toward a belief
in social responsibility and reliance on government."[17] They were confident
that things were moving their way, for the market is now the sphere of freedom in which self-serving, autonomous, individual decision-makers act to
better their conditions in conditions of freedom. The welfare state, an outmoded and despotic instrument of meddling bureaucrats, is a dangerous
threat to liberty.

Free to Choose turned out to be an effective piece of political propaganda—partly because of the nature of the times and partly because Milton
Friedman had a considerable body of important economic work to his credit.
It summarized a comprehensive worldview and amplified Hayek's and Kristol's earlier positions. As familiar as they were, the book's arguments against
equality and the welfare state were couched in a reasonably restrained manner, accorded a certain legitimacy to opposing viewpoints, and reflected an
academic open-mindedness and willingness to debate. Its partisan propagan-
dizing was supported by a seriousness of purpose and a genuine intellectual
pedigree that stood in stark contrast to William Simon's *A Time for Truth*.
Friedman was a politically engaged intellectual who made serious arguments.
The former Secretary of the Treasury under Presidents Nixon and Ford was
an indignant, angry, and aggrieved warrior.

Written two years before *Free to Choose*, Simon's screed was a furious
claim that Washington's "death grip" over the economy is at the root of
America's most important difficulties.[18] "This country is in desperate trouble," Simon grimly announced, and he warned that if the egalitarian dreams
of today's humanists continue to drive public policy, American society will
be ruined, the economy will wither, and democracy will yield to tyranny.[19]
Like Hayek, Kristol, and Friedman, he proposed to save the country by helping his readers understand how closely economic liberty is connected to

political democracy. He drew a bead on freedom's most dangerous enemy. "No economy can survive a structural war conducted against it by the state," he warned.[20] And that "war" consisted of federal social spending—particularly the redistributionist policies of the New Deal and the Great Society. They have undermined productive citizens, rewarded the undeserving, raised taxes and public debt, lowered profits, investment, and capital formation, hobbled businessmen and entrepreneurs, produced inflation, and increased unemployment. No good has ever come of it. The welfare state is the scourge of modern society, and FDR was its Attila. The American people have venerated their greatest President for far too long. They don't realize how much damage and ideological confusion he inflicted on the uniquely American cause of liberty.

> FDR actually redefined that concept, corrupting it so hopelessly that, save for a few philosophical diehards, succeeding generations were never again clear as to what it meant. Political freedom means only one thing: freedom *from* the state. FDR, however, invented a new kind of 'freedom': a government guarantee of economic security and prosperity. He thus equated 'freedom' with cash. However desirable economic security may be—and it is profoundly desirable—it is *not* the same thing as political freedom. By equating the two, FDR corrupted the philosophical concept of freedom. In fact, by calling cash a 'freedom' in a society where the state was pledged to protect freedom, he converted 'freedom' into a monetary claim on the state. By this single ideological switch, FDR caused a flat reversal of the relationship between the individual and the state in America. The state ceased to be viewed as man's most dangerous enemy, to be shackled forever by constitutional chains. It was henceforth proclaimed to be the precise *opposite*; it became man's tenderhearted protector and provider. Statism and collectivism were brought into this country by the back door—and, ironically, were heralded thereafter as the saving of free enterprise.[21]

As crazy as he sounded, Simon was no outside crank. A powerful Wall Street figure before entering the Nixon administration, he served successive Republican presidents as Deputy Secretary of the Treasury, "energy czar," Secretary of the Treasury, head of the powerful Economic Policy Board, the East-West Trade Board, the Council on Wage and Price Stability, and a host of other official bodies. In addition to his long service at the very center of national politics, he was an important figure in the development of the contemporary Right. President of the John M. Olin Foundation, co-founder with Irving Kristol of the Institute for Educational Affairs, President of the Richard Nixon Presidential Archives Foundation and the United States

Olympic Committee among others, Simon was a sophisticated, experienced, and powerful political ideologue. He certainly knew who his enemies were. The heart of America's problem is the drive toward equality and redistribution, the historic enemy was FDR and the New Deal, and the immediate threat was social democracy and mixed economies. The "heresy" that threatened to infect American society is "the belief that the state, under an FDR-type leader, has both the moral obligation and the competence to 'run' the economy and guarantee its citizens economic security."[22] Simon wanted to make sure that Americans would never be tempted again. The third of Roosevelt's Four Freedoms of speech and expression, religion, freedom from want, and freedom from fear—the great, unfulfilled promise of American democracy—was now a treasonous and dangerous fantasy.

Simon's white-hot anger wouldn't have been so destructive if he hadn't been able to put it to good use. But New York City had the profound bad luck to run into a severe economic crisis while he was Gerald Ford's Secretary of the Treasury, and he worked hard to starve the nation's greatest urban social democracy to death. Increasing city budgets and deficits during periods of decreasing or flat tax receipts had been perfectly acceptable to the city's creditors for many years, but the mid-70s precipitated an unprecedented squeeze as major banks, the United States Treasury, and a host of other creditors now demanded austerity. Laying off thousands of city workers, increasing their "productivity," reducing capital spending, restricting city services, and raising fees and taxes would bring New York to heel and eviscerate her unique standing as the nation's preeminent example of social welfare. A sustained attack on the city's proudest accomplishments—its cheap public transportation, municipal hospital system, public housing, free university system, extraordinary public schools, rent control, and many other institutions—did enormous damage to the idea and the reality of an expansive, democratic public sector. When the *Daily News* summarized the situation with its famous headline, "Ford to City: Drop Dead," it could just as well have named Simon.

The fiscal crisis gave the banks their opportunity to restructure New York to their liking, and they were happy to take it. They insisted on less government activity in their areas of interest, called for fiscal "restraint," and demanded the privatization of services that served and protected the city's working class, unemployed, and poor. Weakened labor unions and changed work rules would deprive public employees of the comparative advantage they had over workers in the private sector, and as the city began sliding toward bankruptcy Wall Street saw its opportunity. It was simple: the banks simply denied the city money by refusing to buy or underwrite municipal bonds. When Washington declined to guarantee loans in face of Wall Street's capital strike, it became clear that a wider political project was at work. A right-wing effort to make New York a national example of liberal excess would be a useful cautionary tale against future projects to extend the welfare state. When Wall Street and Washington took over the city through the Municipal Assistance Corporation and the Emergency Financial Control Board, a comprehensive assault on New York's social democracy unfolded.

William Simon was at its center. Attacking high municipal worker salaries and generous pensions, cutting back on the labor movement, restricting subsidies to the City University, and gutting middle-income housing, rent control, and similar programs would paralyze New York's civic liberalism and deter anyone from ever trying to imitate it. Gleefully refusing Mayor Beame's urgent request for a federal loan guarantee, Simon knew that attacking New York was a perfect way to attack the welfare state. Political leaders, public intellectuals, labor leaders, and the population as a whole had become accustomed to the idea that progress meant continuously expanding services for the city's middle and working classes. Better public housing, more rent control, world-class faculty for CUNY's working-class students, first-rate municipal hospitals, expansive educational opportunities at the public schools—it sounded great, said Simon, but the hard truth was that they were profoundly destructive. Luckily, New York could no longer afford them. Now an opportunity had come along to set things straight and reassert what America really meant. The time had come to say no.

Simon moved ruthlessly to impose draconian spending restraints on New York's political leaders and their labor allies. The city had too many workers on its payroll, their salaries were "absurdly" high, and their pensions were "appalling."[23] "How did the unions run off with the New York budget?" he asked rhetorically, answering that what had really happened was that the city's middle class had formed an unholy alliance with the municipal bureaucracy to enrich themselves at the expense of the productive population and the genuinely poor. The salaries, pensions, and fringe benefits paid to government workers, the social welfare programs from which they benefited, the middle-class housing projects and free tuition at CUNY—all of these unnecessary expenses were responsible for the city's fiscal collapse. Charging tuition at CUNY, ending rent control, privatizing health, sanitation, and other services—even default if it came to that—was the way out of the crisis, the first painful step toward a national accounting with the liberalism that had brought the nation's greatest city to its knees.

Simon knew an opportunity when he saw it and he moved quickly to broaden his attack. The regulatory state, he announced, has had "a devastating impact on investment, price stability, productivity, and economic development."[24] Businessmen are suffering under a tyrannical regime that has become parasitic, arbitrary, and dictatorial. Corporate taxes are too high, bureaucracies have too much power, and the state now threatens to destroy the country's economic fabric. Everything of value comes from the market, the only sure foundation for political democracy. Freedom means freedom from the state, capital must be protected, wealth is a virtue, and poverty is not to be rewarded. A rigidly individualistic Social Darwinism lay at the center of all this. "There is no such thing as the People; it is a collectivist myth," announced Simon. "There are only individual citizens with individual wills and individual purposes. There is only one social system that reflects this sovereignty of the individual: the free-market, or capitalist, system, which means the sovereignty of the individual 'vote' in the marketplace and sovereignty in the political realm."[25]

Like other right-wing propagandists, Simon paid a lot of attention to ideas. It was important to convince Americans about the evils of the welfare state, remind them of what had happened to New York, and reassure them about the virtues of the market. It was important to depress their expectations that were born of their ties to others and reinforce their readiness to stand alone. It was important to help them understand that egalitarianism was the origin of totalitarianism, that leveling encouraged mediocrity, and that inequality was the condition of progress. Most of all, it was important to make them understand that they shouldn't expect too much. Ideas were powerful things, as potentially dangerous as they were comforting. As angry as he was, Simon didn't ask his readers for too much—just to accept his argument that the welfare state was founded on a lie and that it led to the concentration camps and the gulag. The lie was the "rationalist perversion in modern politics" that Jeanne Kirkpatrick defined as "the determined effort to understand and shape people and societies on the basis of inadequate, oversimplified theories of human behavior."[26] Ever since Plato had insisted that the statesman knew more than anyone else about the good society, she said, this "perversion" has animated all of history's tyrants and murderers. When it takes shape as a statist, egalitarian political doctrine, it reveals the common heart of Nazism, Communism—and liberalism. Kirkpatrick was astounded at how little had been learned from history's mistakes. "The most extraordinary fact about our times," she said, "is the tenacity with which persons who pride themselves on being rational and scientific hold to a mystical faith in political propositions which are demonstrably false and unreasonable. A good example among the beliefs which have been repeatedly demonstrated to be false but which nonetheless continue to command the assent and faith of educated men of goodwill is the belief in absolute equality as an operational social good." And, cutting to the heart of the matter, she named the problem. "One of the most widespread notions of our age is that justice requires egalitarian allocations of wealth, opportunity, and other social goods."[27]

The state as such was never the Right's target, since it had no objection to militarism, moral authoritarianism, tax cuts, direct handouts, and more. It was always the welfare state and economic equality that it had in mind. All that mattered was convincing the country that the real story of American freedom was written in the brave struggle of its citizens to maintain their liberty against a national government that was always tempted to impose tyrannical notions of equality on a free people. And no one knew better how to use state power against the welfare state than the Great Communicator himself. "It's been said," claimed President Reagan, "that government performs its highest duty when it restores to its citizens taxes oppressively collected."[28] He didn't identify precisely who equated taxation with oppression, but it wasn't important. He'd made the point.

The Enemy of Prosperity

It was one thing to portray the welfare state as a tyrant, quite another to call it an obstacle to progress. Conservative spokesmen did both. For years the Right had been the backward-looking and marginalized defender of wealth and privilege, but its *faux* populist attacks on the state now allowed it to step forward as the forward-looking and respectable defender of wealth and privilege. Its traditional arguments that any restriction on property was tantamount to tyranny had been given a new lease on life by changed economic conditions and a broad social crisis, but they would never have carried the day unless something was added. That crucial something was its new-found ability to convince a lot of people that the welfare state was the parasitical representative of the past, the obsolete defender of unproductive "special interests," and the enemy of economic growth. This made it possible to claim that cutting back on regulation and redistribution would unleash the forces of entrepreneurship and innovation that had been restricted by unnecessary political restrictions for far too long. Inequality, environmental damage, unemployment, poverty, racism, urban decay, moral collapse—all these problems would be resolved, the Right claimed, once the suffocating hand of the welfare state was lifted from the throats of the entrepreneurs and innovators who would usher in a new age of prosperity and freedom.

The Right's attack was initially expressed as a series of demands for lower taxes, less regulation, and fewer bureaucrats. But it soon became clear that it really wasn't crafting a *laissez faire* position about state activity in general. Its assault on equality, regulation, and redistribution was a disguised one, for American history made it easy to develop broad "populist" arguments against central authority. But this required a new way of thinking. On December 11, 1974, Jude Wanniski, a young writer for the editorial page of *The Wall Street Journal*, published a column called "It's Time to Cut Taxes." It turned out to be the opening salvo in the drive to legitimize "supply-side economics." Keynesianism had suggested that there was a trade-off between inflation and unemployment, that state macroeconomic policy should stimulate demand, and that a little inflation wouldn't be a catastrophe if it encouraged consumption and raised employment. This position was about to come under a sustained attack that acquired credibility because of the period's seemingly intractable economic crisis. Supply-side's fundamental claim—that lower taxes would actually yield higher government revenues because they would stimulate a new round of economic growth—was not new. What was new was a more hospitable environment for a doctrine that turned out to be little more than a "scientific" rationale for reducing taxes on business and the rich.

Wanniski's column introduced the world to Robert Mundell and Arthur Laffer, two economists at Columbia and the University of Chicago who sought to change the mix of monetary and fiscal policies that federal authorities deployed to combat inflation and unemployment. They argued that tight money should be used to control inflation and that lower taxes should provide enough stimulus to increase employment. Only when the economy began to respond should the government allow the money supply to grow. "Real economic growth would be stimulated by the big tax cut on both personal and corporate incomes," announced Wanniski. Lower taxes would stimulate demand but, more importantly, would simultaneously encourage production and increase supply. "With lower taxes, it is more attractive to invest and more attractive to work; demand is increased but so is supply."

Wanniski's column soon attracted attention and he got a $40,000 grant from William Simon's Richardson Foundation to write a book. The modest title of *The Way the World Works* was an early indication of how confident Wanniski was and how ambitiously he defined his project. The book introduced "supply-side" economics to the Right's stable of arguments against the welfare state, but its position was a carefully nuanced one.[29] Wanniski wasn't alone in recognizing that demand-stimulus strategies could neither explain nor resolve the twinned evils of unemployment and inflation that hobbled the Carter administration. The dilemma facing Keynesianism was apparent to everyone, but Wanniski joined the rest of the Right in arguing that the welfare state's misbegotten tax policies explained why it had become so destructive of economic progress. His general argument for reducing taxes and other forms of state regulatory and distributive activity revolved around his claim that they act as powerful disincentives to production. The Right was poised to steal Keynesianism's thunder and come across as the voice of sustained economic growth and broad prosperity.

Ever since the Great Depression, it had been a staple of economic thought that if tax rates fell too quickly, the government might not have the resources to stimulate demand and revive the economy. The Right had never been able to effectively counter this argument, but Proposition 13 swept to victory in California in the same year *The Way the World Works* appeared and the persistence of stagnation and inflation created the opening that legitimized long-standing right-wing arguments for tax cuts. The "Laffer Curve," which Wanniski was instrumental in popularizing, made the counter-intuitive case that lower tax rates need not mean lower governmental revenues. Taxes and productivity exist in inverse relation to one another, it suggested, and lower tax rates would actually stimulate production. Once the optimal point is reached, increased activity would actually mean higher governmental revenues.

Demand-side economists suggested that increased demand will call forth increased supply and hence tended to favor consumers. The new supply-siders, on the contrary, insisted that increasing production will stimulate consumption and regarded investors as the most important actors in the economy. Their timing was propitious, for Keynesianism had become paralyzed by a pair of mutually contradictory impulses. Its commitment to increasing purchasing power drove it toward policies that put more money into consumers' pockets. But this impulse blunted its ability to limit the money supply and control inflation. Late-70s Keynesian theory was never able to square this particular circle, and this is what led Wanniski and others to call it an outmoded hindrance to economic growth. "It is possible to say that the supply model is generally superior when the policy-maker's objective is economic growth; the demand model is relevant when the policy maker is compelled to consider first the needs of the consuming public," he announced. "Both basic models are 'legitimate' and have been around since the dawn of civilization, but it is not possible to say that one is superior to the other, except at a particular time. Policy makers make the choice when confronting the economy that they must deal with—one that invites expansion or one that seems intractably in decline."[30] Confident that the "demand model" could not remedy a situation in which stagnation and inflation came together, Wanniski claimed that supply-side economics was the new future-oriented science of growth and innovation.

Keynesians had thought that lower taxes could stimulate production most effectively if they were concentrated on those more likely to spend. This is why the welfare state was built on progressive taxation and tended to favor the many who were in the middle and at the bottom of the income scale. Its redistributionist and egalitarian thrust explains why the Right has always found it so objectionable, and Wanniski made certain that there be no misunderstanding about what he had in mind. Like Gilder, he argued that regressive tax cuts aimed specifically at investors and employers would stimulate growth and increase government revenue.

This was—and remains—the Right's core economic argument about why helping the rich would be good for everyone else. After all was said and done, the sum and substance of supply-side economics was cutting taxes on wealth. The claim that one could simultaneously raise defense spending, cut income taxes, and balance the budget—the seductive siren-song of what the press began calling "Reaganomics"—was always nonsense, and only the terminally naive were surprised when Reagan's budget director David Stockman confessed that supply-side economics "was always a Trojan horse to bring down the top rate."[31] But there was nothing fraudulent about its other claims: that holders of private capital should be restored to their paramount position, that governmental policy should be oriented to the needs of investors, and that social spending and economic regulation should be restricted. Soon a new phrase appeared to describe the Right's new approach, one that was a far more accurate description than its predecessor. "Trickle-down economics" summarized the net effect of the regressive tax cuts.

For all its pandering to wealth, supply-side economics carried the day—but that was due less to its intrinsic power than to a changed ideological environment. Keynes had rejected the emphasis that Say's Law put on the needs of entrepreneurs and its related claim that supply would stimulate demand. Concentrating even more income and wealth in the hands of the rich didn't necessarily work, since there was a limit to what even the very wealthy could absorb and put to productive use. Keynes had explained what egalitarians had always believed: that spreading money around was the key to prosperity. His emphasis on stimulating mass purchasing power undermined the simplistic right-wing claim that the government should always act like a household and demonstrated that deficit spending was often better for the economy than balanced budgets. The price might be a little bit of inflation, but its mildly redistributive implications would stimulate consumer spending and few doubted that economic growth would make it worthwhile.

When stagflation made it impossible for the government to use the "pump-priming" strategy that had been its most powerful stimulative tool, the way was open for conservative economists—and particularly for Milton Friedman. His monetarism held that restricting the money supply was the most powerful weapon against inflation. That was a fairly orthodox claim, and Keynes had approved of it when used in tandem with other monetary and fiscal measures. But controlling the money supply was only one of many interlocking strategies, and Keynes had never elevated it to a good in and of itself. Taken by itself, it risked choking off economic growth. Paul Volcker's tenure at the head of the Federal Reserve System made the danger clear, and the sharp recession that marked Reagan's first term reminded everyone how severely orthodox hostility to inflation could bite.

Supply-side economists wanted to combine the monetarists' tight money with a policy of "fiscal ease"—that is, they wanted to combine high interest rates and tax cuts. Their preference for the holders of capital was clear, but it needed a "technical" explanation. Say's Law made the claim that supply, not demand, was the economy's most creative economic force. Where demand-side economics had a powerful egalitarian impulse and spread purchasing power around, supply-side economics consciously embraced inequality. "Trickle-down" economics had a simple set of related goals: to lighten the burdens on capital, concentrate wealth upward, reward investment, and encourage savings. If Keynes's heroes were the political leaders and the planners who kept business healthy by taxing, spending, and redistributing, Wanniski's heroes were the entrepreneurs and investors who started the businesses and invested the capital that kept people employed. It seemed simple enough, but the supply-siders faced an ideological problem. They had to convince the citizens of a democratic polity that everyone would benefit from a set of policies that were explicitly committed to assisting wealth and protecting property.

It proved easier to do so than one might have thought—partly because lower taxes are always popular, partly because trickle-down economics had a set of talented propagandists to make the case, and partly because no one proposed a credible alternative. Its most effective spokesman, of course, was the President of the United States. "Like Federal employees, taxpayers also work for the Government—they just don't have to take a civil service exam," said Reagan as he seamlessly accused the welfare state of being viciously tyrannical and hopelessly obsolete. "Here in America, land of opportunity, governments at all levels are taxing away 40 percent of our nation's income. We've been creeping closer to socialism, a system that someone once said works only in heaven, where it isn't needed, and in hell, where they've already got it."[32]

Supply-side really conquered political power in 1980, but its breakthrough victory had come two years before Reagan's election. When the Democratic Congress and a Democratic President agreed to cut the capital gains tax in 1978, they did so after careful prodding. Wanniski made the crucial argument—not that the rich deserved to be rewarded because they were rich, but that concentrating even more money in the hands of those who already had it would benefit everyone. If taxes on capital were lowered, then investments would rise. If investments went up, then productivity and production would also rise. If productivity and production rose, then more jobs would be created. Tax cuts for the rich would be good for everyone, the supply-siders said, since high tax rates discourage work, investment, and growth. Lowering them would stimulate economic activity across the board, create more jobs, improve productivity, help the poor escape from poverty, make American products more competitive, and assist the cities—all at the same time. These arguments enabled the Right to portray the 1978 cut in the capital gains tax, an action that benefited only the rich, as a populist bow in the direction of the hard-working, overtaxed, and underemployed working and middle classes. The other supply-side argument—that the government would actually gain revenue, and hence would have more money to spend, if it cut taxes—was a bit more unsettling to the hard-core conservatives who didn't want to do anything to strengthen the public sector. The claim turned out to be a false one, but balancing the budget was never the central goal of the supply-siders. As Stockman confessed, they achieved their goals with the era's dramatically regressive tax cuts.

It's astonishing how quickly all this became the new orthodoxy. Trickle-down economics stood behind Reagan's optimistic claims that there was nothing wrong with the country that couldn't be cured with lower taxes, less government spending, and fewer regulations. "The people" could solve their own problems, he repeated endlessly; all the government had to do was get out of the way. It was soon clear just what he meant: the best way to help everyone was to reduce taxes on the rich. By the time his first administration had ended, three enormous regressive tax cuts had built on the 1978 cut in the capital gains tax to begin directing historic amounts of wealth and power upward. That's really what the Right had wanted all the way along. The sum total of "Reaganomics" was little more than crushing budget deficits, massive increases in the national debt, and accelerating inequality.

The tax revolts that made all this possible predated Reagan's election and lent powerful support to his repeated claims that briefcase-toting bureaucrats were stealing the people's money and using it for sex education, abortions, and immoral school curricula. When endlessly repeated and exaggerated, these alleged assaults on ordinary people confirmed the Right's portrait of a welfare state that had spun out of control and was rewarding the lazy at the expense of the hard-working, "welfare queens" over national defense, offensive museum exhibitions over the "family values" of ordinary citizen taxpayers in the nation's "Heartland." The picture also served as an outlet for subtle forms of racial hostility, allowing the Right to appeal to the resentment of white voters with claims that welfare, public housing, and aid to cities were nothing more than thievery and extortion. As demographic and political power shifted to the South and the Southwest, contempt for the "nanny state" served as the flip side of an appeal to the market and reverence for the manly virtues of economic competition.

Reagan was convinced that American recovery and renewal required a broad attack on the core institutions of the welfare state and on the attitudes that supported them. The Carter administration, he declared during his 1980 campaign, had cooked up "a new and altogether indigestible economic stew, one part inflation, one part high unemployment, one part recession, one part runaway taxes, one part deficit spending seasoned with an energy crisis. It's an economic stew that has turned the national stomach."[33] He proposed to put the country on a diet. It required an attack on a government that taxed too much, spent too much, regulated too much, and meddled too much. This meant three things: cutting more taxes on wealth, deregulating business, and privatizing as many public services as possible.

Although the Right led the charge, the attack on equality and the welfare state that marked Reagan's first term was a bipartisan one. Passed with significant Democratic support, the "Economic Recovery Act" of 1981 was the first step in a long and successful campaign to reorient federal tax policy away from the progressivity that had been in place since the New Deal. Taxation had never been particularly popular of course, but Americans were prepared to accept it if government was able to deliver important social goods and if it imposed some limits on the wealth and influence of the very rich. Reagan transformed the terms of the debate. Instead of taxes being about equity and justice, they were now about tyranny and efficiency. Instead of allowing Americans to talk about class and power, they now allowed them to talk about big government and oppressive bureaucrats. All of this had very direct results. The top income tax bracket was 70% when Reagan was elected President—already significantly lower than it had been for decades. By the end of his presidency, it was down to 28%. Corporate, inheritance, and capital gains taxes also fell dramatically. The small gains that taxpayers of moderate incomes saw were soon erased by dramatically higher Social Security taxes. Most of the deregulatory and privatizing measures that Reagan proposed were also voted into law, often with indispensable Democratic support. The terms of the country's politics and ideology were violently changed as old assumptions yielded to new realities. Attacking progressive taxation, cutting back on the welfare state, deregulating business and capital, and encouraging privatization initiated the most dramatic upward redistribution of wealth and power in the country's history. Where poverty and inequality had been seen as social illnesses and the welfare state as the cure, Reagan lauded entrepreneurship, growth, and innovation and made the welfare state the enemy.

Gilder and Murray provided valuable material to Reagan's speechwriters. *Wealth and Poverty* tried to link "futuristic" supply-side ideas with a frankly anti-modernist and authoritarian set of social values. Its central claim—that much of the disorder and rebellion in domestic and public life was caused by inflation, high taxes, egalitarian ideas, and government regulation—spoke to the period's anxieties and hostilities. High taxes on those who worked and wrong-headed egalitarian government programs penalized the family, weakened men, and hurt the economy. If policy-makers want to address the causes of social breakdown, Gilder announced, they will have to organize more support for capitalism's core values and give fuller rein to market forces. Murray's attacks on egalitarian social policies and the welfare state had the same effect. Investors and entrepreneurs were the new heroes of the age, more wealth for the few was good for the many, inequality served everyone's interests, and self-reliance gave meaning to life. The welfare state was the corrupt and inefficient instrument of "special interests," bureaucrats were self-serving parasites, equality was the politics of envy, and solidarity was mushy-headed cowardice.

Supply-side's attack on equality came with Reagan's drive to replace Keynes and the welfare state with the Laffer Curve and tax cuts for the rich. Gilder called for a reorientation of federal policy so the real sources of national wealth could benefit the entire economy. Lower taxes can stimulate investment, business, and innovation. Resources can be shifted to centers of activity that will create more jobs and bring in more tax revenue instead of flowing to the unproductive and parasitical. But this would take considerable effort, for social policy was encouraging the very behavior it was supposed to discourage. The welfare state had degenerated into a dangerous threat to social health, the very embodiment of the law of unanticipated consequences.

Reagan's constant repetitions of Gilder's arguments announced supply-side's ideological victory. Inefficiencies are built into the very fabric of the welfare state, both announced, because its core project is defending people from the very market forces that guarantee their prosperity and freedom. The claim that state policy should nurture and protect wealth, that entrepreneurship, investment, and production should be accorded pride of place and that everyone will benefit from tax cuts on wealth, deregulation, and privatization has shaped the Right's public face for years. When he wrote a new introduction to the tenth anniversary edition of his original attack on the welfare state, Murray could accurately say that "much of what was controversial when *Losing Ground* first appeared has since become conventional wisdom. It is now accepted that the social programs of the 1960s broadly failed; that government is clumsy and ineffectual when it intervenes in local life; and that the principles of personal responsibility, penalties for bad behavior, and rewards for good behavior have to be reintroduced into social policy."[34] Almost everything he said about the Great Society was false, but that was beside the point. The welfare state has gotten everything backward, said Murray, for it institutionalizes the view that worthy objectives required the transfer of resources from the haves to the have-nots. This is exactly the wrong policy. Before Reagan's first term was very old, he had brought Murray's and Gilder's attacks on the welfare state and their defenses of inequality to the center of legitimate political discourse and official state policy. He told the nation where stagflation came from with the disarming clarity that became his stock in trade. "It's been nearly 6 months since I first reported to you on the state of the nation's economy," he said. "I'm afraid my message that night was grim and disturbing. I remember telling you we were in the worst economic mess since the Great Depression. Prices were continuing to spiral upward; unemployment was reaching intolerable levels, and all because government was too big and spent too much of our money."[35] It was time to lower taxes, reduce spending on social programs, take "our" money back, deregulate, and privatize. Good intentions were no longer enough. Solving the nation's social problems would require hard work and force difficult choices.

> We got in trouble when we started looking to government for too many answers, when we listened to those who insisted that making a government bigger would make America better. Well, forgive me, but I happen to believe that the best view of big government is in the rearview mirror as you're driving away from it.
>
> I know they were well-intentioned with all the social experiments, but too often their cure only led to despair and dependency for the very people that needed genuine opportunity. The era of rising savings, investment, productivity growth, and technological supremacy that we once knew somehow seemed to slip further from our grasp. Did we forget that government is the people's business, and every man, woman, and child becomes a shareholder with the first penny of tax paid? Did we forget that government must not supersede the will of the people or the responsibilities of the people in their communities? Did we forget that the function of government is not to confer happiness on us, but just to get out of the way and give us the opportunity to work out happiness for ourselves?[36]

It had been a long time since an American president had talked like this. The essential purposes of human life, said Reagan, are to be found in private life and the sphere of economics. Any attempt to improve the existing order that originates from outside the logic of the market will fail. Trying to impose political or moral categories on economic life will always make things worse, end in failure, and jeopardize the economic freedom on which democracy rests. Societies are structured on a small set of invariant principles and it is futile to try to impose reforms on a social order that will always rebel against outside interference. This is particularly true of the United States, said the President. The country's history demonstrates that the market will always defeat the welfare state and assert its primacy as society's central organizing logic, but if liberal excess is indulged for too long it will damage economic growth, public welfare, and freedom. It was time to learn the lesson of the past thirty years. The welfare state is the voice of reaction. Progress requires giving free rein to capital.

If New York City had once been the nation's chief example of what an enlightened welfare state could do, Reagan now served notice that urban liberalism had failed. The real history of the nation's cities, he announced, was that they relied too much on Washington and failed to pay enough attention to market forces. "Clearly, decades of spending programs have done little more than subsidize the status quo and make wards of the government out of citizens who would rather have a job than a handout," he said. "It's time for us to find out if two of the most dynamic and constructive forces known to man—free enterprise and the profit motive—can be brought to play where government bureaucracy and social programs have failed."[37] The private sector is the most important and dynamic source of progress, the guardian of liberty, the guarantor of everything that makes America great. "You know," he dreamily said in his classic line, "there really is something magic about the marketplace when it's free to operate."[38]

It's true that Reagan didn't preside over the dismantling of the welfare state, as many on the Right hoped he would. It's true that, in endorsing Social Security, he protected the New Deal's largest and most important single initiative. It's true that the state consumed a larger share of the national economy at the end of his presidency than it had at the beginning and that the civilian federal workforce had grown by 150,000. In the end, Reagan didn't make much of a dent in the size of the federal government. He had slowed its domestic growth, but its military side had increased dramatically. The "Reagan Revolution" really meant deregulation, lower taxes, higher defense spending, and huge deficits.

To leave matters here is to miss the importance of Reagan's presidency. Even as he expanded its role in many ways, his constant warnings about the federal government encouraged a broad change in public perceptions of the welfare state. Consumption, not welfare, was solidified as the foundation of American social cohesion and the meaning of its citizenship. The contemporary period's disenchantment with politics, cynicism about reform, pursuit of individual advancement, and acceptance of historic levels of inequality could not have developed without Reagan's ideological preparation. Even now, the Right parrots his old arguments because twenty-five years of accelerating inequality, tax cuts, deregulation, and privatization aren't enough. Taxes are still too high, government regulations are still too intrusive, and there are still too many obstacles to rational investing. Lifting all these onerous burdens from the rich will still benefit everyone and will still increase government revenues at the same time.

The Right's twenty-five-year assault on equality, welfare, and solidarity has entered a new stage. Its reach once limited by a widespread acceptance of the core institutions of the New Deal, it objected to progressive taxation but never seriously tried to destroy it, railed at economic regulations but never convinced the country to dismantle social limits on capital, complained about corporate, estate, and capital gains taxes but never tried to abolish them. Those days are over. For the first time in seventy years, the United States has a government that openly intends to destroy what remains of the welfare state. Its plan to privatize Social Security, lower taxes, and deregulate even more has to be seen as part of a larger project that includes even more rewards for saving and investment and a full-court assault on the basic principle of progressivity that has guided federal tax policy for many years.

> And in many respects, the replacement is already well under way. After four rounds of largely Republican-inspired tax legislation, today's code is a profoundly different instrument than the one that existed when Bush first took office. And though the White House has never publicly laid out a common rationale for its policies, Bush's changes—which have cut income taxes on high earners, reduced rates on capital gains and dividend income, temporarily eliminated the estate tax and allowed businesses to write off the cost of new capital purchases more quickly—depart drastically from the old model of reform. Bush's cuts have greatly reduced the costs formerly borne by corporations and the wealthy, leaving the tax code considerably less progressive than it once was. Instead of getting rid of loopholes so that fewer businesses can escape paying taxes, conservatives have essentially set out to universalize those loopholes, aiming for a day when corporations won't have to pay taxes at all.[39]

The Right State

The triumphant Right is not opposed to the state as a matter of principle. It is opposed to the *welfare state* as a matter of principle. All its positions about militarism, authority, race, and politics pivot around its attack on equality. They depend on popular acceptance of a set of highly debatable assertions that has been evolving since the Reagan presidency and shows no sign of slowing down. Its claim that American history is uniquely marked by a suspicion of the federal government willfully ignores the country's long tradition of using political power to advance economic equality, social justice, and political democracy. Its claim that the welfare state is an unjust transfer of wealth from the productive to the parasitical willfully ignores the economic and moral price of inequality. Its claim that regulation and redistribution distort the economy willfully ignores the effects of Washington's wealth-serving activities. Its claim that inequality will benefit everyone in the long run willfully ignores the enormous cost of reduced family incomes, stagnant wages, fewer governmental services, poorer physical health, more stress, lower benefits, and longer work weeks. Its claim that economic equality will destroy freedom willfully ignores the obvious fact that equal opportunity requires adequate housing, healthy diets, good health care, a decent education—the very definition of social democracy.

To a greater extent than ever, the Right's ideological coherence and political power will depend on how it manages to explain the way wealth is distributed. Americans have traditionally been willing to accept higher levels of inequality than their peers in other advanced industrial societies, but they have to be convinced that everyone has an equal chance to get rich, that most people are benefiting to some extent, and that the distribution of wealth isn't coming at their expense or hurting the country. The Right's alarmist warnings about military vulnerability, eroding authority, rebellious women, unruly blacks, and an intrusive welfare state have disguised and supported its long campaign against equality. As successful as they've been, though, they haven't been successful enough. No ideology can thrive if all it does is complain and attack. Unlike its carping predecessors, the contemporary Right has been able to make a convincing "positive" claim. National restoration and individual prosperity, it says, require that the market be recognized as the central organizing principle of modern life. An explicit defense of inequality wasn't far behind. Once again, a cynical betrayal rested at the center of all this sunny optimism. Accelerating inequality isn't what millions of citizens who were offended by welfare, convinced that the government was wasting their money, and worried about the nation's cities had in mind, but here too it's what they got.

Notes

1. See Bruce J. Schulman, *The Seventies: The Great Shift in American Culture, Society, and Politics* (New York: Free Press, 2001).

2. See Seymour Martin Lipset, *American Exceptionalism: A Double-Edged Sword* (New York: Norton, 1997).

3. Larry M. Bartels, "What's the Matter with *What's the Matter with Kansas?* paper presented at 2005 Annual Meeting of the American Political Science Association, Washington DC, September 1–4, 2005.

4. "Tocqueville's Mistake: A Defense of Strong Central Government," *Harper's*, August 1984, pp. 70–74. See also Eric Foner, *The Story of American Freedom* (New York: Norton, 1999) and John Ehrenberg, *Civil Society: The Critical History of an Idea* (New York: New York University Press, 1999).

5. Friedrich Hayek, *The Road to Serfdom* (Chicago: University of Chicago Press, 1944), p. vii.

6. *Ibid.*, p. 35. His emphasis.

7. *Ibid.*, p. 72.

8. *Ibid.*, p. 79.

9. *Ibid.*, p. 101.

10. *Ibid.*, p. 106.

11. *Ibid.*, p. 205.

12. *Two Cheers for Capitalism* (New York: Basic Books, 1978), p. 190. His emphasis.

13. *Ibid.*, pp. 191–92.

14. *Ibid.*

15. Milton and Rose Friedman, *Free to Choose: A Personal Statement* (New York: Harcourt Brace, 1980), p. 11.

16. *Ibid.*, pp. 148–49.

17. *Ibid.*, p. 286.

18. William Simon, *A Time for Truth* (New York: McGraw Hill, 1978), p. 4.

19. *Ibid.*, p. 11.

20. *Ibid.*, p. 97.

21. *Ibid.*, p. 113. His emphasis.

22. *Ibid.*, p. 116.

23. *Ibid.*, p. 136.

24. *Ibid.*, p. 188.

25. *Ibid.*, p. 221.

26. Jeanne Kirkpatrick, *Dictatorships and Double Standards: Rationalism and Reason in Politics* (New York: Simon & Schuster, 1982), p. 11.

27. *Ibid.*, p. 14.

28. See http://www.reagan.utexas.edu/resource/speeches/1981/72481a.htm.

29. Jude Wanniski, *The Way the World Works* (Washington: Regnery, 1978).

30. *Ibid.*, p. 116.

31. William Grieder, "The Education of David Stockman," *The Atlantic Monthly* 247 (December 1981), p. 46.

32. Radio Address to the Nation on Federal Income Taxes, April 9, 1983. See http://www.reagan.utexas.edu/resource/speeches/1983/40983a.htm.

33. http://www.americanrhetoric.com/speeches/ronaldreagan1980rnc.htm.

34. Charles Murray, *Losing Ground: American Social Policy, 1950–1980* (New York: Basic Books, 1995), p. xvi.

35. Address to the Nation on Federal Tax Reduction Legislation of July 27, 1981, http://www.reagan.utexas.edu/resource/speeches/1981/72781d.htm.

36. Remarks at a Meeting With Chief Executive Officers of National Organizations To Discuss Private Sector Initiatives, March 24, 1982, http://www.reagan.utexas.edu/resource/speeches/1982/32482a.htm.

37. Remarks on Signing a Message to the Congress Transmitting Proposed Enterprise Zones Legislation, March 23, 1982. See http://www.reagan.utexas.edu/resource/speeches/1982/32382a.htm.

38. Radio Address to the Nation on Taxes, Tuition Tax Credit, and Interest Rates, April 24, 1982. See http://www.reagan.utexas.edu/resource/speeches/1982/42482a.htm.

39. Nicholas Confessore, "Breaking the Code," *New York Times Magazine*, January 16, 2005.

CHAPTER SIX

Defending Inequality

In March 2002, President George W. Bush traveled to Mexico so he could tell the International Conference on Financing for Development how concerned he was about inequality. No stranger to working both sides of the plate, the former baseball owner spoke as a sincere man of faith and a principled defender of the status quo. "The growing divide between wealth and poverty, between opportunity and misery, is both a challenge to our compassion and a source of instability," he solemnly informed his listeners. "We must confront it."

Bush soon had the chance to put his money where his mouth was and it didn't take him long to clarify what he really meant. When United Nations Secretary General Kofi Annan asked the world's richest countries to come up with an additional $50 billion a year to meet the Conference's goal of halving the number of people living on less than $1 a day by 2015, Washington hastened to assure him that economic development required free trade and private investment. The President's sincerity could be measured by the distance between his proclamation of concern and the staggering reality of global inequality.

By 2000, the richest one percent of the world's population earned substantially more than the poorest half; indeed, the combined wealth of the world's 200 richest individuals—more than a trillion dollars—was greater than the combined annual income of the poorest half of the world's population.

The amounts of money necessary to end this deprivation were, by industrial-country standards, trivial. Experts estimated that $80 billion a year would provide every inhabitant of the developing world with basic food needs, health care, education, water, and sewers. This was a trivial amount, three cents of every ten dollars of the rich world's income, less than $100 a year for the average inhabitant of the developed world, less than 8 percent of the combined wealth of the world's 200 richest individuals. The price of ensuring that everyone in the world had basic nutrition and health was less than the amount Americans and Europeans spent on pet food in an average year.[1]

It's no secret that capitalism produces poverty and inequality, nor is it a secret that countries with weak public supervision of the market produce more of both than those with vigorous regulatory and welfare states. Even so, some very successful societies have existed for a long time with great disparities of wealth and income. They might have been racked by frequent civil wars and their history might have been shaped by intense class struggles, frequent insurrections, and ferocious repression, but they didn't rely on coercion alone. Egypt, Rome, China, India, and feudal Europe survived for so long partly because they developed convincing ideologies that justified inequality and explained the status quo. These explanations of why things had to be the way they were often attained great depths of analysis and heights of sophistication.

More recent defenses of inequality have often been effective for some time, but popular demands for equity, democracy, and security have steadily made it more difficult to justify great inequality in living conditions. Democratic ideologies, egalitarian social movements, and modern states developed in large measure because large numbers of people entered public life demanding that the fruits of the earth—and of their labor—be distributed more equally than they had been. This has certainly been true of the United States. Her original sin of slavery notwithstanding, many took American history as a sign that freedom, equality, and opportunity in the new world could redeem inequity, hierarchy, and arbitrariness in the old. "The general spread of the light of science," said Thomas Jefferson in his last letter, "has already laid open to every view the palpable truth, that the mass of mankind has not been born with saddles on their backs, nor a favored few booted and spurred, ready to ride them legitimately, by the grace of God."[2]

Jefferson didn't extend this argument to slaves of course, but a little bit of hypocrisy is still the homage that vice pays to virtue. Political leaders can justify, ignore, or deny inequality all they want, but popular impatience with great extremes of income and wealth has often threatened the stability of even the most legitimate and long-lived of polities. "The freest government cannot long endure when the tendency of the law is to create a rapid accumulation of property in the hands of a few, and to render the masses poor and dependent," warned Daniel Webster. The contemporary Right knows this very well and has crafted a series of arguments that explain how policies that benefit a tiny minority of the population aren't really what they seem. It has learned to appeal to a country that still adheres to a broadly democratic ethos by arguing that equality applies to opportunity alone, that economic differences are accurate reflections of contributions to the general welfare, and that making the rich even richer will benefit everyone.

The old Right had defended inherited wealth and established power by looking backward to a time when people knew their place and deference organized the relations between inferiors and their betters. But this sort of argument won't work any longer. The contemporary Right broke out of its earlier isolation because it learned how to articulate a "positive" program that goes far beyond nostalgia and complaint. An aggressive and forward-looking conservatism has stepped forward as the agent of revitalization and the voice of the future. It has convinced many people to entrust it with the task of organizing a regime that is supposedly organized around personal liberty, individual opportunity, and economic growth. Its impressive success in shaping the terms of public debate helps explain how historic levels of inequality have become acceptable or irrelevant to a wide section of the population.

Two strands of arguments have come together. Public policy, conservative spokesmen have insisted, must restore the market to its rightful place as the central organizing principle of a free society for reasons of both morality and efficiency. A moral claim asserts that markets are indispensable requirements of individual opportunity and political democracy. They are, so goes the argument, the best grounding for individual autonomy, the most reliable defense against tyranny, and the only arena in which people have an opportunity to contribute to the public good as they seek to better their own condition. This politico-ethical justification of the market is accompanied by a second and more pragmatic set of efficiency arguments claiming that economic freedom will stimulate such a broad economic expansion that the welfare state will become unnecessary. Liberating the market from the arbitrary requirements of equity, the Right says, will solve all the problems that Keynesianism had tried to address through state action in an earlier period. The results will be good for everyone. A rising tide will lift all boats, even if it lifts some more than others. As for popular nervousness about inequality and residual longings for economic democracy, the Right was confident that combining its moral claim of liberty and opportunity with its efficiency claim of growth and prosperity would carry the day.

There's more to this argument than meets the eye. Conservative defenses of the market have become much more substantial and sophisticated than the moral platitudes, angry grievances, and wistful nostalgia of earlier periods. As the Right developed an optimistic market populism to supplement its indignant cultural populism, it learned to speak the language of the future and articulate the promise of a better tomorrow. All social ills can be solved if there's more wealth creation, it assured skeptical citizens who had thought of Keynesianism as the ideology of fairness and growth. The free market became the agent of efficiency, innovation, and progress, the brave innovating CEO was the democratic hero of the age, the pursuit of prosperity expressed the American Dream, and a yuppie T-shirt announcement that "he who dies with the most toys wins" summed up the meaning of life. No one expressed the new period's unconcealed worship of money better than Ronald Reagan. When the newly-elected president said that "more than anything else, I want to see the United States remain a country where someone can get rich," he summarized the Right's intention to frame the market as the sphere of freedom, self-determination, and individual choice on the one hand and the sphere of efficiency, economic expansion, and social progress on the other.

The appearance of a conservatism that looked to the future signaled how dramatically things had changed. The announcement was a simple one: freeing the market, cutting back on regulation, and channeling more wealth to those who would invest would open the path to a utopian future of rapid innovation, new markets, more jobs, greater productivity, and a free nation full of upright and prosperous citizen-consumers. "There is a legitimate role for government," Reagan said, "but we mustn't forget: Before the idea got around that government was the principal vehicle of social change, it was understood that the real source of our progress as a people was the private sector. The private sector still offers creative, less expensive, and more efficient alternatives to solving our social problems. Now, we're not advocating private initiatives and voluntary activities as a halfhearted replacement for budget cuts. We advocate them because they're right in their own regard. They're a part of what we can proudly call 'the American personality.'"[3]

Reagan was free to define the "American personality" any way he wanted of course, but what's noteworthy is the suggestion that market-driven private initiatives are ethically superior to anything that comes out of the public sector or results from state initiative. An individualistic moral principle that was articulated by the head of state explained how policies that strengthen the private sphere are "right in their own regard." Solidarity and mutual support had been public goods for decades, but the Great Communicator was confident that he could redefine a problem that had bedeviled conservatives for generations and help them reposition themselves on the right side of history. He was at the beginning of all this, but it's moved far beyond any single spokesman by now. Speaking to the citizens of a democratic republic whose dedication to equity and justice remains strong, the Right continues to explain how the market can make us all free, equal, and rich. Equality has disappeared as a legitimate goal of public life, swamped by individualistic appeals to freedom, broad claims about personal opportunity, and breathless expectations that prosperity will make everyone happy.

The heady claim that the United States had solved all of mankind's important problems and was the living incarnation of "the end of history" received formal expression from an unknown minor official in the State Department toward the end of Reagan's presidency. Writing in a 1989 issue of *The National Interest*, Francis Fukuyama gave full voice to a confident right-wing triumphalism as he announced that the struggle between ideologies that had marked human history had come to a definitive end with the final victory of consumerist liberal democracy. He was happy to sign onto British Prime Minister Margaret Thatcher's famous claim that "there is no alternative" to the Anglo-American model. The collapse of the Berlin Wall and fall of the Soviet Union were closer than anyone imagined, and Fukuyama's essay captured the spirit of the moment as it expressed the Right's confidence that the world was being reordered to its liking. "The twentieth century saw the developed world descend into a paroxysm of ideological violence, as liberalism contended first with the remnants of absolutism, then bolshevism and fascism, and finally an updated Marxism that threatened to lead to the ultimate apocalypse of nuclear war," he said. "But the century that began full of self-confidence in the ultimate triumph of Western liberal democracy seems at its close to be returning full circle to where it started: not to an 'end of ideology' or a convergence between capitalism and socialism, as earlier predicted, but to an unabashed victory of economic and political liberalism."[4] The implications of this were positively Hegelian, Fukuyama assured his readers. "What we may be witnessing is not just the end of the Cold War, or the passing of a particular period of postwar history, but the end of history as such: that is, the end point of mankind's ideological evolution and the universalism of Western liberal democracy as the final form of human government."[5]

Fukuyama was certain that the American system—"liberal democracy in the political sphere combined with easy access to VCRs and stereos in the economic"—would solve all social problems.[6] The only two ideologies that had given it a run for its money were fascism and communism, and the twentieth century had managed to discredit both. The United States provides the only credible alternative to medievalism's concentration of wealth and communism's leveling totalitarianism, he said. Echoing similar claims made in a variety of areas, Fukuyama proclaimed that inequality is no longer a serious problem because the state doesn't officially discriminate; "the egalitarianism of modern America represents the essential achievement of the classless society envisioned by Marx. This is not to say that there are not rich people and poor people in the United States, or that the gap between them has not grown in recent years. But the root causes of economic inequality do not have to do with the underlying legal and social structure of our society, which remains fundamentally egalitarian and moderately redistributionist, so much as with the cultural and social characteristics of the groups that make it up, which are in turn the historical legacy of premodern conditions. Thus black poverty in the United States is not the inherent product of liberalism, but is rather the 'legacy of slavery and racism' that persisted long after the formal abolition of slavery."[7]

For Fukuyama and the rest of the triumphalist Right, inequality became a political issue only when officially codified or explicitly sanctioned by the state. As long as the country's formal legal structure didn't explicitly favor any particular class of people, then "the system" couldn't be blamed for what the market produced. Residual "cultural and social characteristics" were to blame. Besides, things were getting better. If race continued to be a problem, it wouldn't be for long. The same was true of economic inequality. So long as there was equality before the law and the state didn't openly discriminate, what the market did was immune to ethical judgment or political remedy.

Even if inequality was a non-problem, Fukuyama did acknowledge that wealth and power were becoming more concentrated and that the momentum of upward redistribution had accelerated dramatically during the "morning years" of Reagan's America. The Right is still sure that there's nothing to worry about. Its official policies have reflected its confidence that it could serve the rich without paying an important political price, stimulating a populist reaction, or calling its ideological claims into question. So long as it could promise that wealth would trickle down, it could avoid angering too many people. It began twenty-five years ago. Reagan's tax cuts, disinflation, and deregulation favored wealth of all kinds, particularly that of the "paper entrepreneurs" described by Robert Reich. "Between 1979 and 1989," reports Kevin Phillips, "the portion of the nation's wealth held by the top 1 percent nearly doubled, skyrocketing from 22 percent to 39 percent, probably the most rapid escalation in U.S. history."[8] Some people certainly got rich in Reagan's America, but a rhetoric of freedom and opportunity defined the problem in such a way as to take equality off the table.

In his 1964 nominating speech for Goldwater, Reagan had declared freedom the central value of American life and identified two threats to its survival: communism abroad and big government at home. As President, he conducted a rhetorical Cold War against both. The 'free market' took its place alongside the free world as the essence of freedom. Reagan's administration marked the end of the New Deal as a politically dominant set of public policies, ideas, and political alliances. Like Roosevelt and Johnson before him, Reagan spoke of 'economic freedom' and proposed an 'economic Bill of Rights.' But in contrast to his predecessors—who used these phrases to support creating jobs, combating poverty, and enhancing social security—economic freedom for Reagan meant dismantling economic regulations and reducing the power of unions, all to ensure the individual's right 'to contract freely for goods and services.' The key to 'economic freedom,' however, was a radical reduction in taxes. High taxes, said Reagan, produced 'servitude' to government, while 'the right to earn your own keep and keep what you earn' was 'what it means to be free.' The cuts not only reduced the level of taxation, they all but eliminated the principle of progressivity, one of the ways twentieth-century capitalist societies have tried to redress the unequal distribution of incomes produced by a market system. The result was a massive shift of wealth from poorer to wealthier Americans. By the mid-1990s, the richest 1 percent of Americans owned 40 percent of the nation's wealth, twice their share of twenty years earlier.[9]

The astonishing thing about all this is that the Right's intention to organize the modern version of a Roaring Twenties political economy came dressed up in the emperor's new clothes of optimistic faith in the future. But it would take more than assurances about the End of History to convince a democratic citizenry that orienting state policy toward wealth and property would be good for everyone. As the population stubbornly held on to the country's egalitarian ethos, it became clear that an ideological campaign would be needed to persuade broad swaths of the population that morality and efficiency demanded that the market be made the central organizing institution of American society.

The Moral Market

The Right had plenty to work with. If the European social contract is built around solidarity and welfare, the American leans toward individualism and opportunity. That has been particularly true in recent years, largely because the Right has worked hard to develop a market-based understanding of freedom that defines democracy as cutting taxes on wealth, deregulating corporate behavior, and privatizing as many governmental functions as possible. The market is the only dependable foundation of liberty, it repeatedly says, adding Gilder's claim that it is also the sphere in which a moral social order is built on the basis of individual creativity and genuine concern for the welfare of others. The picture is a relatively simple one and relies on a mutually reinforcing set of claims that build a case against equality in the name of freedom and opportunity. Necessarily indifferent to status, race, gender, or other limiting qualities, we are told, the market confers rewards that faithfully and justly record contributions to social welfare. Working without central direction, its equilibrating mechanism has to be impartial because it can recognize only what one does rather than who one is. Past accomplishments, present identity, historic wrongs, paranoid fantasies, fraudulent dreams, self-important puffery don't matter—nothing can compromise the market's requirement for accurate and untainted information. When allowed to work without any outside direction, the market rewards truth and punishes falsehood, recognizes contribution and is blind to bombast, protects freedom and ignores demands for unearned privilege, encourages productive work and rejects idleness. Its natural end-point is a pure meritocracy of self-serving equals whose liberty is protected by equality of opportunity and the right to participate or leave.

Jude Wanniski's announcement that the market is always right and provides the only dependable grounding for justice stood behind the Right's eagerness to sacrifice equality of outcome to an individualistic claim of equal opportunity. A powerful efficiency argument has also emerged to supplement its moral argument about markets. Acquisition and wealth now represent the optimistic future, while equity and solidarity are either the remnants of an unproductive past or the malignant threat of a totalitarian future. A wider social theory has come to support the Right's optimistic picture of political democracy, individual opportunity, and limitless growth—all coming at the expense of the common ties, mutual responsibility, and social welfare that is just so much feel-good meddling.

This identification of the market with morality, freedom, and autonomy has been successful for a variety of reasons, not the least of which is its ability to appeal to a powerful American ethic of individual achievement, self-determination, and opportunity. The more the Right has framed the issue as an ethical one of choice and mobility, the more successfully it has marginalized once-powerful concerns about welfare and equality. Its most sophisticated ideologues have worked hard to reconcile individual interest and social welfare. Reagan, George Gilder, Charles Murray, Newt Gingrich, and others argued forcefully against the lingering suspicion that the market encourages selfishness by claiming that it forces people to satisfy others' economic interests before they can satisfy their own. Markets are moralizing institutions, Reagan said repeatedly, because they provide a way for us to help one another while we help ourselves. Gilder's Golden Rule makes it possible to do well and do good at the same time. Plutocracy was good for all, and the rich could rest content that a state whose first order of business was protecting their wealth would serve others as it did so.

For Gilder, Reagan, and others on the Right, the market was pretty close to the voice of God. But no one summarized the economics and politics of the Great Awakening better than Michael Novak. Published at the very beginning of Reagan's presidency, *The Spirit of Democratic Capitalism* was a direct response to Irving Kristol's call for a spiritual defense of capitalism. Seeking to fill the void left by Catholic theologians' failure to justify American history in an appropriately conservative fashion, Novak collaborated with William Simon in attacking the American bishops' powerful 1984 pastoral letter that criticized the American economy in the name of social justice and economic equality. All this activity provided a religious anticipation of Fukuyama's announcement that the End of History had arrived.[10] None of this was especially new, particularly in the United States. American Calvinists had often tried to marry God and Mammon by suggesting that worldly success is a sign of heavenly love, a theme that conveniently married religious enthusiasm with the more profane goal of getting ahead. Novak's Catholic-inspired statement that economic success need not come at the expense of spiritual ideals supplemented the Reverend Falwell's assurances that God so loves the rich that he wants their taxes cut and the thieving welfare state destroyed.

What set Novak's argument apart was its grand ambition, even if he struck an appropriately humble note. The central control and organization of virtue, he began, is neither possible nor desirable. A distinctly Friedmanite theology assured readers that God made each soul free to choose and that the market-bounded interplay of uncoerced people is the only dependable basis of virtuous behavior. Capitalism encourages, organizes, and rewards ethically upright behavior, and Novak's book proposed to examine the "the life of the spirit which makes democratic capitalism possible. It is about its theological presuppositions, values, and systemic intentions."[11] Novak's ambitious project wasn't much different from what secular defenders of inequality had been saying for some time. What was new was his attempt to give it some theological armor and his strong suggestion that God made his people free and wanted them to be rich.

Since capitalism and democracy share a set of moral foundations that are grounded in generosity and kindness, it stands to reason that they also share institutional foundations. "In the conventional view, the link between a democratic political system and a market economy is merely an accident of history," said Novak. "My argument is that the link is stronger: political democracy is compatible in practice only with a market economy."[12] The position that markets make democracy possible because property protects individuals from state power and provides a zone of privacy is a fairly orthodox one. So was Novak's expectation that markets stimulate economic expansion. More productivity and greater abundance were indispensable to personal liberation and carried the solution to poverty, ignorance, war, and the other afflictions that deform human potential and distress a loving God. Economic growth will make the interventionist and redistributive politics of the past unnecessary. Markets no longer meant greed, exploitation, and poverty. They might produce inequality, but Novak knew that justice would not suffer and that those with talent and wealth were safe.

> Democratic polities depend upon the reality of economic growth. No traditional society, no socialist society—indeed, no society in history—has ever produced strict equality among individuals or classes. Real differences in talent, aspiration, and application inexorably individuate humans. Given the diversity and liberty of human life, no fair and free system can possibly guarantee equal outcomes. A democratic system depends for its legitimacy, therefore, not upon equal results but upon a sense of equal opportunity. Such legitimacy flows from the belief of all individuals that they can better their condition.[13]

Social inequality will always reflect the wide range of natural human capacities, but under certain conditions it can serve God's purposes. Protecting liberty makes the exchange worthwhile. The market may produce inequality, but that's because it's the home of genuine individuality and service to humankind. Tyranny cannot take hold, the self-interested works of sinful people serve the public good, individuals are protected, acquisitiveness serves virtue, and decency and compassion mark the work of God's imperfect creatures.

The spirit of democratic capitalism, Novak repeatedly assured his readers, is one of charity, generosity, faith, trust, and dreams. Inequality is a permanent feature of the human condition because people are different, but inequality in market conditions of freedom makes possible a fully redemptive life of the spirit. Capitalism creates a community out of countless individual acts of self-improvement, for markets tie individuals together in a moral nexus despite their ever-present inclination to selfishness. Increased prosperity for some means increased prosperity for all in a mutually beneficial realm where no one loses when others win.

The market is the way God knits free individuals together in a network of voluntary transactions. It requires—and rewards—autonomy, judgment, choice, responsibility, optimism, inventiveness, energy, and a commitment to the individual as "the main source of social energy." Equality, regulation, redistribution, democratic supervision—they're all out because they interfere with God's purpose. The moral market prizes peace, encourages unity, grants power to those who don't have it, opens doors of opportunity to the most humble, makes it possible for sons to do better than their fathers. The moral market is the friend of the poor, rewards humility, punishes arrogance and greed, and recognizes innovation while elevating the humble and the meek. The moral market might need guidance from religion, humanism, and the arts—it might even require taming by the state from time to time—but Novak was certain that "an economic system without profit is merely spinning its wheels, providing neither for the unmet needs of the poor nor for progress."[14] The moral market relies on trust, protects the weak, rewards risk, and makes individuals attentive to the worth of others. Charity, generosity, faith, hope, and dreams drive the behavior of individual actors as they celebrate the good fortune of others that makes possible their own welfare. Exploitation disappears because the new wealth that's created does not come at anyone's expense, all participants benefit, and it becomes clear that "the hopes for a good, free, and just society are best reposed in a system which gives high status to commerce and industry."[15] Novak couldn't deny that markets channel wealth to those who already have it, so he dressed inequality in the clothing of selflessness, generosity, and concern for others. Hopes for security and equality fuel a desire that "runs counter to the human condition. No individual or society is secure in a world of emergent probability and sin; and the talents with which human beings are endowed are unequal."[16] The understandable hope to eliminate poverty, reduce inequalities in wealth, and meet basic needs must take account of the dangers posed by the state, the importance of freedom of opportunity, and the understanding that the general good, if it exists at all, is best organized by the infinite number of private decisions made by free consumer-citizens. The welfare state restricts liberty, strengthens the bureaucracy, puts the cart of distribution over the horse of production, leads to stasis and stagnation, breeds divisive sullenness and resentment, rewards the group at the expense of the individual, and sets loose a never-ending search for security that undermines social order even as it fails to deliver protection. Egalitarian social policies must elevate the arbitrary state over the free market, impose an unnatural uniformity on people of different aptitudes, and raise those of lesser talent over those with more. "By contrast," says our theologian of wealth, "democratic capitalists hold that *every* person of talent—musical, intellectual, economic—should have every opportunity to develop his talents. They hold, further, that natural and developed inequalities enhance the common good of all."[17]

So inequality nurtures morality and is good for everyone. Novak knew precisely to whom he was appealing, and he made the argument explicit. His good news to the rich assured them that God approved of, and society was served by, their money and property. After all, they support charities, patronize the arts, dabble in inventions, and dispose of social resources in a far more trustworthy manner than any bureaucrat or politician. The trust that wealth requires—trust in the stability of the currency, in the quality of information, in the human desire for self-improvement—enriches modern life and explains how brotherhood arises from individualism and greed. Indeed, Novak placed inequality at the center of a new market theology and located both in God's appearance in history. The community, individuality, and humility to which he rendered lip service were bit players by comparison. If the market is to organize social life, then its consequences were part of a divine plan. Novak's God is a Social Darwinist God, and his Scripture justifies inequality. "The Jewish and Christian view shows that God is not committed to equality of results. One steward differs from another in his performance; some virgins are foolish, some wise. The faithful son receives no celebration comparable to the one given by his father for the prodigal. Workers who arrive at the eleventh hour receive the same wage as those who bore the whole day's heat. St. Paul bids all to compete, to measure themselves as he measures himself, and to outdo him if one can; God will be the judge. Religious compassion does not entail leveling."[18] Augustinian that he is, Novak announced that sin brought judgment and inequality into the world and made of both an opportunity as well as a curse. Life was what the individual made of it.

Democracy demands that we not put too much stock in our own abilities or expect too much of one another, but it also enjoins us to do the best with what we have. It reminds us that our energies are limited and our vision faulty, but it recognizes individuality, supports plurality, and makes it possible to extract the good from our evil tendencies. Reagan's mystical sense of the market's magic now had a solid theological foundation, for Novak was sure that man's God-given desire for self-improvement drives toward market economies and the unlimited accumulation of wealth. "It does not seem to be inconsistent with the gospels," he said, "for each human being to struggle, under the spur of competition with his fellows, to become all he can become."[19] It's nice to see that the Army's advertising slogan has a biblical warrant, all the more so because God's love extends even unto money.

Investors are the new carriers of virtue and the agents of morality. Markets that enable free individuals to choose are the visible manifestation of divine love, the sign of *caritas* and God's sacrificial love for man. The entire history of the race finds its culmination in democratic capitalism, Fukuyama's secular conviction that the United States represented the End of History echoing Novak's earlier theological conviction that God makes capitalism, individualism, and choice serve justice, love, and brotherhood. Life might be a vale of tears and Original Sin may stain the works of man, but things are bound to be better in conditions of plenty than of equality. If trickle-down economics sought to provide a "scientific" account of how enriching the wealthy would be good for everyone, Novak provided its "theology."

Novak gave old claims a particularly vulgar pseudo-religious gloss, but he doesn't occupy some sort of fringe position. Indeed, the theoretical foundations of his argument are widely shared. Once he saw the light and gave up a youthful flirtation with progressive politics, the George Frederick Jewett Scholar in Religion, Philosophy, and Public Policy at the American Enterprise Institute spent a career safely ensconced at the heart of the modern Right. He served on Reagan's oddly-named "Presidential Task Force on Economic Justice," was the American ambassador to the United Nations Human Rights Commission and to the Conference on Security and Cooperation in Europe, and after a number of other assignments now sits on the Board of the National Endowment for Democracy. His most recent assignment was a trip to Rome at the behest of George W. Bush to explain the invasion of Iraq to a pope who clearly opposed it.

Ever since it made its reluctant peace with formal political democracy, the American Right has argued that equality should be limited to opportunity. Any social commitment to equality of condition, it says, will always be arbitrary, reward the undeserving, make it impossible for the market to recognize contribution, destroy any incentive to improve one's prospects, strike at the core principles that organize an ethically responsible meritocracy, and begin a slide down the slippery slope that leads to the gulag of the welfare state. It's an argument that has draw upon deep roots in modern history. The promise that individuals could find recognition and success through their own efforts was an important galvanizing force in the struggle against the timeless claims of feudal power, inherited property, and patriarchal families. Removing the hidebound obstacles to individual achievement and social progress became part and parcel of the long struggle for democracy and opportunity. Only if access were free, open, and equal could the deserving hope for individual prosperity and serve social progress at the same time. Justice had to be blind if the market was to be impartial.

It was always clear that substantial inequality of condition would result when equality of opportunity was combined with free markets, but the trade-off was so clearly superior to feudal irrationality and arbitrariness that the New World could claim to have redeemed the promise of the Old. Slavery, the systematic oppression of women, the destruction of small farmers, and the exploitation of workers called all of this into question from time to time, but powerful social movements moved history along and prosperity enabled American optimists to paint a picture of expansion and inclusion. Eliminating official discrimination in state and society, weakening the power of inheritance, encouraging industrialization and urbanization, organizing public education—the country's history seemed to be moving smoothly along a path of recognition for those who deserved it, justice for those who contributed, and wealth for those who helped others.

The relationship between equality of opportunity and fair competition on the one hand and social justice and distributive equality on the other is one of the most persistent fault lines of American life. The Right has worked carefully to exploit it, rooting the first in a partisan reading of the country's history and the other in a narrative of alien influence. The roots of this argument go back to the anti-French agitation of the late eighteenth and early nineteenth centuries. Powerful movements for economic reform have been central to American history from the beginning, but a quarter of a century of right-wing ideology has had a dramatic effect. "Compensatory programs" like Head Start enjoy wide support, but "affirmative action" is said to violate the principle of fair competition. Americans spend more money on education than Europeans but are willing to live with far stingier welfare systems. They are less likely than Europeans to support economic redistribution, social welfare programs, wage and price controls, government intervention in the economy, reduction of the workweek, wearing seatbelts, providing jobs, guaranteeing a basic income, and a host of other "positive" measures. They are willing to accept far higher levels of economic inequality than Europeans, tend to see welfare as a matter of individual failure rather than social responsibility, and insist that the rules of fair competition and equality before the law be respected. A wide respect for work, effort, and achievement indicate the extent to which "Americans remain much more individualistic, meritocratic-oriented, and anti-statist than peoples elsewhere."[20]

The Right's position that a free market will distribute society's goods in a more equitable and just fashion than is possible with any politically-driven or morally-defined program draws on this tradition. Its claim that merit means innate ability, hard work, and a measure of luck—and the twin assumption that this "merit" will be recognized and rewarded by a properly-functioning market—seem to run directly counter to the desire to eliminate the estate tax, but easy assumptions often obscure difficult questions. After all, how is one to measure "merit"? Is generosity a component of "merit?" How about education, imagination, intelligence, kindness, or sympathy? Where do honesty, bravery, respect, or competence fit in?

From Hayek and Kristol to the Friedmans, Gilder, and Novak, the Right says that merit is what the market says it is. Since the market can confer only one sort of reward, wealth becomes the visible manifestation of merit. And this contemporary gauge is also a measure of inequality, since nothing is truer than to say that people are unequal in their endowments and that those endowments will find their just reflection in market processes. How a trite observation should translate into a principle of distribution is ultimately a political matter—but it's certainly not a godly one. For the Right, the obvious fact that people are born with unequal capacities justifies economic, political, and social inequality. Inequality should be acceptable just so long as people "play fair," make contributions to the wider society, and don't harm others as they do so. The notion that some social goods should be distributed equally because they are required for a decent life, and not because they're "earned," has no place in an ethical universe that's organized by market categories. Since stratification by merit is not arbitrary but reflects real capacity, it follows that the rich are rich because they're meritorious.

Alarmed by a broad crisis of confidence, Kristol had urged business to establish a moral argument for property and profit. Novak and others took up his call and tried to go beyond the Right's vulgar celebrations of money and tradition. As they identified the market with democracy, creativity, autonomy, and freedom they developed a parallel claim that it was the greatest wealth-creating mechanism ever developed. In doing so, they undermined one of the key arguments that had supported the modern welfare state. The Keynesians had demonstrated that important measures of state regulation and redistribution were required if economic expansion was to serve stability, benefit the middle and working classes, and strengthen democracy. Militarism was an important part of all this, but the general prosperity of the postwar period seemed to neutralize Eisenhower's famous warning about a "military-industrial complex." The return of free-market fundamentalism—in matters of ideology if not in practice—helped the Right steal Keynesianism's thunder and announce itself as the guarantor of economic expansion, wealth creation, and all-round prosperity.

The Wealth Creator

Like postwar liberalism, the contemporary Right depends on economic expansion to lend legitimacy to its political economy and coherence to its ideology. When the Carter stagflation began to call Keynesianism into question, conservative ideologues began their long effort to supply an alternative to the principles that had guided American social policy since the end of World War II. Kristol's early claim that income redistribution cannot eliminate poverty marked the beginning of the unfolding argument, but it took a while for a set of supporting claims to take shape. In the meantime, *Two Cheers for Capitalism* announced that economic growth would solve the country's most important problems and simultaneously enable conservatives to escape their ideological isolation. Kristol wasn't the first right-winger to claim that poverty could be ended without egalitarian social policies, of course. What was relatively new, and proved to be of decisive importance, was his accompanying claim that conservative economic principles could restore sustained economic growth and that general prosperity would address the social problems to which liberalism had addressed itself. Keynesian economic policies weren't just authoritarian. They were also obsolete.

Kristol's early call to reform a welfare state that he did not oppose in principle would be transformed into open hostility before long. For the moment, he contrasted the vast amounts of money spent and the growth of the Great Society's size and reach with its allegedly meager results and concluded that "the welfare state, over the past 25 years, lost its original self-definition and became something more ambitious, more inflated, and incredibly more expensive." Kristol knew what that something was. "It became the paternalistic state, addressing itself to every variety of 'problem' and committed to 'solving' them all—committed, that is, to making human life unproblematic."[21] The slow expansion of liberalism's regulatory and redistributive activities had overwhelmed its initial intention to provide a modest degree of social insurance. Modern welfare policy, Kristol said, had skidded off the tracks of sensible social reform and had become a many-headed hydra that sought to end pollution, reform education, solve problems of mental health, police family life, and organize urban revitalization with such an intrusive level of state activity that liberty was compromised and prosperity endangered.

Kristol wanted to restate Hayek's principle that any effort to prescribe a set of social goals guided by claims from outside the logic of the marketplace was morally suspect and economically disastrous. This was particularly true when it came to the more sensitive areas of social policy, he said—especially the matter of inequality. The idea that society—or the state, which is how "society" speaks—should have an important say in determining the distribution of wealth violates the elementary rules of political economy, jeopardizes democracy, and runs counter to the country's history. "The social order we call 'capitalism,' constructed on the basis of a market economy," Kristol said, "does *not* believe that 'society' ought to prescribe a 'fair' distribution of income." Since no sound morality allows an outside observer to privilege one set of private goals over another, society can efficiently recognize talent and reward contribution only if organized around the market's blind neutrality. Individuals are the only reliable guides when it comes to setting goals and making plans, and the summation of their preferences provides policymakers with all the information they need to organize social life. Justice is served even if equality is denied, and Kristol's readers could rest content in the knowledge that his five "bedrock truths" about economics permit only one form of social organization:

(1) the overwhelming majority of men and women are naturally and incorrigibly interested in improving their material conditions; (2) efforts to repress this natural desire lead only to coercive and impoverished polities; (3) when this natural desire is given sufficient latitude so that commercial transactions are not discouraged, economic growth does take place; (4) as a result of such growth, everyone does eventually improve his condition, however unequally in extent or time; (5) such economic growth results in a huge expansion of the property-owning middle class—a necessary (though not sufficient) condition for a liberal society in which human rights are respected.[22]

Milton and Rose Friedman also worked hard to establish the principle that the market was a progressive and forward-looking institution that represented the future. It was time to break with the dead hand of the statist past and recognize the connection between freedom and prosperity, they announced. From education and environmental protection to Social Security, the Friedmans were clear that the future belonged to the market. They urged Americans to break with the stultifying past and move toward a future of greater liberty and wider prosperity. "Whenever we find any large element of individual freedom, some measure of progress in the material comforts at the disposal of ordinary citizens, and widespread hope of further progress in the future, there we also find that economic activity is organized mainly through the free market."[23]

The Right announced that Keynesianism's reliance on state activity to stimulate demand, distribution, and employment had become obsolete fetters on growth and prosperity. Now capital is the progressive, creative, and democratizing force of the future. "This country is bursting with energy, but a government run by central decree has no way to respond," announced Reagan as he asked the 1981 Annual Meeting of the National Alliance of Business to support his tax cuts and revenue proposals. He knew who his friends were, and so did they. "So, our message today is simply help us pass these incentives so we can help you. We want nothing more than to turn you loose so you can make the 1980's the most exciting, successful decade our nation has ever known—years of renaissance for American entrepreneurs, years when millions of free men and women went out and found the energy to make us secure and created a revolutionary technological breakthrough on every front, years when they rebuilt our cities and, in the process, created millions of new jobs, stronger families, and a real hope for young Americans everywhere. That's the kind of country I want to leave for our children, and I know it's what you want, too."[24] Times had changed. Reagan used to claim that he was the only President who had been a member of a trade union as he pursued the most relentlessly anti-labor policies in a generation. Now the erstwhile New Dealer announced that he had seen the future. He was sure that it wouldn't be like the past and equally sure that he could help it along.

> With the same energy that Franklin Roosevelt sought government solutions to problems, we will seek private solutions. The challenge before us is to find ways once again to unleash the independent spirit of the people and their communities. That energy will accomplish far, far more than government programs ever could. What federalism is to the public sector, voluntarism and private initiative are to the private sector.[25]

Reagan prepared the ground for every subsequent effort the Right has made to identify the state with the past and the market with the future. His endless repetitions of a few central claims pictured a country composed of individual consumers who knew what they wanted, a forward-looking market that was the source of all progress and innovation, and a reactionary state that had been captured by unproductive "special interests." Markets, he said over and over again, unleash human creativity and reward genuine social contributions. If the state wanted to help usher in the new world of freedom and prosperity, it should get out of the way, get off people's backs, and take its hands out of their pockets. These arguments lent credibility to Reagan's enthusiastic use of state power to lower taxes on wealth, attack labor, roll back economic regulations, and privatize governmental functions.

Wanniski helped popularize the view that the market is never wrong because it represents everyone and knows everything. The most democratic and efficient way of expressing individual preferences and organizing general principles, it is the most powerful template for the modern state and the calculation of individual advantage the best framework for the modern citizen-consumer. Indifferent to any considerations beyond immediate efficiency and thoroughly uninterested in any set of questions that arise from outside its own logic, the market provides perfect information if all its rules are followed. This would require a whole new set of beliefs and practices. "Think of the market as an instrument that has a mind of its own, over and beyond the total of minds participating in it," Wanniski urged. "The market is the most accurately programmed computer on the planet, the closest expression of the mind of the electorate itself."[26] Such a position could be applied to the most basic institutions of a political democracy.

> The results of an election represent the best judgment of the body politic in accommodating the interests of its individual parts. Insofar as elections are honestly conducted, *they always turn out right*. No individual, no philosopher king, could possibly be a superior judge of the interests of the electorate than the electorate itself. To put it even more emphatically, barring fraud, the winners of every election are superior to those who lose. Every referendum, every bond issue that goes to the voters turns out correctly. And in every national or local election, each and every citizen who is elected to the Presidency, the Congress, or City Hall is the optimum reflection of the national or local interest, given the choices available to the electorate.[27]

Tampering with the market will destroy democracy, announced Wanniski. Keynesianism has failed as a theory of growth and a guide to policy. Now it is more suited to contraction than to expansion. Its refusal to take account of the power of self-interest or to place the individual at the center of its analysis means that it cannot connect private impulses to the common good. It's time to reorganize social life based on a new set of understandings. The market is the register of the popular will, the summarizer of private interests, the model democratic institution, and the great wealth creator. Like all the supply-siders and Reagan himself, Wanniski repeatedly argued that it is more important to stimulate growth rather than to rearrange distribution, more important to encourage private wealth rather than to equalize conditions, more important to favor entrepreneurs and investors than to protect workers and consumers. Redistribution and regulation aren't just immoral, unjust, and arbitrary. They are also inefficient, outmoded, and obsolete. The Right has held on to this argument for a long time. Years after Wanniski introduced the world to supply-side economics, Republican Representative Dick Armey summarized matters with his customary clarity. As he prepared to retire from his post as House Majority Leader, the Texan ruminated about all that he and Newt Gingrich had accomplished. Proud of the "axioms" he had developed to guide the congressional Right, the former professor of economics was asked to name his favorite. He didn't hesitate. "The market is rational; the government's dumb."[28]

The contemporary Right's market-worship has often been observed more in the breach than in reality, but there's no denying its ideological appeal to a country of strivers. Markets offer consumers broad choices, bring buyers and sellers together, provide measures of value, apportion economic resources, and drive toward greater levels of efficiency. When they work well, they allocate resources, refine information, and purge economies of failure. But that's not enough for a decent society, for the price system doesn't care about measures of worth or merit that can't be expressed in economic terms. Only those with resources that the market can recognize will benefit if its values are regarded as ends in themselves rather than as limited means to ends that are defined by outside standards. It's no accident that UNICEF's project on Child Poverty in Rich Countries reported that the United States has one of the highest rates of child poverty among the world's wealthiest societies. In February 2005, the survey found that 22% of Americans under eighteen were living in households with a per capita income below 50% of its national average. Of all the countries surveyed, only Mexico was worse. UNICEF's regional director knew why the United States fared so poorly and why the Nordic social democracies had the world's lowest rate of child poverty. "Higher government spending on family and social benefits is very clearly associated with a lower level of child poverty," said Philip O'Brien as he made it clear that market forces could not lift children out of poverty and that systematic government intervention is indispensable.[29] Efficiency is one thing, decency quite another.

None of this has prevented the Right from endlessly repeating that the market is the voice of the people, the faithful register of popular desires, and the fundamental principle of healthy social organization. The market recognizes wants, punishes and rewards according to what people actually do, encourages self-expression, organizes an efficient democracy of buying and selling, destroys hierarchies, works on the people's behalf, protects autonomy and eliminates unproductive activities of all sorts. It is the twenty-first-century model for elections, the creator of citizens, defender of liberty, organizer of societies, *vox populi*. These claims are so striking not because they're so original but because they're so radical. American populism had been organized around defending small property, limiting concentrated wealth, protecting the poor, and respecting labor. It recognized that democracy required that market efficiency had to be subjected to important measures of democratic accountability and political supervision. It understood that markets would inflict enormous harm on society if uncontrolled by outside, non-market limits and expectations. The notion that there are some fundamental social goods that originate from outside the logic of the marketplace is an ancient one.[30] But the Right has stood these old democratic arguments on their heads. Its new economic populism dresses up in the clothing of opportunity and George W. Bush's new "ownership society," but it's the same old defense of wealth, property, and inequality.

The Source of Freedom

There's nothing wrong with opportunity, autonomy, or ownership—unless they're used as slogans to disguise something else. That's exactly what's been happening for twenty-five years. A consciously right-wing political program has facilitated an historic shift of wealth toward American families with annual incomes above $200,000 and away from almost everyone else. The result is a level of inequality not seen in this country since the Gilded Age and the Roaring Twenties.

Seen in retrospect, it all happened pretty quickly and proceeded pretty smoothly. As the 1970s drew to a close, the Republicans came to power as a middle-class, anti-elitist correction to fifteen years of disorder, permissiveness, and decay. Beginning with Reagan's presidency, an increasingly conservative GOP has been the engine for capitalist revitalization and, not coincidentally, has also been the organizer of historic levels of inequality. The orientation of federal policy toward the country's corporations and super-rich began with a series of regressive tax cuts, attacks on federal programs for the poor, economic deregulation, and a supply-side "trickle-down" economic program that was designed to reward wealth and investment. Ever mindful of ideology, Reagan worked hard to convince millions of middle-class Americans that their interests were with the wealthy and against the poor. His successors have continued what he began.

For a quarter of a century, the American Right has said that policies aiming at tax equity and the moderate redistribution of wealth had to yield to the realities of a new world. Claiming that it wanted to increase the amount of money available for capital formation, to reward work, savings, and investment, and to facilitate the transition to a more efficient global marketplace, it has insisted that everyone would benefit if public life were organized around the requirements of the market. Behind the lofty rhetoric and the appeal to individual self-reliance, though, one could find the traditional program of defending wealth and property. George W. Bush's attempt to build support for privatizing Social Security with talk of an "ownership society" of autonomous investor-owners is a perfect case in point, and it's not likely to be the last. His assault on the New Deal's most successful program of universal social insurance is now being described as an equal-opportunity chance to make a buck. The attempt to undermine Social Security's founding premise of mutual responsibility and a shared future with the language of self-reliance and the promise of personal autonomy has fallen on deaf ears so far, but the Right is not about to abandon such an ambitious attack on the heart of the welfare state anytime soon.

A much more important long-range purpose is driving Bush's appeal to individual interest and the lure of Wall Street. The Right hopes that encouraging people of middling income to see themselves as small proprietors will help create a huge new investor class whose individual ownership of small private retirement accounts will unite them with the richest 1% of Americans—the million families with an average income of $1 million and an average net worth of $8–10 million. It was this group that took 42% of all the stock market's advances during the last four years of Clinton's bull market and now owns more stock than 90% of the rest of the country. The Right's heady talk of a Republic of Shareholders and 401(k)s For The Masses is designed to persuade a large stratum of the general population that its interests are with established wealth and that trial lawyers, government regulation, corporate taxation, and trade unions are threats to their security. If it can do so, Americans are likely to become even more skeptical of the idea that government should work for the common good and that civilized societies require an expansive social contract.

Bush has attacked Social Security with the language of choice and opportunity, but the Right's assault on social welfare is far broader than this or that particular fight. As it shrinks federal support of Medicare and Medicaid, undermines public education with talk of school vouchers, touts "health savings accounts" as an alternative to comprehensive health insurance, continues to deregulate as much as it can, eviscerates public housing, privatizes public services, opens the door to "faith-based" initiatives, and insists on even more tax cuts for wealth and property, the administration continues the Right's long attempt to change the way Americans think of themselves and of the society in which they live. Instead of talking the language of producers and citizens, its public discourse is shaped by the categories of owners, consumers, and taxpayers. When Milton Friedman assured readers that "the market can transform our schools" with the old Right's old saws about competition, fairness, and justice and added that vouchers would actually "narrow the income gap between the less skilled and more skilled workers," he testified to how radically things had changed.[31]

An important strand of such thinking goes back to the nineteenth century, but much of its recent version originated in Nixon's talk of a "silent majority" of white middle-class suburbanites and urban workers whose property, "values," and patriotism were under assault by the spoiled sons and daughters of an arrogant liberal elite. His dark warnings about hordes of self-indulgent youth who scorned hard work, religious faith, and the nuclear family initially focused on what we now call "culture," but few were naive enough to believe that Nixon's claims were ever free of political calculation. The Right has moved far beyond his early attempt to articulate a conservative cultural populism. Now it's been extended to the economic sphere, all organized around Kristol's claim that all attempts to interfere with the market's moral and efficiency imperatives are elitist by definition. The Right continues to insist that overbearing and out-of-touch bureaucrats are wedded to economic regulation and redistribution because they just don't trust ordinary people. What's new is that it has broadened its attack on elitist "social engineering" from busing, abortion, and affirmative action to virtually all efforts to supervise the market. Conservative populism has migrated from the initial "cultural" attack on liberals, intellectuals, and the social movements of the 1960s to the economic sphere of regulation, redistribution, and welfare. Arrogant, contemptuous liberal enemies of ordinary people's "values" have been strengthened by arrogant, contemptuous liberal threats to their economic well-being. Morality and efficiency require the market. Right-wing populism has come full circle, its work done.

Appeals to individual opportunity and private interest have redefined some of the country's basic ideological categories. The persistent claim that "liberty" and "freedom" are incompatible with regulation, redistribution, and equality of condition has helped reconcile the Right's formal notion of political democracy as equality before the law with historic levels of economic inequality. None of this an accident, nor does it stand apart from other claims the Right has been making for years. If getting rich is the central purpose of life and serves as the standard by which public affairs are measured, then a democratic government need do little more than guarantee equality of opportunity and let the market organize everything else. If the market's economic processes and the rule of law summarize the requirements of political democracy in the twenty-first century, then we needn't worry about inequality. It just comes with the territory and strengthens society to boot.

The Right has worked for a long time to legitimize the idea that markets are democratic institutions that are responsive to popular desires, precise in registering social worth, and fair in allocating rewards. But there's more. Now they organize consent, incarnate the Golden Rule, and provide the only dependable ground for the free exercise of autonomous choice. Since they articulate the will of the people, right-wing spokesmen say, any scheme to limit their reach, control their effects, or operate outside their boundaries is an elitist and undemocratic attack on opportunity and mobility. People buy Microsoft operating systems because they freely choose to; they go to work every morning because they freely choose to; they smoke cigarettes because they freely choose to; they are even homeless—in President Ronald Reagan's infamous formulation—because they freely choose to be.

Markets and their inhabitants—producers, consumers, corporations, investors, executives—are now more legitimate and socially useful than governments and their bureaucrats. Entrepreneurs and investors have replaced citizens as the engines of progress and change. The political sphere has been systematically hollowed out, replaced by economic categories, subverted by private calculation, and paralyzed by unprecedented levels of inequality. None of this happened spontaneously. As the historic foes of the country's business community withered and collapsed, a newly emboldened Right developed an aggressive campaign to channel wealth upward and worked to convince broad sections of the population that economic equality was neither possible nor desirable. Eviscerating the trade unions, undoing government regulations, attacking the welfare state, and rewarding wealth and property are the core projects of its new democracy—and all require substantial state action. Democracy no longer means a reasonable standard of living, substantial economic equality, and widespread social welfare. Now it means equal opportunity, the free market, and inequality of condition.

It's no accident that President Bush suggested that Americans demonstrate their political strength and patriotic resolve in the weeks after September 11 by going shopping.[32] As family, self, and community become defined through the ownership of goods, equality of opportunity defines a society of wannabe millionaires, Lotto winners, day traders, and American Idols. Citizenship no longer requires political knowledge or action. Consumer aspirations, display, and consumption have replaced the old idea that democracy meant respect for labor, a measure of economic security, social solidarity, the dispersal of property, and substantial economic equality. The Right's notion of democracy is unfettered consumption, its public life is spent as a member of the consuming crowd, its individual judgment is consumer choice, and its self-fulfillment comes from being part of a society dedicated to owning things. It has used this idea to redefine opportunity, participation, and solidarity in ways that do not require public activity that takes people outside the mall.

The Right has worked for twenty-five years to reverse the old notion that regulation, redistribution, and progressive taxation could serve democracy, stability, and efficiency. It had a lot to work with, and much of it predated its rise to power. After all, postwar American prosperity made it possible to organize a democratic republic of consumers without redistributing wealth or threatening property in any important ways. As long as production was increasing and everyone was spending, then attempts to subject consumption to the needs of the environment, social justice, or other values could be reconciled with the existing distribution of wealth or safely ignored. By the middle 1970s Americans spent four times as many hours shopping as did Europeans, a figure that has remained fairly constant for the past thirty years.[33] In the absence of any public recognition of inequality as a problem, the Right advances consumerism and the market as the lodestars of an American citizenship that locates inequality at its root and announces irresponsibility as its mantra. A society that reduces everything that's important to the market must divide those who can buy from those who can't. It cannot fail to undermine equality and eviscerate shared responsibility as it does so.

The Right's campaign to define democracy in the language of economic mobility, consumer choice, and individual opportunity has paralyzed Americans' ability to understand the consequences of the country's historic levels of inequality. Its upside-down populism has persuaded many ordinary citizens that they will benefit by helping the very wealthy with even more tax cuts, deregulation, and privatization. A recent survey shed some light on how a population that retains a general commitment to equality and is distressed about accelerating economic divisions can be convinced to support policies that will strengthen exactly what it opposes. It revealed that middle- and lower-income Americans initially supported President Bush's highly regressive tax cuts even though they knew that the rich would make off with the lion's share of the wealth and that inequality would be intensified. These larger concerns didn't seem to matter. They supported lower taxes, not because they were ideologically committed to cutting federal spending or because they felt that inequality was a good thing, but because "they thought they, too, would benefit, if only by a small amount, and because they failed to connect the tax cuts to rising inequality, their future tax burden, or the availability of government services." Knowing that inequality was far worse than it had been twenty years ago didn't substantially affect their own hopes that policies targeted toward the richest sector of the population might help them too. If the rich were getting richer, then maybe they could share in some of the fun.

> For example, most Americans will never have to pay the estate tax, yet 70 percent expressed support for eliminating it anyway. Support for eliminating the tax was nearly as great—66 percent—among people who had strong reasons to favor keeping it: namely, those in families earning less than $50,000 a year who said that the increase in income inequality was a bad thing, that government policy contributed to differences in income, and that the rich pay less than they should in taxes.[34]

It seems that "most Americans support tax cuts not because they are indifferent to economic inequality, but because they largely fail to connect inequality and public policy." But as successful as the Right has been in convincing people that inequality resulted from automatic market processes rather than from political policy, it knows that it has to be careful. Plutocracy will be far more palatable to Americans if cloaked in the language of individual freedom, liberty, and opportunity. It's no longer necessary to defend inequality by appealing to history, tradition, genetics, or Darwin. It's enough to invoke the arrogant liberal elite, "family values," a God who wants all his children to get rich, and the magic of the marketplace. Inequality is now the friend of the downtrodden, the disrespected, and the forgotten. Deregulation, privatization, cutting taxes, and rolling back the welfare state is the path to prosperity and progress for all. Defending the little guy now means serving wealth and property.

Now that the United States has been forced to rejoin history and Fukuyama's confident optimism lies buried in the sands of Iraq, it might be wise to reexamine the claim that democracy requires free markets, that justice stops at equal opportunity, and that the welfare state is the first step down the slippery slope of stagnation and impoverishment. Irving Kristol was sure that the United States was a pretty egalitarian society when he uttered his *Two Cheers for Capitalism*, but the political forces he helped set in motion have changed all that. It's no accident that the broad indices that measure quality of life began to fall in the late 1970s—just when the Right came to power and began tilting state policy toward capital and property. They've continued to decline over the entire period as the United States has been transformed from a high-wage and best-working-condition society to one that is increasingly middling in its wages, harsh in its hours worked and conditions of employment, and stingy in its benefits. According to the Organization for European Cooperation and Development, the typical employed American works 315 more hours a year than his French counterpart—that's nine weeks, or the period from the last week of October to the end of the year. Comparisons with almost every other West European country are similar. The eight-hour day, that signature victory of the labor movement, is becoming a thing of the past, since one American in three now works more than fifty hours a week. Americans get the industrialized West's least amount of vacation time, shortest maternity leaves, and shortest average notice of termination. They endure higher rates of infant mortality than West Europeans and have more general poverty and a lower life expectancy than any other major advanced nation. That's not all. The United States shares with South Africa the dubious distinction of being the only developed society without universal medical coverage—as a result of which 45 million Americans have no health insurance at all, the United States spends more per person on health care than any other country in the world, and the World Health Organization's 2000 World Health Report ranked the overall quality of the country's enormous medical industry 37th in the world, trailing behind the likes of Andorra, Cyprus, Colombia, Malta, and Oman.[35] In a country where the richest 1% of the population holds over 40% of the wealth (up from 20% in 1979) and the average chief executive makes a staggering 475 times as much money as the average manufacturing employee (up from 40:1 in 1980 and compared with 24:1 in Britain, 15:1 in France, and 13:1 in Sweden), it seems fair to question the claim that everyone will benefit from organizing social life around the needs of capital.[36]

Kristol had derided regulation and redistribution as the self-serving work of elitist authoritarians who wanted to organize social life around their own understanding of the high ideals and grand plans that organizing the common good—and giving them jobs—would require. He was convinced that their disdain for the ordinary lives of ordinary people provided an opportunity for the Right to craft a populist attack on the "new class" and would place the market at the center of social life. "Individual liberty and security—in the older, bourgeois senses of these terms—and increasing material prosperity are still goals that are dear to the hearts of the working classes of the West," he announced. "They see nothing wrong with a better, bourgeois life: a life without uncommon pretensions, a life to be comfortably lived by common men."[37]

Kristol might have been right, but his promise has proved to be a false one. Americans are often willing to tolerate more inequality than Europeans because they hope that they'll be able to benefit as well. The rich might be getting richer, but many Americans seem to feel that's because they're more talented or lucky. There's no reason to punish them for their success, particularly if it's not hurting anyone. But there are limits to all this, and the contemporary Right knows full well that things can get tricky when people begin to suspect that the wealth of the super-rich is coming at their expense, that it's not good for the country—or both. On March 8, 2005, five of the most important Protestant clergymen in the country issued a "Joint Ecumenical Statement on Bush's 2006 federal budget." In it, the leaders of the Episcopal Church, the Evangelical Lutheran Church, the Presbyterian Church, the United Church of Christ, and the United Methodist Church made it clear that inequality had become a religious issue of the highest order. "Jesus makes clear that perpetrating economic injustice is among the gravest of sins," they said, adding that "when we see injustice, it is our duty to say so. The 2006 Federal Budget that President Bush has sent to Capital Hill is unjust."

> According to the White House's own numbers, this budget would move 300,000 people off food stamps in the next five years. It would cut the funds that allow 300,000 children to receive day care. It would reduce funding for Medicaid by $45 billion over the next ten years, and this at a time when 45 million Americans—the highest level on record—are already without health insurance.

These cuts would be alarming in any circumstances, but in the context of the 2006 budget, they are especially troubling. For even as it reduces aid to those in poverty, this budget showers presents on the rich. If passed in its current form, it would make permanent tax cuts that have bestowed nearly three-quarters of the "relief" on one-fifth of the county. If passed in its current form, it would include whopping new cuts that would benefit, almost exclusively, those with household incomes of more than $200,000 per year. If passed in its current form, it would take Jesus' teaching on economic justice and stand it on its head.

Some contend that these cuts will stimulate the economy and improve life for all Americans, but we believe that stocking the rich man's larder is a peculiar strategy for getting Lazarus more food. Not only does this policy rest on dubious economic assumptions, but it asks the poor to pay the cost for a prosperity in which they may never share.

Frankly admitting that no combination of private efforts could "fill the gap created by the government's retreat," the statement called on all people of faith to oppose the administration's budget. "Join the organizations working to obtain justice for the 36 million Americans living below the poverty line, the 45 million without health insurance and the unknown millions struggling to keep their families from slipping into these ever increasing ranks," it urged. "Together, let us pledge ourselves to creating a nation in which economic policies are infused with the spirit of the man who began his public ministry almost 2,000 years ago by proclaiming that God had anointed him 'to bring good news to the poor.'"[38]

The Right's twenty-five-year campaign to reward wealth and property has come at an enormous price for the "common" people in whose welfare it has long claimed to be interested. Stagnating wages, family breakups, heightened stress on the job, vanishing leisure, falling retirement benefits, persistent unemployment, disappearing pensions, and costlier health insurance now describe the lives of millions of Americans who were supposed to benefit from all that wealth flowing upward. But maybe things are changing. When the country's most important Protestant leaders publicly and directly contested the Right's claim that inequality is an inevitable and beneficial accompaniment of markets and democracy, they focused attention where it belongs: on ideology and politics. Just three years after George W. Bush preached the gospel of tax cuts, privatization, and deregulation in Mexico, they put him on public notice that bringing good news to the poor didn't mean enriching the wealthy, protecting their property, and creating even more inequality. In doing so, they directly addressed the country's historic level of inequality and made it clear that government policy was directly responsible for making it worse. This isn't what millions of Americans who had been attracted to the Right's rhetorical defense of freedom and opportunity had wanted, but once again it's what they got.

Notes

1. Jeffrey Frieden, *Global Capitalism: Its Fall and Rise in the Twentieth Century* (New York: Norton, 2006).

2. See http://www.loc.gov/exhibits/jefferson/214.html.

3. Remarks at the Annual Meeting of the National Alliance of Business, October 5, 1981, http://www.reagan.utexas.edu/resource/speeches/1981/100581a.htm.

4. Francis Fukuyama, "The End of History?" *The National Interest* 16 (Summer 1989), p. 3.

5. *Ibid.*, p. 4.

6. *Ibid.*, p. 8

7. *Ibid.*, pp. 13–14

8. Kevin Phillips, *Wealth and Democracy: A Political History of the American Rich* (New York: Broadway Books, 2002), p. 92.

9. Eric Foner, *The Story of American Freedom* (New York: Norton, 1998), pp. 321–22.

10. Michael Novak, *The Spirit of Democratic Capitalism* (New York: Madison Books, 1982).

11. *Ibid.*, p. 14.

12. *Ibid.*

13. *Ibid.*, p. 15.

14. *Ibid.*, p. 121.

15. *Ibid.*, p. 89.

16. *Ibid.*, p. 124.

17. *Ibid.*, pp. 203–4. His emphasis.

18. *Ibid.*, p. 345. See, by contrast, Jim Wallis, *God's Politics: Why the Right Gets It Wrong and the Left Doesn't Get It* (New York: HarperSanFrancisco, 2005).

19. *Ibid.*, p. 348.

20. Seymour Martin Lipset, *American Exceptionalism: A Double-Edged Sword* (New York: Norton, 1996), p. 22.

21. *Two Cheers for Capitalism* (New York: Basic Books, 1978), p. 247.

22. From "The Crisis in Economic Theory," a 1980 special issue of *The Public Interest*. Quoted in E. J. Dionne Jr., *Why Americans Hate Politics* (New York: Simon & Schuster, 1991), p. 71.

23. Milton and Rose Friedman, *Free to Choose: A Personal Statement* (New York: Harcourt Brace, 1980), pp. 54–55.

24. See http://www.reagan.utexas.edu/resource/speeches/1981/61181c.htm.

25. *Ibid.*

26. Jude Wanniski, *The Way the World Works* (Washington: Regnery, 1978), p. 135.

27. *Ibid.*, p. 6. His emphasis.

28. Quoted in Jake Tapper, "Retiring, Not Shy," *New York Times Magazine*, September 1, 2002.

29. See http://news.bbc.co.uk/1/hi/world/4307745.htm.

30. See, among others, Karl Polanyi's classic *The Great Transformation: The Political and Economic Origins of Our Time* (Boston: Beacon Press, 2001).

31. "The Market Can Transform our Schools," *New York Times*, July 2, 2002.

32. See Lizabeth Cohen, *A Consumers' Republic: The Politics of Mass Consumption in Postwar America* (New York: Vintage, 2003) and Gary Cross, *The All-Consuming Century: Why Commercialism Won in Modern America* (New York: Columbia University Press, 2000).

33. Gary Cross, *The All-Consuming Century: Why Commercialism Won in Modern America* (New York: Columbia University Press, 2000), p. 170.

34. Alan Krueger, "Cloudy Thinking on Tax Cuts," *The New York Times*, October 16, 2003. See Larry Bartels, "Unenlightened self-interest: The strange appeal of estate tax repeal," *American Prospect*, June 2004. See also Larry Bartels, "Homer Gets a Tax Cut: Inequality and Public Policy in the American Mind," *Perspectives on Politics* 3:1 (March 2005), pp. 15–31.

35. See http://www.who.int/whr/2000/en/index.html.

36. Tony Judt, "Europe vs. America," *New York Review of Books* LII (2), February 10, 2005, pp. 27–41 and Thomas Frank, *One Market Under God: Extreme Capitalism, Market Populism, and the End of Economic Democracy* (New York: Doubleday, 2000), pp. 7–8, 96–97. See also Peter Kilborn, "Census Shows Bigger Houses and Incomes, but Not for All," *New York Times*, May 15, 2002, and Kevin Phillips, *Wealth and Democracy: A Political History of the American Rich* (New York: Broadway Books, 2002), p. 107.

37. Irving Kristol, *Two Cheers for Capitalism* (New York: Basic Books, 1978), p. 180.

38. See http://www.wisethoughts.com/article_detail.cfm?articleID=21. See also "Economic Justice for All," the 1984 Pastoral Letter on Catholic Social Teaching and the U.S. Economy" by the U.S. Conference of Catholic Bishops at http://www.osjspm.org/cst/eja.htm.

CHAPTER SEVEN

~

Democracy and Equality

For twenty-five years now, the Right has used the rhetoric of freedom and democracy to build support for the politics of wealth and privilege. It's traveled a long way from earlier appearances as the marginalized defender of an idle and backward-looking upper crust and the patriotic champion of an aggrieved and ignored majority. It has come to dominate national politics because it has taken advantage of opportunity with patient organizing and close attention to a distinct set of core ideas. As it rose to power, it constructed a formidable mass base, built an impressive set of institutions, and developed a coherent ideology that wasn't afraid to address problems that were troubling millions of people. But everything that the Right has had to say about world affairs, authority, race, morality, the state, and the economy has been organized to serve its single core project. Above all else, the Right has sought to eliminate social equality as a legitimate aim of public policy. Its success in doing so has facilitated one of the most dramatic, undemocratic, and dangerous transfers of wealth and power in recent American history.

Its long march to power notwithstanding, the modern Right is not a monolith. Like any coalition, its constituent parts coexist in an often-unstable alliance. Libertarian attacks on intrusive government often run up against neo-conservative demands for enormous expenditures on arms and an imperial foreign policy. Calls for individual self-reliance and attacks on welfare don't go very well with massive government assistance to corporations. The Christian Right is often uneasy about the market's selfishness, destructiveness, and amorality. Nationalists worry about Wall Street's cosmopolitanism. Sometimes these differences break out into the open, but for the most part the Right has been able to develop a consistent set of core positions. This has helped it contain the contradictory impulses that tug at its political coherence and threaten its organizational strength.

Loosely organized around themes of military strength, moral restoration, self-reliance, equal opportunity, and individual freedom, the modern Right has matured from its earlier focus on fear, insecurity, and resentment. It has learned how to craft a positive, optimistic, and forward-looking program that's very different from the backwardness and complaining that marked earlier forms of political conservatism. The particular themes are familiar enough, but their overall impact has shaped a whole historical period. Neo-conservative demands that the country rearm so as to conduct a more aggressive foreign policy have been succeeded by calls to spread "democracy" everywhere and wage an endless "war on terrorism." Defenses of individual opportunity and personal freedom mask attacks on the welfare state's foundation in solidarity and mutual support. The "free market" has been defined as the essence of Americanism and social justice as a dangerous flirtation with alien forms of totalitarianism. Collective nostalgia and individual piety have been married to astonishing levels of personal consumption and ostentatious displays of wealth. Calls for a "color-blind society" have blended into attacks on affirmative action that quote Martin Luther King. None of this is particularly new. What is different is that millions of Americans have been persuaded that individual prosperity and national renewal justify historic levels of inequality.

As important as they were, neither tactical flexibility nor well-funded institutions are enough to explain the Right's triumph. Its real strength derives from its close attention to ideas that remain powerful long after the material conditions that incubated them have disappeared. A low-tax, small-government nineteenth-century agrarian democracy rooted in decentralized local connections, small property, restricted production, and limited markets generated an authentically American democratic ideology that has served as an ironic backdrop to the development of an equally authentic twenty-first-century American plutocracy. These ideas continue to resonate in conditions shaped by a powerful central government, an aggressive and militarized foreign policy, an increasingly globalized world system, and enormous concentrations of economic power. Two years before Osama bin Laden proved Francis Fukuyama wrong and thrust the United States back into the real world of historical conflict and ideological struggle, the editors of *Policy Review* celebrated the Right's ideological triumph and looked to the future.

> The period of intellectual ferment is over. In a way, that is a tribute to its success. One can say of ideological conservatism nowadays that, in general, it knows what

the important questions are and it knows the answers to those questions. There remains much detail to work out, but the outlines are clear. Conservatives resolve arguments in favor of the individual rather than the collective, of clear standards of judgment rather than relativistic measures, of personal responsibility rather than the interplay of vast social forces, of the market rather than government economic intervention, of international strength rather than empty promises of security. The federal government is, in general, too big, taxing too much of the wealth of Americans, doing too many unnecessary and unproductive things that get in the way of economic growth, to say nothing of personal liberty. Even as it has indulged in frivolity, the federal government has been neglectful of the security of Americans in its rush to disarm after the successful conclusion of the Cold War. Meanwhile, a debased high and popular culture shows few signs of recovery.

Among conservatives, one is hard-pressed to find any disagreement on these basic issues. The real questions, instead, are whether, when and how the American political process will make good on the promises of conservatism.[1]

Terrorism usually strengthens the existing regime, and it didn't take long for George W. Bush to address the Heritage Foundation's "real questions." Capitalizing on the opportunity that Al Qaeda so brutally presented, his administration quickly orchestrated a belligerent nationalism that swept memories of its illegitimate birth off the table and created an opening for its own version of the Right's aggressive program to reorganize American life. A concentrated attack on the basic institutions of the welfare state announced the political maturation of an ideologically focused, politically radicalized Right that was ready to use state power in a final assault on the consensus that had informed American politics for two generations.

From the Depression until the political crisis of the mid-70s, it had been broadly assumed throughout the industrialized West that one of the state's essential functions was to protect its citizens from the cruelties, irrationalities, inequities, and arbitrariness of the market. The extent to which it did so—and whom it excluded—varied from country to country, but a relatively broad political understanding recognized that economic growth, social health, and political stability demanded important measures of regulation and redistribution. The period's broad social compact came under heavy pressure during the late 1970s as the "Golden Age" dissolved into stagflation and crisis, but even as a new breed of conservative political leadership preached austerity and tried to lower expectations it seldom claimed that the welfare state was illegitimate on the face of it. For all his talk of "family values" and his attacks on liberalism's "culture of dependence," Ronald Reagan didn't try to destroy Social Security, cripple economic regulation as such, or eliminate all taxes on wealth. As important as he was in popularizing the Right's suspicion of the welfare state, he accepted the period's fundamental premises.

George W. Bush's clear intention to destroy what remains of the New Deal is a measure of how radical the Right has become. It sets him apart from every postwar Republican president—even Reagan. Neither economic difficulties nor terrorist attacks are enough to explain his administration's extremism. They certainly account for many of its specific policy initiatives, but the country's dramatic motion toward a Southern regime of low taxes, reduced public services, aggressive religiosity, and bellicose jingoism is as much a matter of ideology as of anything else. A generation of right-wing ideas, regressive tax cuts, direct handouts to the rich, deregulation, privatization, and accelerating inequality shows no sign of slowing down. The Democratic Party's bankruptcy, the long stock market boom of the 1990s, and the residual effects of September 11 have strengthened the Right's long effort to convince white working- and middle-class Americans that their interests are with the wealthy. It's possible that millions who don't benefit from any of these policies somehow hope that they'll share some of the money going to the very rich. It's equally possible that they're deeply unpopular and can be explained by a political offensive by the wealthy, the collapse of democratic control, and heightened levels of political partisanship in general.[2] There's plenty of empirical evidence to support both interpretations, but there's not much doubt that twenty-five years of right-wing attacks on equality and solidarity have had a dramatic effect. Even as the white working class continues to support the welfare state and resists the Right's calls to substitute "values" and "culture" for economics and politics, there's little indication that Americans care very much about inequality at the moment.[3]

It's the more affluent whites who have been most responsive to the right, but even this was never inevitable—nor will it last forever. The country's history has always been marked by sharp disagreement about how political democracy and the distribution of wealth affect one another. The Right's project to dismantle the welfare state draws on a particular reading of American history, but it also stands in violent contradiction to powerful domestic traditions that have fought for equality of condition for over two hundred years. Speaking of the Gilded Age's greed and corruption, the great journalist Henry Demarest Lloyd carried those traditions into the modern age more than a century ago. "If our civilization is destroyed, it will not be by barbarians from below," he warned. "Our barbarians come from above."

Repairing the damage that inequality has inflicted on millions of people will require renewed attention to politics, something that was very familiar to citizens at earlier stages in the country's history. Americans might be willing to accept gross disparities in economic resources if they're reasonably confident that everyone has an equal and reasonable chance to prosper, but even this isn't always dependable. Long before it became fashionable to believe that liberty and self-determination were to be found in the marketplace, many citizens knew that maldistributions of wealth resulted from unfair political advantage and constituted a profound threat to democracy and republican self-rule. Thomas Paine, Samuel Adams, Thomas Jefferson, James Madison, Andrew Jackson, Ralph Waldo Emerson, Walt Whitman, and Abraham Lincoln all believed that a republic's free citizens could defend their public virtue and political freedom only if they could remain economically independent in an environment of substantial economic equality. This always meant more than formal equality before the law. As notions of free labor developed during the 1830s and 40s, it was assumed that social mobility, personal merit, political democracy, and economic justice required that people be able to directly appropriate the fruit of their own labor. This conviction rested at the heart of a real, if limited, American agrarian republicanism. It was not extended to women yet because their labor was confined to the private sphere, nor to slaves because they were not free and hence they could not be "productive," nor to Indians because they were simple plunderers—but when applied to free citizens, it proved to be of enormous significance. It carried forward the traditional view that inequality distorted justice, threatened democracy, and was incompatible with republican self-rule because a small, parasitical, and idle class used political power to rob its productive neighbors and unjustly transform natural equality into social inequality.

This native republicanism had important consequences. It fueled the intense public debate about Hamilton's economic program and was at the heart of future struggles over foreign policy, slavery, tariffs, westward expansion, internal improvements, and civil war and reconstruction. Its early egalitarian impulse was limited because it applied only to free white men at first, but property was widely dispersed, there was a lot of free land, and the labor theory of value provided a potent foundation for reform. The continuing power of this republican tradition expressed the widespread belief that a free press, legal protections, the franchise, and other political instruments could help the country's smallholders protect themselves against the wealthy and defend democracy for everyone as they did so. The material conditions that generated the country's petty-bourgeois democratic republicanism have long since died away, but it survives as a reminder of the country's history and is an important source of contemporary ideas as well.

The emergence of a national economy, enormous centers of industry and finance, huge cities containing millions of propertyless urban workers, a vigorous foreign policy, great waves of immigration, and a stronger national political apparatus signaled an end to an entire period in American history. A new one developed quickly as unprecedented levels of economic inequality and political strife accompanied the country's new economic regime. Faced with the dramatic concentration of wealth that marked the Gilded Age and sparked Lloyd's warning, the emergence of a more active "positive state" signaled that government intervention in the economy would now receive a wider ethical sanction than earlier. As the 19th century's agrarian republic died, so did the assumption that the equitable distribution of wealth was a natural phenomenon that could be undone only by the arbitrary use of political power. Since the market was the main engine of inequality, reformers looked to the public sphere. From the 1892 Populists until the present, all egalitarian and democratic trends in American thinking have been statist and interventionist.

By the time a stock market bubble introduced the Roaring Twenties and announced the birth of the modern consumers' republic, it was clear that gross inequality was the "normal" result of market forces. The pressing need to control the railroads, trusts, and monopolies, and to tax the incomes and inheritances of the very rich, ushered in important democratic restrictions on property during the Progressive Period. The Right continued to demand a restrained government and sometimes went so far as to say that inequality was inevitable, efficient, and just. Its public position that government regulation would distort the "natural" operation of the market, reward the undeserving, and give rise to the politics of envy didn't address the way state policy encouraged the concentration of wealth. For a while it seemed that the Depression had swept these positions away, but they've reappeared with a vengeance. Just as the martinis, jazz, Art Deco, oysters, bridge, cigars, ballroom dancing, and golf of contemporary America illustrate how historical periods often imitate their predecessors in matters of social fashion, so does the contemporary Right's defense of inequality harken back to the disparities of the Roaring Twenties.

Today's mansions, yachts, servants, limos, and private jets announce the momentary collapse of American egalitarianism as surely as their earlier versions spelled the end of the agrarian republic and Progressivism. From 1973 to 2003, the income of the median American family rose only 22% after doubling between 1947 and 1973. But the average income of the richest 1% of the country has more than doubled in the same period, and that of the richest 0.1% has tripled. There's a connection between these phenomena. The concentration of wealth that has developed over the past generation cannot be understood apart from the collapse of the social mores and the commitment to solidarity and mutuality associated with the New Deal and the post–World War II middle-class republic.[4]

There's nothing natural about contemporary inequality; the explosion of income at the top of the scale been consciously prepared, encouraged, and defended by the Right for the past twenty-five years. And, just as it was politically created, so it can be politically undone—but that will require a new way of thinking about democracy that draws strength from deep American roots and great contemporary danger. Just as the ideology of formal equality and individual freedom has been used to organize the unprecedented enrichment of a tiny minority, so a public commitment to more economic equality and political democracy will require limits on capital and restrictions on property. It's no longer sufficient, if it ever was, to limit freedom to equal opportunity.

This is why expropriations of property and restrictions on wealth have often been central to democratic revolutions. Indeed, the constant plebeian drive to extend equality from formal guarantees to substantive results is one of the subtexts of all the great democratic revolutions. The lower one descended in the social ladder, the clearer it was that equality requires more than free markets and the rule of law, that citizens are more than producers and consumers, and that a decent society requires more than the politics of self-interest. It is evident that the level of contemporary polarization has gotten so extreme that it degrades the entire social order, eats away at political democracy, and directly threatens the well-being of millions. It is manifestly unjust and deeply immoral that the trivial desires of a small minority should be addressed before the urgent needs of the great majority. Democracy now requires that we define those public goods that are essential to a decent life for all, raise the general level of culture, contribute to social welfare, and do not have to be "earned."

Equality, Citizenship, and Freedom

It's not hard to understand the logical and historical connections between opportunity and outcome. One's ability to make full use of the chances provided by formal equality depends in large measure on one's access to resources. Logic, ideology, and history demonstrate that equality is indivisible, but one particularly apt example will illustrate the problem. As the Civil Rights Movement drove toward winning equality before the law, it became clear that the vote would be the crowning victory in the long effort to freely ride buses, go to school, shop in stores, hold decent jobs, drink at water fountains, and even walk on sidewalks. Jim Crow rested on black political disenfranchisement, and this is why the Civil Rights Act of 1964 had to be strengthened by the Voting Rights Act a year later before the most elementary level of political democracy could take root in the South. But there is more to democracy than what the law says. Made possible by the epic struggles in Birmingham and Selma, the movement's two legislative victories, great as they were, have to be seen as steps along the road rather than the end of the trail. Just as Reconstruction failed and land reform was abandoned when democracy's substantive core began to press up against private property, so the promise of political democracy has often been betrayed by the reality of economic inequality. Many Americans know from personal experience that structural obstacles persist long after the law declares that everyone is equal, and it's not too much to demand that the state remain active in the effort to democratize political and social life even after the formal battle has been won. Sitting back and declaring that legal proclamations are all that's needed to establish a democratic political order has become little more than an excuse for inequality. This is particularly true at the present juncture of American history. Social welfare is considerably more than extending charity, heading off extreme deprivation, providing payback, giving in to extortion, or providing a "safety net." It's an indispensable requirement of political democracy, individual freedom, and a civilized social order. Democracy means enriching people's life chances across a wide range of areas. It requires substantial equality in politics, society, *and* economics.

It's perfectly reasonable that unequal access to economic resources should mean unequal degrees of political power, no matter what the law says. A raft of empirical and theoretical studies support this position. Political participation in all areas of American public life has been heavily biased upward for many years, and the situation is getting worse as the concentration of economic wealth accelerates. From voting in elections to writing letters, running as candidates, joining political organizations, giving money, and going to demonstrations, politics in this country is marked by significantly higher levels of inequality than most other forms of public activity.[5] And almost all the factors that explain differences in political influence are generated by economic disparities. The rich vote more, donate more money, write more letters, and contact government officials more frequently than their fellow citizens. That means they're listened to more attentively and their concerns are more likely to be acted upon. It's not hard to understand why: they have access to more time, money, education, connections, and informal resources. "It is well known that the United States lags behind other democracies in voter turnout," observe three knowledgeable analysts. "What is less frequently acknowledged, however, is that when it comes to other forms of political activity—for example, campaigning, becoming active in the local community, or contacting government officials—Americans are as active as or substantially more active than citizens elsewhere. Compared to other democracies, however, participation in America is very unequally distributed, hewing closely to the fault line of social class. The bias in participation toward the well educated and the well heeled is evident around the world, but it has been particularly pronounced in the United States."[6] It is preposterous to suggest that inequality can be limited to economic matters without affecting other spheres of life.

It's true that most forms of overt and legally enforced discrimination against women, blacks, and others are things of the past. It's no less true that the United States stands alone among all industrialized societies on the planet in the maldistribution of its economic resources. There's no contradiction here; indeed, the two phenomena are two sides of the same coin. After twenty-five years of conscious political policy, the percentage of national income and wealth going to the top 0.1% of the population has exploded since the end of the 1970s after remaining about the same as other industrialized societies for most of the twentieth century.[7] The *New York Times* describes how this happened with dramatic clarity. "One way to understand the growing gap is to compare earnings increases over time by the vast majority of taxpayers— say, everyone in the lower 90 percent—with those at the top, say, in the uppermost 0.01 percent (now about 14,000 households, each with $5.5 million or more in income last year)," it reported. "From 1950 to 1970, for example, for every additional dollar earned by the bottom 90 percent, those in the top 0.01 percent earned an additional $162, according to the *Times* analysis. From 1990 to 2002, for every extra dollar earned by those in the bottom 90 percent, each taxpayer at the top brought in an extra $18,000."[8] These numbers put to shame all the Right's horror stories about welfare queens, intrusive bureaucrats, dirty movies, gay predators, and politically correct college professors. The real threat to American democracy is American inequality. It's important that women and minorities have achieved formal equality with white men and that millions of people have entered public life, but the median white household still earns 62% more income and has twelve times as much wealth as its black counterpart. History, education, technology, family structure, globalization, and "culture" may account for a certain amount of this, but twenty-five years of deliberate governmental policy have been devastating for both economic equity and political democracy. Given the enormous role that money plays in American politics, the fact that the 12% of American families with incomes of more than $100,000 accounted for 95% of all substantial campaign contributions in 2000 must have a dramatic effect on the political system.[9] Almost all the figures for other forms of political participation tell the same story of economic inequality, political helplessness, and the cynical disengagement that inevitably follows.

Americans tend to be more likely than others to believe that economic differences reflect different levels of effort, talent, and luck. But their trust in the market has never been unlimited, and popular resistance has attacked the accumulation of wealth when people lose confidence that everyone has an equal chance to get ahead, the wealth of the rich does not come at the expense of others, and the wider society is not being harmed. The country has come to such a pass several times, the Progressive Era and the New Deal taking shape as populist correctives to years of economic inequality and political corruption. The contemporary period's long-overdue political reckoning has been temporarily delayed by the Right's effective use of ideology, economic transformations, the collapse of an alternative vision, and bin Laden's gift to wealth and privilege. The Bush administration's astute use of fear and insecurity doesn't change the fact that years of right-wing assaults have narrowed access to political power as they have accelerated economic inequality. "Skewed participation among citizens and the targeting of government resources to partisans and the well-organized ensure that government officials disproportionately respond to business, the wealthy, and the organized and vocal when they design America's domestic and foreign policies," reports a committee of respected and alarmed political scientists.[10] As important as it is, democracy requires more than equal opportunity. People don't become equal just because the law says they are. Supreme Court Justice Louis Brandeis penned an appropriate warning years ago. "We can either have democracy in this country or we can have wealth concentrated in the hands of a few, but we can't have both," he told his fellow citizens.

The Right claims to represent the central narrative of American history and has effectively used a self-serving account of the past to legitimize its current position. But history is contested and open to many interpretations. The country's history has been as committed to the common good, social cooperation, and economic security as to individual advantage, competitive striving, and private property. Much of the country's central republican ideal was built around the idea that self-government is a requirement of virtuous citizens and decent societies *as such*. Politics is more than a competition between formal equals who share a desire to get ahead and a commitment to their private possessions, but the Right has worked hard to tarnish collective public life with danger, irresponsibility, and parasitism. One of the most notorious early formulations of this position came from across the Atlantic, but British Prime Minister Margaret Thatcher certainly spoke for many American rightists in 1987. "I think we've been through a period where too many people have been given to understand that if they have a problem, it's the government's job to cope with it," she said. " 'I have a problem, I'll get a grant.' 'I'm homeless, the government must house me.' They're casting their problem on society. And, you know, there is no such thing as society. There are individual men and women, and there are families. And no government can do anything except through people, and people must look to themselves first. It's our duty to look after ourselves and then, also to look after our neighbor. People have got the entitlements too much in mind, without the obligations. There's no such thing as entitlement, unless someone has first met an obligation."[11] Hurricane Katrina exposed the brutality of this position with a clarity that shocked tens of millions.[12]

It didn't take long for the Right to change the United States from a land born of democratic revolution and characterized by broad economic equity into the country with the industrialized world's biggest fortunes and its largest gap separating the rich from everyone else. The reformist administrations of Theodore Roosevelt, Woodrow Wilson, and Franklin D. Roosevelt marked the nation's most powerful twentieth-century turn away from great wealth and historic inequality, but the tradition they represented has fallen victim to the same attacks that have opened up such enormous economic divisions. The Right's ascendancy started as a reaction to the disorder of the Sixties, but it's been acquiring momentum and becoming more aggressive for thirty years. Its initial drive to impose order has become part and parcel of a political offensive by the rich. In 1960, the top 1% of the population owned about 34% of the country's wealth; by 1972 its share had fallen to 20%. Since 1968 also saw the crest of the "Gini Coefficient"—the standard index of income equality—it's reasonable to see the late-70s political offensive of the rich as a full-throated attack on thirty years of Keynesian economic leveling. It wasn't long before they began to turn things around. Reagan's attacks on inflation, his regressive tax cuts—particularly reducing the top income tax bracket from 70% to 28%—and his stepped-up defense spending and deregulation increased the portion of the nation's wealth held by the richest 1% from 22% in 1979 to 39% in a decade.[13] The reversal was almost complete, for the convergence of income tax rates for the top 1% and for the median family illustrates the full dimension of the Right's attack on the 20th century's middle-class republic. With the rich still on the defensive during the 1950s, the largest proportion of the postwar period's income gains had gone to the middle of the population. By the 1990s, a decade during which everything was turned on its head, the vast majority was falling behind the top fifth, the top 1%, and particularly the top 0.1%, of the income and wealth distribution. By 1999, the real after-tax income of the middle 60% of the American population was *lower* than it had been in 1977. That's not all. Where the bottom third of all Americans had more than ten times as much income as the richest 0.01% of the population in 1960, things had been reversed forty years later. By 2000, the 28,000 Americans in the top 0.1% of the population had as much income as the 96,000,000 people at the bottom. A more graphic demonstration of this will help. From 1970 to 2000, "the bottom 99 percent of Americans had an average increase in total income of $2,710. That is an annual raise of less than $100 per year, the equivalent of a nickel an hour raise each year for 30 years. The super-rich did fabulously better, their average incomes rising $20.3 million to an average of $24 million each. Plot these figures on a chart and the results astound. If the increase for 99 percent of Americans is a bar 1-inch high, the bar for the super rich soars heavenward 625 feet."[14]

Wealth in America has always depended on who controls the government, and none of this could have happened without sustained ideological help and active political encouragement. The history of the past twenty-five years gives the lie to the Right's claim that wealth reflects merit. Indeed, it is becoming clearer that the wealth of the super-rich is the chief reason for the increasing distress of the middle and the unending poverty of the poor. The distribution of wealth has become this country's most important democratic issue. The very real gains made by middle-class women and blacks fade by comparison.

Barbarians from Above

The past twenty-five years have been shaped by the political, social, and economic triumph of upper America. Well served by a radicalized political apparatus, the very richest elements of the population have used state power in a skillful and relentless effort to permanently restructure American society.

They've gone a long way. Saddled with one of the most right-wing governments in the country's history, the United States has become the most
unequal and unjust advanced society on the planet. We are well on the way
toward a plutocratic regime of systematic social cruelty and endless foreign
war.

This had been developing for many years before George W. Bush elbowed
his way into history. What's new is the uneasy realization that the Right's
drive for even lower taxes, even less regulation, and even more privatization
shows no sign of slowing down. One wonders how much is enough. After
taking so much of the country's wealth, rolling back so much of its regulatory
protection, and eviscerating so much of its welfare state, what else do the
corporations and the rich need? There's no easy answer to this question, for
the country's recent past gives little reason to hope that the Right's political
offensive will run into some sort of natural limit. "You know, the only trouble
with capitalism is capitalists," observed a former president who knew what
he was talking about. "They're too damn greedy." Herbert Hoover had an
old conservative's sense of ethical limits, but the contemporary Right will
stop at nothing in his service to wealth. Even in the aftermath of Hurricane
Katrina, leading Republicans hastened to assure the country that more tax
cuts and continued deregulation would stimulate economic growth and help
New Orleans recover from devastation. "Raising taxes in the wake of a
national catastrophe would imperil the very economic growth we need to
bring the Gulf Coast back," said Indiana Congressman Mike Perce. The co-
chair of the Conservative Caucus of the House of Representatives had a good
old populist trickle-down claim to make it clear who would continue to bear
the burden of the Right's program. "I'm mindful of what a pipe fitter once
said to President Reagan: 'I've never been hired by a poor man.' "[15] Sure
enough, after authorizing an additional $50 billion for the occupation of
Iraq, the Congress and the President made it clear that Katrina-related
recovery efforts would be financed by further cuts in domestic programs. This
might help explain some of what's been happening, but Hoover had it only
partly right. The Right's single-minded determination can't be entirely
explained by subjective preferences. After all, important elements of business
and finance supported the welfare state for many years. Something deeper
has to be at work to explain why a small class that has systematically
despoiled so many for so long continues to insist on doing so.

Inequality is reshaping a wide swath of American society, a process all the
more pernicious and anti-democratic because it's so often hard to see. The
small insults of everyday inequality are nothing compared to the great dangers embedded in the response to Katrina and the USA Patriot Act, but they

cut deeply all the same. After all the calls to patriotic unity, it turns out that even the most basic costs imposed by the government's "war on terrorism" are imposed unequally. It's all very well to ask people to sacrifice at a time of national tragedy, particularly since millions have shown themselves willing to give up a bit of personal convenience for collective security. But here too, the extension of good will and the presumption of honesty were prematurely granted. The population's willingness to shoulder a group of general burdens might not be so freely given if it were known how unequal they really are—and who's paying for them.

> Interminable security lines have become a routine part of air travel. The inconvenience seems a small price to pay for increased safety. After all, we tell ourselves, it's a burden all passengers share.
>
> But this isn't quite true. At some of the busiest airports in the country, including ones in New York City, Miami, and Los Angeles, passengers with premium-class tickets or upper-level memberships in airline clubs are now able to cut the line.
>
> When they show their boarding passes and identification these passengers are directed into a separate luxury line to be screened by Transportation Security Administration employees. The person checking boarding passes is often an airline employee. The security screening personnel and equipment are part of the federal agency and are financed in part by a flat fee added to the purchase price of your airline ticket.
>
> The agency exists because in the wake of the Sept. 11 attacks, Congress no longer trusted the airlines with the critical job of balancing security and convenience. By administering special lanes for airlines' most favored customers, the agency is serving the wrong master. At Los Angeles International Airport for example, Transportation Security Administration representatives say that if an airline requests, the agency will provide a dedicated security checkpoint for its luxury lane, or allow them to escort those passengers to the front of the line while economy class passengers creep along behind them.

"Increased security protects us all and the inconvenience it requires is a trial we all must share," adds Daniel Squadron. "No one should be able to buy his way out of it." And, noting that the federal government has organized the airlines' favors to wealth, he calls on the White House to rectify the situation. "President Bush," he gamely says, "should insist that the agency start treating all the people that it was created to serve equally."[16]

There's not much in the country's recent history to suggest that this is any more likely than it's been in other areas of public life. Nor is there any evidence that the Democratic Party, the bearer of the New Deal, the home of liberalism, and the traditional party of government, is about to step forward to defend the most basic principles of equality. Indeed, part of the reason for the Right's victory is that the Democrats have been its silent partner. The Republicans have been explicit in their intention to enrich the wealthy and reward the privileged, but they have been assisted by a Democratic Party that has been unable to adapt to a new environment for which it was unprepared and with which it is still uncomfortable. If the GOP has ended up as the party of the radical Right and has abandoned the pretense that its "moderates" have any real influence, the Democrats have been immobilized by civil war, ideological confusion, and political paralysis. Their gradual abandonment of social justice and economic equality is a bitter reminder of how accurate Kevin Phillips was when he called them "the world's second most enthusiastic capitalist party."

The GOP suffers from little of the confusion that has marked the Democrats' recent history, for its Right wing swept to victory years ago. But history played itself out somewhat differently for the party of liberalism. As the economic difficulties of the late 1970s became a general crisis of economic Keynesianism, they precipitated an internecine struggle that the Democrats have still not settled. Even as he tried to offer some relief from the Right's continuous attack on living standards, Bill Clinton served as a powerful reminder of the price that many are paying for his party's failure to construct a real alternative to the GOP's program of cutting taxes, deregulating, and privatizing.

Part of the problem is that the Democrats were growing more uncomfortable with ideas just when the Republicans began developing new ones. As the Right became more excited and politicized during the late 1970s, party leaders decided that ideology was an obsolete and divisive remnant of the recent past. Michael Dukakis, Paul Tsongas, and Gary Hart began to move away from redistribution and regulation, but they were thoroughly overmatched by a highly ideological Republican opposition that knew exactly what it wanted to fight for. Unable to match Reagan's rhetorical anti-statism, the Democrats vainly tried to articulate a new approach to the coming postindustrial economy. Nothing worked, and they quickly collapsed. It was President Carter who deregulated the trucking and airline industries, and it was Congressional Democrats whose assistance made possible the original financial deregulation of 1980 and Reagan's regressive tax cuts. And it didn't end with the Great Communicator. Even after eight years of the most ideological president in a generation, presidential candidate Michael Dukakis's claim that the 1988 election "isn't about ideology. It's about competence" didn't inspire much hope—particularly since polling data demonstrated that, while American voters liked Reagan the man, they disagreed with most of his political positions and had little use for his Vice President.

Running against George H.W. Bush proved little. The Democrats' evolving theory of the state turned out to be a bloodless, cumbersome, and unconvincing managerialist response to crisis and confusion. They knew that wide sections of the electorate had tired of conflict and their response was a general position that the national government should dampen social divisions, tone down the level of partisan disagreement, and unify the country. A distaste for adversarial processes, a desire to rise above "politics as usual," and an aversion to disruptive "big ideas" led them to avoid conflict just when the Republicans were gleefully fanning the fires of racial backlash, organizing tax revolts, embracing bitter religious fundamentalists, and loudly complaining about the federal government. But the "new" Democrats kept to the high ground. Searching for ways to bring people together, move past conflict, and build community, they tried to articulate a "national interest" and a "common good" that would convince people to accept a regimen of shared sacrifice and modest expectations. Just when the Republicans were rejecting the notion of American decline and were stepping forward as the party of wealth creation and economic growth, the Democrats proposed to target particular economic sectors for state support. Where the Republicans made clear their intention to support capital in general and encourage market forces to organize the future, the Democrats began to explore an "industrial policy" that they hoped would persuade the electorate to let them manage the transition to a post-industrial economic order. Accusing Reagan of simply wanting to reward the rich so they could do whatever they wanted, Democratic spokesmen claimed to offer a more palatable alternative that would temper reliance on the market with modest central planning, looser regulation, and less social protection. Targeted economic growth was the primary means, investors and entrepreneurs the favored agents, and an end to the politics of division and competition the final goal.

Democratic leaders repeatedly claimed that guided growth would create so much new wealth that past conflicts would fade into memory. Everyone would have more than enough, the divisive politics of race and class would fade away, and social peace would be the happy consequence of general prosperity. This would require "flexibility" in the short run and a willingness to modify old positions in the light of new realities. If wages were too high, work rules too restrictive, and benefits too expensive, they would have to yield to the new requirements of an economy that needed a mobile, trained, flexible, compliant, and—if necessary—unorganized workforce. Party spokesmen began to gingerly suggest that social equality might be too costly, the welfare state might be too burdensome, and more equality might be undesirable. In the end, the imperatives of business expansion, economic growth, capital accumulation, and freedom of investment took the same pride of place for them as it did for the Right. The major differences between the two parties were not programmatic but were driven by the Democrats' lack of coherence. Where the Republicans were preparing themselves for battle, the Democrats were looking for a way out. Their exit was their abandonment of their party's traditional commitment to economic equality, regulation, and redistribution. In the end, little separated them from the Republicans except the Right's skill, determination, ideas, and clarity. That's been more than enough.

And so the Democrats began to develop an alternative to themselves long before George H. W. Bush made the "L-word" a curse. Having decided that it was suicidal to oppose the new age of post-industrial abundance that was just around the corner, "centrists" like Arkansas Governor Bill Clinton organized the Democratic Leadership Conference in 1985. The new organization took it for granted that expanding the welfare state was neither possible nor desirable. Democrats could still win national elections but had to prove to the country that they were open to debate and capable of change. In concrete terms, this meant appealing to moderate white suburbs, talking less about cities, workers, and minorities, and moving away from big ideas. The DLC was the American version of the "Third Way," a British trend that had urged the Labour Party to break with its social-democratic past and embrace much of Thatcher's attack on social solidarity and the welfare state. The old boundaries between left and right are becoming obsolete, the Third Way suggested. It proposed to split the difference, adopting the Left's verbal reformism and retaining the Right's refusal to pay for it. Third Way theorists suggested that economics no longer had much to do with democracy. As a "post-industrial" world moves toward a "post-material" politics, it would be wise to place a premium on personal autonomy, individual expressiveness, tolerance of new lifestyles, and the healing power of family and community. Just when the Republican Right was starting to come together around an aggressive and focused political program, the Democrats began to suspect that their old model of social justice and economic equality was obsolete.

The DLC organized itself around the Third Way proposition that people were better educated and more prosperous, less political and more self-absorbed, less inclined to support grand schemes of social renewal and more focused on "lifestyle" choices than they had been. That made sense to the Democratic centrists, for this entire position assumed that the important problems that people are facing do not originate in economics, are no longer expressed in political terms, and are no longer susceptible to solution with the instruments of an earlier period. Although more people are informed about public matters than ever, general prosperity will inevitably weaken public life, erode strong central authority, and fragment unitary ideologies. It is time to move away from the state and its embrace of politically-driven regulation and redistribution, the DLC announced. Freeing up market forces will ease the transition to the post-industrial future that will benefit core constituencies in the long run even if they have to make painful choices in the short. "Progressive" social policy ought to focus on ways to make economic resources available to those on the bottom of the ladder so they can compete more effectively in a market open to all with talent and good ideas.

The "new" Democrats suggested that their party's commitment to economic equality had become politically dangerous and economically disruptive because it was intimately connected to a "Fordist" program of some central direction of the economy, a restributionist state, and an emphasis on production and expansion. Equality remained an important rhetorical goal, but it had to be redefined so it did not require access to economic resources. It was important not to alarm centrist constituencies with talk of regulation, equality, and redistribution. The DLC announced that the economically secure, socially tolerant, and morally upstanding middle class was the Democratic Party's future. The goods that make possible the pursuit of happiness—security, self-respect, and self-actualization—were now a set of "post-material" values that would allow the Democrats to compete with the GOP for the allegiance of suburban white voters. The DLC was sure that this new understanding of equality as equal access and social toleration fitted the country's new economic and political realities and would permit them to compete in the South. The American polity had been fractured, the politics of social class were dangerous and obsolete, and moderate social movements that did not call for regulation or redistribution represented the Democratic Party's future.[17]

Some of this came from pragmatic political calculations about what it would take to get elected, but the party was rotting at the core. Its abandonment of equality was a matter of "principle," but few could see the abject surrender that lay at the heart of the DLC's activity. At a time when the Right was deliberately using state power to organize an historic upward transfer of wealth, it was hard to tell the programmatic difference between the country's two major parties. But there was a big difference between the loud, coherent clarion call of the Republican right and the flabby, moralizing pseudo-sociology of the DLC. The GOP was absolutely clear about what it wanted and whom it served. But the more these "new" Democrats claimed that American politics was becoming "postmaterial," that social movements of identity and recognition were the force of the future, and that economic issues of justice and fairness were rooted in a dying industrial past, the quicker they abandoned the field before the battle had even begun. Seeking to find a politically viable middle ground between the victorious Republican right and the welfare state's past, the DLC's "New Democratic Credo" celebrated New Year's Day 2001 by announcing that

> The Third Way philosophy seeks to adapt enduring progressive values to the idea that government should promote equal opportunity for all while granting special privilege for none; an ethic of mutual responsibility that equally rejects the politics of entitlement and the politics of social abandonment; and, a new approach to governing that empowers citizens to act for themselves.

> The Third Way approach to economic opportunity and security stresses technological innovation, competitive enterprise, and education rather than top-down redistribution or laissez faire. On questions of values, it embraces "tolerant traditionalism," honoring traditional moral and family values while resisting attempts to impose them on others. It favors an enabling rather than a bureaucratic government, expanding choices for citizens, using market means to achieve public ends and encouraging civic and community institutions to play a larger role in public life. The Third Way works to build inclusive, multiethnic societies based on common allegiance to democratic values.[18]

Carefully crafted to be as reassuring as possible, this "credo" has been supplemented by the DLC's grandly named Hyde Park Declaration of August 1, 2000. Calling itself the "Declaration of the Suburban South" would probably have been more accurate, but its thinly-veiled suggestion that the Third Way is the legitimate successor to FDR's now-unacceptable program announced its general position clearly enough. True to form, the document claims to represent the "modernizers of the American progressive tradition" and announces "a new politics for a new America." Tailored to a country that is being transformed by information, technology, and globalization, it speaks to "a population that is rapidly becoming more diverse, more affluent, more educated, more suburban, more 'wired,' less political, and more centrist." The "new" Democrats' target audience is younger, more skeptical about poli-

192 ~ Chapter Seven

tics and government, and more open to a "'higher politics' of moral purpose." So it follows that the Democrats should become less political as well.
At a time when the country's super-rich have been systematically appropriat-
ing an enormous portion of the country's wealth, the DLC embraces "a Third
Way that rejects the old left-right debate and affirms America's basic bargain:
opportunity for all, responsibility from all, and community of all." A laundry
list of positions centers on the suggestion that "the Democratic Party's mission is to expand opportunity, not government" and announces its belief in
"shifting the focus of America's anti-poverty and social insurance programs
from transferring wealth to creating wealth." In the end, the document
embraces much of the Right's core positions, offers to ameliorate some of
their harshest effects, and says nothing about equality that goes beyond
equality of opportunity.[19]

Since it makes an apolitical and moralistic appeal to moderate voters, the
Third Way goes out of its way to be non-controversial. Clinton used it to win
over white suburbanites to an economically safe Democratic program, Tony
Blair used it to assure southern English commuters that the Labour Party was
ready to abandon its trade unionist base, and Gerhard Schroeder used it to
flatter the German middle class by calling it the New Center. All three
rested their appeals on the tacit understanding that their core constituencies
would not be taxed for the benefit of the less industrious and less worthy.
Economic growth would soften the edge of class conflict and social strife.
The more radical claims of the cultural and political Right would be diffused
by an ethic of toleration, calls for unity, and support for achievement and
accomplishment.

This meant abandoning the ideals of social equality that have driven progressive politics for hundreds of years. Reorienting the Democratic Party
toward creating and supporting a meritocracy turned out to be perfectly compatible with the Right's claim that political power should go no further than
equality of opportunity. "Merit" turned out to be particularly attractive
because it would enable the Democrats to avoid the stigmas of their statist
past and rise above the Right's charge that they were little more than the
party of "special interests." And, since almost all measures of "merit" corre-
late very closely with social class, what was exciting, innovative, and subver-
sive turned out to be a moderately less direct endorsement of inequality than
that of the increasingly aggressive and hard-edged Right. The Democrats
could be the good guys who cared about people's pain rather than the mean-
spirited Republicans. It didn't matter much. Systemic problems of historic
inequality were ignored by both.

The significant advantage that "merit" seemed to offer was that it appeared objective, flexible, and fair. It offered a path upward for those who were smart, willing to work hard and a little lucky. Merit had a good pedigree, for it had helped organize the long struggle against aristocratic privilege that had marked the modern era's great revolutions. Napoleon's declaration that "every soldier carries a marshal's baton in his pack" helped bring hundreds of thousands of French peasants to the Revolution and illustrated the tremendous liberating potential of upward mobility and formal equality, even if more substantial matters like the destruction of the estates and land reform played a more direct role. Equal opportunity before the law also legitimized taxes on inheritance and "unearned income," laws against entail and primogeniture, free public schools, bans on nepotism, measures against housing discrimination and the like all over the world. The more the world was opened up, the better it was.

Taken by itself, though, "merit" never meant substantive economic equality, for a level playing field accepts social classes and inequality. The gradual shift from blood to achievement as the criterion of social position turned out to be as firmly rooted in substantive inequality as its feudal predecessor, since nothing is truer than to say that people are unequal in their endowments. Removing irrational barriers to the recruitment of new elites is not the same as improving the quality of life for all. Opportunities for individuals to rise are no substitute for a general diffusion of the means of civilization and a public commitment to provide the dignity and culture that are needed by all, whether they "rise" or not and whether they are "meritorious" or not. Equal opportunity is certainly a necessary condition of freedom and democracy, but it's just as certainly not a sufficient one. The increasing withdrawal of the wealthy from any sense of general responsibility illustrates that "the rich have decided that, since they don't use public services any more, they shouldn't have to pay for them"[20] At the same time that they are happy to pay for their private schools, private police forces, private systems of garbage collection, volunteer fire departments, and gated communities, the super-rich continue to demand lower taxes and frankly deny any obligation to contribute to the national treasury. Given their massive enrichment over the past quarter of a century and the general sense that they somehow "deserve" all this new-found wealth, equality of opportunity has turned out to mean equality of opportunity to be unequal.

The Republican Party has been perfectly clear about where it stands for some time, but the Democrats are still stuck in an ideological swamp. The Third Way's politics of self-esteem can't recognize inequality as a political problem, doesn't see it as a threat to democracy, and won't confront it on the general and comprehensive level that only politics makes possible. It can't address the urgent problems created by the right's deliberate encouragement of inequality because it wasn't designed to. Its weak, small-bore moralizing is demonstrably inadequate to the tasks at hand. It has shut the Democratic Party out of national politics because it has consistently chosen safe, small measures that it imagines will demonstrate its good intentions and get people to like it. Its cautious offer of symbolic gestures, its determination to avoid fights over fundamental principles, and its aversion to big ideas has unilaterally disarmed a powerful American tradition of republicanism and democracy. The country's victorious right wing has been offering real proposals, is willing to fight, and has a broad and comprehensive picture of the society it wants to organize. No wonder people like it better, even if they disagree with it more deeply. At least it stands for something.

President Clinton's early attempt to address the crisis in American healthcare was an uncharacteristically "big" idea. After it was defeated and the Republican right swept to Congressional victory in 1994, he reverted to retreat and compromise. Hemmed in by huge inherited budget deficits and famously beholden to Wall Street's bond traders, his hopes for a middle-class tax cut and higher domestic spending led him to low interest rates, spending cuts, attacks on welfare, embrace of globalization, deficit reduction, deregulation, and privatization. Toleration and openness of mind were important in the "culture wars" led by an aggressive and politicized Christian right, but Clinton was constrained by underlying economic forces and the inexorable demands of central bankers and global bond markets. And so the "long boom" of his second term was limited to the stock market and contributed to the rapid acceleration of inequality. As Washington became more dependent on upper-bracket wealth concentration and high stock prices, banks, securities markets, investors, corporations, and exports became the privileged darlings of federal policy. Increasing the market value of society's productive assets was the chief aim, the needs of investors and holders of capital trumping those of everyone else. Little wonder that the upward transfer of wealth continued during the only Democratic administration of the last twenty-five years. "Of the stock market gains between 1989 and 1997, some 86 percent flowed to the top 10 percent of households," reports Kevin Phillips. "Slightly over 42 percent went to the top 1 percent alone. More painfully, according to the Federal Reserve Board's triennial survey of consumer finances, the net worth of the median U.S. household (including home equity) in constant dollars *declined* from $51,640 to $49,900 between 1989 and 1995 because so many Americans had debts growing faster than their assets. Most had little, if any, stock."[21] By the end of the Clinton administration, the United States had gone a long way on its journey toward plutocracy. Even as those on the bottom of the ladder made some modest progress, the basic trend was clear.

Ordinary families gained amid the late nineties boom, but even in 1999, analysts found that the average real after-tax income of the middle 60 percent of the population was lower than in 1977—an extraordinary contrast with the huge gains of the top 1 percent. Some of the first results from a special section of the U.S. Census of 2000 created a stir by showing median family incomes in New York and California, for example, *declining* 5 to 6 percent between 1990 and 2000. Among the major Western industrial nations, it was the United States, its Revolution 225 years distant, that now had the highest levels of inequality.[22]

By systematically ignoring the economics of what's been happening for the past quarter of a century and contenting itself with the safe, harmless language of tolerance, the Democratic Party has abandoned the only field of battle on which it could offer an alternative to the right's politics of plutocracy. It's true that it is just as dependent on the political contributions and general support of the rich as the Republicans, but that's not enough to explain its near-total collapse.[23] The Democrats have sometimes responded to the pressing needs of its mass base, but at the moment they are incapable of initiating any systematic program aiming at economic equality. Perhaps an historical symmetry is at work.

From the Depression through the Civil Rights and anti-war movements, the Democrats have moved forward only when forced to do so by disruptive social movements that they did not create but to which they were compelled to respond. Their paralysis is partly explained by the absence of popular anger about what's been happening to the country. Millions of Americans seem to have bought the argument that the wealth of the super-rich is somehow good for everyone else. But it's not enough to let politicians off the hook because the times aren't right. It's important to defend *Roe v. Wade*, affirmative action, Social Security, clean air, endangered animals, and Charles Darwin. But decades of complicity with the right's core economic project has made the Democrats unable to talk about equality or democracy in a convincing way. Their problem is deeper than money, election strategy, or figuring out how to speak to gun owners and "people of faith." It's ideological first and foremost. Sitting around while equality is swept off the table means that the Democrats can't attack the Right where it is vulnerable.

Given their determination to move away from areas of strength and fight where they are weak, it's no wonder that the Democrats run away as soon as the Right accuses them of waging "class warfare." They've been thoroughly unable to react to the *real* class war that has produced the bloated incomes of America's wealthy and the stagnation of most ordinary families. Under different circumstances, one would expect them to seek votes by proposing to soak the rich. But because they're not being pushed by energetic social movements and have failed to respond to their antagonists in the only way that makes any sense, they've contented themselves with sitting around and waiting for the craziest Republicans to "overreach" and drive the GOP into a ditch. As they wait, inequality accelerates because both parties adopt policies that favor the wealthy.

Powerful currents of American history have been shaped by the old position that individuals cannot claim legitimate entitlement to wealth that is far in excess of their needs. It's not an easy argument to make when the country's service economy seems to provide living proof that wealth does trickle down. After all, the super-rich are willing to pay outrageous amounts of money for their wine, food, art, personal trainers, cars, real estate, nannies, tutors, house cleaners, chauffeurs, and the like. Still, an historically deep and potent understanding that *democracy requires limiting the accumulation of wealth* has produced some of the most powerful reform movements in the country's history. This understanding needs to be put at the center of a new commitment to equality and freedom, even if it will fail to have the support of the Democratic leadership at first. The stakes are as high now as they've ever been. Terrorist attack, foreign war, the Right's arguments, and the Democrats' bankruptcy have made it difficult to address the inequality that deforms American society and threatens its democracy. The relentless enrichment of the few has led to stagnant wages, longer hours, greater stress, disappearing pensions, job insecurity, reduced income, and poorer health for the many. Things have gone far enough. American inequality is a cruel mockery of freedom and a bitter threat to democracy.

It's time to name names. The Right's shameless service to wealth has warped the country, demeaned its history, and betrayed its people. As powerful as it is, its triumph was never inevitable and it doesn't have to continue. American history is a living record of struggles to bring the economy, the state, *and* the society under democratic supervision and control. Elementary decency, democratic politics, and American history provide a simple lesson: the more equality there is, the better. Democracy requires extending the benefits of civilization to all so ordinary men and women can make the most of their common humanity. It can flourish only by reaching into the broadest areas of political, economic, *and* social life. It demands that we speak plainly about who's been winning, who's been losing, and why. It calls for clear and decisive political action to reverse decades of organized robbery. Its unshakeable foundation is the understanding that more equality, rather than less, is the measure of a democratic society and the content of a free one.

Notes

1. Reprinted in Gregory L. Schneider, ed., *Conservatism in America Since 1930* (New York: New York University Press, 2003), pp. 432–43.

2. See Alan Krueger, "Cloudy Thinking on Tax Cuts," *New York Times*, October 16, 2003 and Jacob S. Hacker and Paul Pierson, "Abandoning the Middle: The Bush Tax Cuts and the Limits of Democratic Control," *Perspectives on Politics* 3:1 (March 2005), pp. 33–53.

3. Larry Bartels, "What's the Matter with *What's the Matter with Kansas?*" Paper presented at the Annual Meeting of the American Political Science Association, Washington DC, September 1–4, 2005.

4. Paul Krugman, "Losing Our Country," *The New York Times*, June 10, 2005.

5. See Sidney Verba, Kay Lehman Schlozman and Henry E. Brady, *Voice and Equality: Civic Voluntarism in American Politics* (Cambridge: Harvard University Press, 1995).

6. Sidney Verba, Kay Lehman Schlozman and Henry E. Brady, "The Big Tilt: Participatory Inequality in America," *The American Prospect* 32 (May–June 1997), p. 75.

7. "American Democracy in an Age of Rising Inequality," a report of the Task Force on Inequality and American Democracy of the American Political Science Association. Available at http://www.apsanet.org/.

8. David Cay Johnston, "Richest Are Leaving Even the Rich Far Behind," *New York Times*, June 5, 2005, http://www.nytimes.com/indexes/2005/06/05/national/class/index .html.

9. "American Democracy in an Age of Rising Inequality," p. 7.

10. *Ibid.*, p. 16.

11. Prime minister Margaret Thatcher, talking to *Women's Own* magazine, October 3 1987. See http://www.onlineopinion.com.au/view.asp?article = 2677.

12. John Ehrenberg, "Playing the Blame Game with Katrina," *Logos* 4:4 (Fall 2005), http://www.logosjournal.com

13. Kevin Phillips, *Wealth and Democracy: A Political History of the American Rich* (New York: Broadway Books, 2002), p. 92.

14. David Cay Johnston, "Stroke the Rich: IRS has Become a Subsidy System for Super-Wealthy Americans," *San Francisco Chronicle*, April 11, 2004, http://www.sfgate .com/cgi-bin/article.cgi?file = /c/a/2004/04/11/INGV560VO41.D TL&type = printable.

15. "Liberal Hopes Ebb in Post-Storm Poverty Debate," *New York Times*, October 11, 2005.

16. "United We Stand (In Line)," *New York Times*, June 1, 2005.

17. For a pair of succinct presentations of "the Third Way," see Anthony Giddens, *Beyond Left and Right* (Palo Alto: Stanford University Press, 1995) and *The Third Way* (London: Polity Press, 2000).

18. http://www.ndol.org/ndol_ci.cfm?kaid = 128&subid = 187&contentid = 895).

19. See "Hyde Park Declaration," *ibid.*

20. Ed Finn, Vancouver (British Columbia) Sun, May 16, 1996, http://www.inequality .org/quotes.html. See also Christopher Lasch, *The Revolt of the Elites: And the Betrayal of Democracy* (New York: Norton, 1996).

21. *Op. cit.*, p. 107. His emphasis.

22. *Ibid.*, p. 111.

23. See E. J. Dionne Jr., *Why Americans Hate Politics* (New York: Simon & Schuster, 1991).

Bibliography

Books

Bennett, William. *Why We Fight: Moral Clarity and the War on Terrorism*. New York: Doubleday, 2002.

Bloom, Allan. *The Closing of the American Mind*. New York: Simon & Schuster, 1987.

Bork, Robert. *Slouching Towards Gomorrah: Modern Liberalism and American Decline*. New York: HarperCollins, 1996.

Brinkley, Alan. *The End of Reform: New Deal Liberalism in Recession and War*. New York: Vintage, 1995.

Brzezinski, Zbigniew, ed. *The Crisis of Democracy: Report on the Governability of Democracies to the Trilateral Commission*. New York: New York University Press, 1975.

Cohen, Lizbeth. *A Consumers' Republic: The Politics of Mass Consumption in Postwar America*. New York: Vintage, 2004.

Committee on the Present Danger. *Alerting America: The Papers of the Committee on the Present Danger*. Washington: Pergamon Press, 1984.

Cross, Gary. *The All-Consuming Century: Why Commercialism Won in Modern America*. New York: Columbia University Press, 2000.

Dionne Jr., E.J. *Why Americans Hate Politics*. New York: Simon & Schuster, 1991.

D'Souza, Dinesh. *The End of Racism*. New York: Free Press, 1995.

Edsall, Thomas Byrne. *The New Politics of Inequality*. New York: Norton, 1984.

Falwell, Jerry. *Listen, America!* New York: Doubleday, 1980.

Foner, Eric. *The Story of American Freedom*. New York: Norton, 1999.

Fraser, Steve, ed. *The Bell Curve Wars: Race, Intelligence, and the Future of America*. New York: Basic Books, 1995.

Freeman, Joshua. *Working-Class New York: Life and Labor Since World War II*. New York: The New Press, 2000.

Frieden, Jeffrey. *Global Capitalism: Its Fall and Rise in the Twentieth Century*. New York: Norton, 2006.

Friedman, Milton and Rose Friedman. *Free to Choose: A Personal Statement*. New York: Harcourt Brace, 1980.

Frum, David and Richard Perle. *An End to Evil: How to Win the War on Terror*. New York: Random House, 2003.

Gilder, George. *Wealth and Poverty*. New York: Basic Books, 1981.

Glazer, Nathan. *Affirmative Discrimination: Ethnic Inequality and Public Policy*. New York: Basic Books, 1975.

Hayek, Friedrich. *The Road to Serfdom*. Chicago: University of Chicago Press, 1944.

Himmelfarb, Gertrude. *The De-Moralization of Society: From Victorian Virtues to Modern Vices*. New York: Knopf, 1995.

Himmelstein, Jerome L. *To the Right: The Transformation of American Conservatism*. Berkeley: University of California Press, 1990.

Hirschman, Albert O. *The Rhetoric of Reaction: Perversity, Futility, Jeopardy*. Cambridge: Harvard University Press, 1991.

Kagan, Robert and William Kristol. *Present Dangers: Crisis and Opportunity in American Foreign and Defense Policy*. San Francisco: Encounter Books, 2000.

Kazin, Michael. *The Populist Persuasion: An American History*. Ithaca: Cornell University Press, 1995.

Kirkpatrick, Jeanne. *Dictatorships and Double Standards: Rationalism and Reason in Politics*. New York: Simon & Schuster, 1982.

Kristol, Irving. *Two Cheers for Capitalism*. New York: Basic Books, 1978.

Lipset, Seymour Martin. *American Exceptionalism: A Double-Edged Sword*. New York: Norton, 1997.

McGirr, Lisa. *Suburban Warriors: The Origins of the New American Right*. Princeton: Princeton University Press, 2001.

Murray, Charles. *Losing Ground: American Social Policy, 1950–1980*. New York: Basic Books, 1984.

Murray, Charles, and Richard Herrnstein. *The Bell Curve: Intelligence and Class Structure in American Life*. New York: Free Press, 1994.

Nash, George H. *The Conservative Intellectual Movement in America*. Wilmington, DE: Intercollegiate Studies Institute, 1998.

Novak, Michael. *The Spirit of Democratic Capitalism*. New York: Madison Books, 1982.

Petracca, Mark, ed. *The Politics of Interests: Interest Groups Transformed*. Boulder, CO: Westview Press, 1992.

Phillips, Kevin. *The Emerging Republican Majority*. New York: Anchor, 1970.

———. *The Politics of Rich and Poor: Wealth and the American Electorate in the Reagan Aftermath*. New York: Random House, 1990.

———. *Wealth and Democracy: A Political History of the American Rich*. New York: Broadway Books, 2002.

Podhoretz, Norman. *The Present Danger: Do we have the will to reverse the decline of American Power?* New York: Simon & Schuster, 1980.

Rieder, Jonathan. *Canarsie: The Jews and Italians of Brooklyn Against Liberalism*. Cambridge: Harvard University Press, 1985.

Sanders, Jerry W. *Peddlers of Crisis: The Committee on the Present Danger and the Politics of Containment.* Boston: South End Press, 1983.

Schneider, Gregory L., ed. *Conservatism in America Since 1930.* New York: New York University Press, 2003.

Schulman, Bruce J. *The Seventies: The Great Shift in American Culture, Society, and Politics.* New York: Free Press, 2001.

Simon, William. *A Time for Truth.* New York: McGraw Hill, 1978.

Skrentny, John David. *The Ironies of Affirmative Action.* Chicago: University of Chicago Press, 1996.

Sowell, Thomas. *Ethnic America: A History.* New York: Basic Books, 1981.

Thernstrom, Stephan and Abigail Thernstrom. *America in Black and White: One Nation, Indivisible.* New York: Simon & Schuster, 1997.

Wanniski, Jude. *The Way the World Works.* Washington: Regnery, 1978.

Young, Michael. *The Rise of the Meritocracy.* New Brunswick, NJ: Transaction Publishers, 1994.

Articles

Bartels, Larry. "Homer Gets a Tax Cut: Inequality and Public Policy in the American Mind," *Perspectives on Politics* 3:1 (March 2005): pp. 15–31.

———. "Unenlightened self-Interest: The strange appeal of income tax repeal," *The American Prospect*, June 2004.

———. "What's the Matter with *What's the Matter with Kansas?*" Paper presented at 2005 Annual Meeting of the American Political Science Association, Washington DC, September 1–4, 2005.

Commager, Henry Steele. "Tocqueville's Mistake: A Defense of Strong Central Government," *Harper's*, August 1984, pp. 70–74.

Confessore, Nicholas. "Breaking the Code," *New York Times Magazine*, January 16, 2005.

Ehrenberg, John. "Playing the Blame Game with Katrina," *Logos* 4:4 (Fall 2005), http://www.logojournal.com.

Friedman, Milton. "The Market Can Transform our Schools," *New York Times*, July 2, 2002.

Fukuyama, Francis. "The End of History?" *The National Interest* 16 (Summer 1989).

Grieder, William. "The Education of David Stockman," *The Atlantic Monthly* 247 (December 1981).

Hacker, Jacob S., and Paul Pierson, "Abandoning the Middle: The Bush Tax Cuts and the Limits of Democratic Control," *Perspectives on Politics* 3:1 (March 2005): pp. 33–53.

Johnston, David Cay. "Richest Are Leaving Even the Rich Far Behind," *New York Times*, June 5, 2005.

Krueger, Alan. "Cloudy Thinking on Tax Cuts," *New York Times*, October 16, 2003.

Krugman, Paul. "Losing Our Country," *New York Times*, June 10, 2005.

Suskind, Ron. "Faith, Certainty and the Presidency of George W. Bush," *New York Times Magazine*, October 17, 2004.

Tapper, Jake. "Retiring, Not Shy," *New York Times Magazine*, September 1, 2002.

Verba, Sidney, Kay Lehman Schlozman, and Henry E. Brady. "The Big Tilt: Participatory Inequality in America," *The American Prospect* 32 (May–June 1997).

Websites

President Dwight D. Eisenhower, "Speech to the American Association of Newspaper Editors." http://www.eisenhower.archives.gov/avaudio.htm.

Eric Hobsbawm, "United States: Wider Still and Wider." http://mondediplo.com/2003/06/02/hobsbawm.

http://newamericancentury.org.

http://www.ndol.org.

Speeches of Ronald Reagan. http://www.reagan.utexas.edu/resource/speeches.

http://loc.gov/exhibits/jefferson.

Task Force on Inequality and American Democracy, American Political Science Association, "American Democracy in an Age of Rising Inequality." http://apsanet.org.

Index

www.ingramcontent.com/pod-product-compliance
Lightning Source LLC
Chambersburg PA
CBHW030649270326
41929CB00007B/280